RUNNING
FOR THE HILLS

✖

Growing Up on My Mother's Sheep Farm in Wales

HORATIO CLARE

Scribner
New York   London   Toronto   Sydney

SCRIBNER
1230 Avenue of the Americas
New York, NY 10020

Originally published in Great Britain in 2006 by John Murray,
a division of Hodder Headline

First Scribner edition 2006

This memoir is based on the author's experiences over a twenty-year period.
Names have been changed, characters combined, and events compressed.

For information about special discounts for bulk purchases,
please contact Simon & Schuster Special Sales:
1-800-456-6798 or business@simonandschuster.com

Designed by Kyoko Watanabe
Text set in Garamond 3

Manufactured in the United States of America

1   3   5   7   9   10   8   6   4   2

Library of Congress Cataloging-in-Publication Data
Clare, Horatio, 1973–
Running for the hills : growing up on my mother's sheep farm in Wales /
Horatio Clare. —1st Scribner ed.
p. cm.
1. Clare, Horatio, 1973– —Childhood and youth.
2. Sheep ranchers—Wales—Biography. 3. Wales—Biography.
I. Title.
CT848.C57A3 2006
942.9092—dc22
[B]   2006042351

ISBN-13: 978-0-7432-7427-2
ISBN-10: 0-7432-7427-X

To my parents and Alexander

RUNNING
FOR THE HILLS

Prologue

CLOUDS BOWLED ALONG THE SKYLINE, A PROCESSION OF billowing white shapes, like the sails of yachts I could not quite see. Not far beyond my window the mountain rose, rearing like a vast wave, hundreds of feet above the house. From my bed I gazed up its great green wall of new bracken, which flexed and rippled as the wind brushed it, at the knotty thorn trees that clung on here and there, and I watched the beetling white bands of the mountain ewes, and the blown black sparks that were ravens playing in the winds along the ridge. In the middle of the towering horizon, which darkened where it adjoined the sky, was a single still shape, like a man standing, looking over us. I had once asked my father, when he came to see us, what it was.

"It's a cairn," he said.

"What's a cairn?"

"It's a pile of stones, put there by walkers."

"Why do they do that?"

"Partly for fun, and partly to say they've been there. Cairns are marked on maps, so they help other walkers know where they are. When you pass one, you add a stone to it."

But we—my mother, my brother, and I—were not really in favor

of walkers. When they appeared on summer weekends, stumbling
notches on the horizon, we watched them jealously, daring them to
descend and invade our land. We lived miles up, higher than anyone
else, and we did not like people looking down on us. However, since
my father approved of cairns, I approved of cairns, and when I stared
up at the solitary shape, the watcher on the skyline, as I did every
morning, I thought of him.

"Time to get up, children," our mother said, with lightly forced
gaiety (she loved her bed), her voice coming clearly through the thin
wooden partition that divided our rooms.

"Time to get up! Up, Horatio, up, Alexander!"

"OK, Jenny . . ."

"Yes, Mummy . . ."

(We often called our parents by their first names. Other adults
thought it was some sort of sixties principle but we were never taught
or encouraged to do it: we started because they referred to each other
that way and because Jenny had banned "Mum," which she said was
some sort of deodorant. "You call me Jenny when you're cross with
me," she observed once, "and Mummy when you're being nice! One
day I hope you'll call me Ma-ma, but I should think you'll go straight
to Mother, which sounds so aged.")

My brother appeared in the door of my bedroom, which gave
onto his.

"Come on then, slugabed," he said. "I'm up."

Seven years old, two years younger than me, with an idiosyncratic
vocabulary: "idle slugabed" was one of our father's archaisms. We
remembered and repeated all his sayings.

Now Jenny joined him, on one leg, pulling a long woolen stock-
ing up the other. Her uniform was corduroy britches, a woolly sweater,
and long socks. "Good morning, darlings. Up! Up! Or we'll miss the
best of the day. It looks lovely out there, but pretty cool, I should think.
Warm sweaters."

We dressed. Jenny unbolted the bedroom door and led the way,
stooping, down the little stone stairs, which were chilly through our
socks. The walls were smothered with thick white plaster which flaked
if you touched it and there were gently bending postcards of Florentine
angels on ledges all the way down. She unbolted the door at the bot-

tom: we slept behind a series of rickety but reassuring defenses. The sitting room smelled of dogs and ashes: we had not had a fire since the end of winter but the hearth was huge and drafts from the wide chimney spread its gray smell around the room. Lark's tail beat a dusty tattoo on the old sofa; as she yawned and whined her greeting, her son shrank into himself, "hiding" ineptly by the front door.

"No disgusting little presents this morning, Toss?" Jenny demanded, suspiciously.

Toss snaked forward, head ducked low with shame, muzzle down, licking his lips apologetically, heavy with caution and reluctance.

"Good dog!" Mum said. "You don't have to be guilty if you haven't done anything!"

He always was, though. He associated mornings, not turds, with guilt.

Jenny opened the door to the kitchen. Lark sprang off her sofa; Toss brightened. Jenny pulled the curtains back from the kitchen windows. The dogs sat on their haunches and began scratching madly, heads back, teeth revealed in tight sharky grins as they pursued fleas and the idea of fleas across their chests and around behind their ears. Alexander and I tiptoed across the cold stone of the kitchen floor, gathering bowls, milk, spoons, and cereal, which we doused with delicious and disproportionate quantities of sugar. The radio talked quietly about unemployment figures. Jenny put on some strong coffee, sticking close to the cooker—the one really warm spot in the house— and toyed with her first cigarette. She lit it and pulled open the back door. The dogs dashed out. There was the mountain, bright and sudden. And past the smoke of her cigarette we could smell it, and the long grass out the back, and the new bracken, and all the air.

"Oh! It is a lovely day!" she cried. "Not exactly hot, though."

We finished our cereal and joined her outside, where she sat on a log. Apart from the ash tree, which towered over the house like the mainmast of a ship, there was nothing between us and our infinite view. We looked out at the wide morning, and Jenny shook her head, because there were not really any words for it. We all smiled at one another.

"You off then?" she said later, as we set out. "See you back for lunch, I expect?"

"Yes."

"OK then. I've got a lamb to inject and then Mr. Pugh is coming to see if he wants to buy my ram and then I thought we might go and see Gwyn later and ask him about the shearing. You can take the dogs."

"See you," we said, not really listening to the sheep stuff. Once we had established we were not needed, and were free to go and play, nothing else mattered.

It was late May. The sun on last year's dead bracken made the hill look pink, dusted with the light emerald of the new growth: in ten days, when these fronds had spread and thickened, the flanks of all the mountains would be covered in their heavy, endless green. We went up through the long grass of the back patch, trampling through buttercups—their pollen staining our shoes and the dogs' paws yellow—and climbed out over the hill gate. Here, failing to hold back the unfurling goosenecks and new stalks of the bracken tide, ran the hill fence, the rusty, rickety, collapsing boundary between our land and the mountain. Centuries ago, when the old people first farmed up here, carving pasture out of the hillside, it had been stone-walled. Stacked traces of the wall remained, the stones barely visible under layers of lichens and mosses like seaweed. All along the fence were trees, and we made our way beneath them. Many were ancient birches, their black trunks gnarled, branches ending in bursts of twigs like witches' broomsticks. Among them were old bowed mountain ashes, with peeling silver arms holding out creamy plates of blossom, and one or two oaks. I had been reading *Watership Down,* about wars between tribes of rabbits, so my head was full of territorial battles, rival clans, and wide patrols; I was looking for tracks and signs, droppings, shed feathers, or tufts of hair on the fence. Alexander had been going over Alistair MacLean again, *The Guns of Navarone,* so he carried a stick like a rifle, and occasionally shot down ambushers. To our left side, rising from the soles of our feet into the height of the sky, was the mountain. To our right, dropping away below the hill fence, was the farm. The path we walked between them was one of the few flat ways in our steeply sloping world. We followed it around the angle of the gully, over the stony spread of the stream, and on toward the larch trees that marked the end of our acres. Now we looked back at the house, settled in the crook of the mountain's arm.

Jenny was in the yard. The swallows were nesting in the Big Barn and the sheds; she watched them arrowing in, the rush of their flight dispersing in a rustle of feathers as they reached their building sites. All the world was busy, this May day; the wagtails flitted around the yard in bursts of catching and gathering; the robin followed Jenny down the track as far as the plum tree, carrying a caterpillar in his bill; the hazels bustled with birds. Jenny had noticed something odd about the lamb yesterday, in the Middle Meadow. She had not liked the way it panted and blew. She glanced with pleasure at the choked stream by the meadow gate, which was clotted with myrtles, and let herself into the Middle Meadow, opening and closing the gate gently, so as not to disturb the sheep. A cuckoo called and the sheep nearest her bleated. They came up to her, their warm breath puffing over the backs of her hands. She talked quietly to them and slipped beet-pulp nuts to one or two. They whickered at her, nudging her legs; they sniffed at her pockets. On the edge of the crowd that surrounded her, ewes stood for their lambs, which were big now, butting greedily as they suckled. Jenny stooped, slowly, stroking and talking, then crouched and suddenly lunged, and the sheep jumped and scattered, leaving her and one lamb, kicking helplessly, as she pulled it in by its back leg.

"All right, lamb," she said, "calm down." She turned it onto its back, resting its rump on the ground between her legs, and carefully extracted the syringe and antibiotic from her pocket. She took the cap off the needle and drew 6 cc from the bottle: an adult dose. The lamb's breath came very quickly, and there was a rasp in it.

"Mmm. Maybe a bit of Pasturella. Didn't I vaccinate your mother, then? Lucky I noticed."

She bent over the animal, pulled up its right hind leg, found the muscle, and jabbed the needle in, anticipating and holding back the kick, pressing the plunger down. It was over quickly; she rubbed the place and let the creature go.

"There you go, lamb. Saved your life," she said. "Easy!" She smiled at its mother. Then she heard the engine and turned around. Coming over the crest of the ridge, topping the second of the steep, deadly pitches that separated us from the world, was a Land Rover.

On the hill fence my brother and I were just shaping up to kill a few Nazis when the dogs took off, hurtling madly along the fence, uttering short, explosive woofs and whines, so excited they could hardly bark. We went after them as a wild rattling and shaking in the trees told us what it was.

"Quizzle!" we hissed at the dogs. "Sic 'im, Toss! Get 'im! Get 'im, Larky . . . kill!"

The little animal darted from branch to twigs to trunk, leaping, scrabbling, dashing, faster than Tarzan, quicker than any monkey, as if the trees were a highway through the air and the squirrel a getaway driver. It gained the trunk of a tall ash tree and veered up it, disappearing around the far side in a scrabble of claws. Toss whined and prepared to leap the fence, but we stopped him.

"Come on now, leave it."

"Missed again, Toss."

He had never been known to catch one.

"So, yeah, the Germans are in retreat going that way, and they've got a few troops covering them, and we've got to winkle them out . . ."

But we became distracted by two ravens mobbing a buzzard: we watched as the raptor turned its glide at each last moment, tacking away from the croaking attacks, going higher and higher, silent, apparently calm, as the ravens swore and flapped hectically. "It's a proper dogfight!" Alexander exclaimed as one of the ravens gained height on the buzzard and went for it, and the buzzard abandoned its leisurely maneuvering and tilted backward for an instant, showing the raven its yellow talons.

"Hello, Mr. Pugh," Jenny said, and she opened the meadow gate for him. The Land Rover rolled slowly through and stopped.

"Jump in, then," said Mr. Pugh. He had a long, smiling look about him.

"Oh no, thank you," said Jenny, instinctively, not knowing quite why. "I'll walk up," she said with a smile and a funny little wave of one hand.

The vehicle bumped up the track ahead of her. When she arrived Mr. Pugh was already in the pens, leaning on the gate to the Patch, and staring at the rams.

"It's that one," Jenny said. "What do you think of him?"

"Tell you when I've got hold of him," Mr. Pugh replied.

"I'll get a bag of nuts and they'll come," Jenny said, "Then you can catch him."

"Dogs'll bring 'em now," said Mr. Pugh, and before Jenny could say anything he whistled, and there was a scramble behind them and she turned in time to see the second of two sheepdogs jumping out of the Land Rover through the driver's window. They dived under the gate into the pens, shot past her, flowed through the bars of the second gate, and were out into the Patch in a flash. The rams jumped, Pugh whistled, and the dogs separated, throwing themselves down the field in two intersecting arcs, their tracks like a lasso around the sheep. Pugh opened the gate and stood back. Another whistle, a short rush by one dog and quick dart by the other, and all five rams came tumbling into the pens, flustered and amazed.

"Crumbs!" Jenny cried. "That's just wonderful—what fantastic dogs. Mine wouldn't manage that in a million years."

"Go and lie down," said Pugh sternly, and the dogs did, instantly, flattening themselves against the field, their ears pricked Now Pugh lunged at the ram and caught him. He straddled him, cupped a hand under the animal's chin, lifted his head and peeled back his lips, revealing little teeth and pink gums. He looked for a second. He reached behind him and briefly squeezed the ram's rump Then he let him go. They both watched the animal collect himself, shaking his head at the indignity.

"Well. Nice straight back on him," Pugh said after a moment.

"Yes," Jenny said. "He's not bad, is he?"

"Don't you want him, then?"

"No. I've got enough. Don't want him going with his sisters much."

Mr. Pugh turned around and looked at the view. "Lovely little farm, this, Jenny," he said.

"Yes, it is," she said.

"And it's just you, is it?"

"And my boys," she said quickly. "And Jack Meredith helps me, and there's the dogs—all the animals. We're not lonely."

"Old Jack must be getting on now, isn't he?"

"Well, yes, he is. In his seventies. But strong as an ox."

Pugh tapped the iron of the gate with the flat of his hand and shifted from foot to foot, as though thinking about something. The shift bought him half a yard closer to her.

"Do you think you'll take the ram then?" she asked, briskly.

"What'll you give me?" Mr. Pugh asked, with a lascivious grin.

"Nothing," Jenny said, shortly. Oh no, she thought. Oh, Lord . . .

We fought our way along the fence in a series of rushes, giving each other covering fire. We had to use grenades to clear a couple of strong points.

"Down to your right! In the field—they're trying to flank us!"

We changed magazines, took careful aim, and chopped them down, our volleys mercilessly precise.

"Heavy machine gun—down by the hill fence!"

"I see him . . ." We traded fire, ducking and cursing the incoming rounds, until a lucky shot killed their gunner.

"Fix bayonets! There's a nest of them down there, we've got to hit them before they get that thing going again. Ready?"

We loosed off a few more rounds, rose and charged. Toss and Lark came too. We all hit top speed as we came over the fold in the ground that protected their position. Our mouths were open and we were in full battle roar, but the sudden stink of death and the awful sight of the corpse hit us like a blast, and the attack faltered.

"Yaaaa-urr! Uugh! My God! Yuk."

"Uurch! Shit, that's disgusting."

"Not even a little something?" Mr. Pugh wheedled. His hands came up, palms toward her, and she stepped back smartly.

"No, no. Absolutely not," she said. She sounded arch. Oh, Lord, she thought, he probably thinks it's like Lady Chatterley.

"Bet you'd love a roll in the hay, though, wouldn't you?"

"No, Mr. Pugh, I would not. And neither would you, I promise you. And what about Mrs. Pugh, for goodness's sake?"

"She won't mind. She won't know . . . just quickly . . . a knee trembler!"

"No fear," said Jenny angrily. But Pugh was still grinning, as though she was encouraging him. He was close now, and there wasn't much between her back and the stone wall of the pens. She changed her tone, spoke quietly and in deadly earnest.

Something, dogs or foxes, had torn most of the flesh away from the face, leaving the teeth grinning along the bare jaw. One of the legs had been pulled off; it lay nearby, bone poking through tattered skin. All around our feet was a shell-burst of scraps of white wool, torn from her flanks; it was one of the Norsters' ewes, according to the smear of green paint on the tattered fleece. A stretch of the spine was exposed, as if a ferocious killer had enacted deliberate violence on the corpse, to make its sight more grisly, and there was some yellow and black skin left, stretched tight and stinking over the ribs. The summer's first flies crooned over it.

We looked at each other, our faces puckered in disgust, then leveled our weapons. There was nothing any medic could do for a Nazi in that state.

A couple of quick bursts and we moved on.

"Toss! Come the hell away from there! Oh no, look!"

He had picked up the severed back leg and was prancing along with it.

"Drop it, you horrible animal!" we shouted, laughing. We had to charge him before he complied.

"Look," Jenny said, "I can't, anyway, even if I wanted to. You know when a ewe has a prolapse? How the whole uterus comes out like a big pink balloon and bobs along behind her and gets covered in mud? And you have to get the vet to shove it back in and tie it there, and sometimes it gets infected and she dies? Well . . ."

At first Pugh stayed close, but as she elaborated his smile faded, then he looked sympathetic. By the time she had finished inventing and elaborating, Mr. Pugh looked quite ill.

"Hello, children," she greeted us as we trooped in. She was washing carrots under the tap. "How was your walk?"

"Fine," said Alexander.

"Yeah, nice," I added.

"We found a dead sheep by the hill fence, halfway to the larch trees," Alexander reported.

"Oh, really? How long dead?"

"Don't know . . ."

"Well, was it all blown up—dead for a day or so? Should I go and look at it?"

"No, no, half-eaten," I said, remembering *Watership Down* and the rabbits reporting back after their wide patrols. "Probably an old one. It's just by the fence but it wasn't caught on the wire. You can't tell how it died."

"Whose was it?"

"Derwyn's."

"Oh, right. I see." She went back to the carrots. Derwyn ran hundreds of unvaccinated, semiwild sheep on the mountain and expected them to take their chances.

"I had a pretty successful time," she said. "I caught that lamb and gave him an injection—jolly good thing too, just in time—and I sold that unpleasant ram to Mr Pugh for seventy quid! Aren't I clever!"

"Mmm. Yes, very good."

She sometimes waited years before telling us about her narrower escapes, especially anything frightening or otherwise inappropriate for the ears of children. But the three of us were very close, and she was a wonderful, busy talker. Everything seemed to come out in the end.

✧ ✧ ✧

We had salad for lunch, from Jack's garden (the farm's vegetable patch, which Jenny had turned over to Jack, who tilled and tended it with great skill), with bread and ham from Fine Fare, the little shop in town. Afterward, Jenny invited us to go with her to see Gwyn.

"No thanks, Mummy," I said.

"Will you come with me, Alexander?"

"Um, no, I think I'll stay here."

Our eyes met, both longing to retreat to the attic, where our toys were.

"Oh, come on, boys! Please! Keep me company."

There was a pause.

"Come on! It won't take a minute. Nice for me to have some backup. . . . I'd quite like you to come, if you don't mind."

There was a feather of authority in her tone that we both knew would harden into frustration and disappointment if we thwarted her. It was not worth the argument.

"OK," we sighed with bad grace. But by the time we were in the little car, rattling down the track, with Jenny chatting happily about all the squirrels around this year—and had we noticed the hazelnuts coming?—our resentment had passed. It was a lovely day to be going down the hill and up the valley, and we had chained the dogs up in the yard, to spare us their furious barking when we got to Gwyn's, so perhaps it would not be so bad.

As the eldest I sat in the front passenger seat—except on the rare occasions when Jenny or Alexander made a stand against this routine unfairness—so it fell to me to do the gates. First the Middle Meadow gate, then, after the really rough part of the track, the Far Meadow gate. You could see miles up and down the valley from the exposed corner where it stood; in the winter the east wind waited here, and the freezing iron of the gate licked and scalded the skin of your palms.

Here the tarmac began, and now we rolled down the lane, which turned toward the top of the first pitch. On our left were the shins of the mountain, skirts of ground between us and the view, and it was still our land: these were the Horse Fields, fifteen gently sloping acres tipping over into a deep wooded gully. On our right, above the lane, were the Norsters' fields; mostly empty, except one, covered with droppings and overcrowded with sheep, in which the grass had been picked nearly bare. A cloud crossed Jenny's face.

"They've been standing on nothing for a week," she grated.

The pitch tilted us steeply forward, and we curved down toward the wood. At the bottom we passed our lowest pasture—Ty Newydd, "new house," named after a long-vanished dwelling—a big, dropping field, the quickest route to the valley.

Now the road leveled into a thin ribbon, winding down past an old oak sentry at the start of the wood; then we were into the trees. They closed in suddenly, impenetrably dense above us; thinner, taller, and clinging to a steep slope below: in places it looked close to vertical. The car picked up speed and Jenny kept her gaze ahead, never glancing left: the plunge beyond the thin fence made her feel sick. Our spirits rose with the swoop of the car; sunlight dappled the young leaves and flickered over us as we went; falling in bright showers through the canopy, it pooled and splashed on mossy trunks and silvered branches, scattering light all through the jumbled wood.

We passed the ruined cottage where Derwyn Norster was said to take refuge when his mad wife and son ganged up on him, then the road fell again, the trees thinned, and we were at the head of the second pitch. The turning at the top of it is as steep as a car can manage, and we dreaded the day we would meet Derwyn in his tractor anywhere on its savage slide. (Coming back up we would all will the car around that corner; it never failed, but there was always a moment when you thought it might.) Ahead were the upper reaches of the valley, hills like a circle of old friends with their arms around one another's shoulders, a choppy sea of fields and woods slipping and sloping between them, animated by the shift of cloud shadows and the dimming and brightening of the light.

It was another quarter mile down to the village from the bottom of the pitch, but instead we turned right along the back lane, one of the old roads up the valley. The gentle climb was interrupted every half mile or so by the edge of one of the mountain's toes; suddenly the road would dip down to cross a stream and loop steeply up again on the other side. Here and there were farms, most still working, some ruined: I remembered going to one, when I was a toddler, with my father and the owner, who had sold us a load of stone tiles.

We came to Emrys's place, slowing at the sight of him in his yard. Jenny and Dad had bought our farm from him, and Emrys in turn had bought this farm from Jack, when Jack and his brother Alfie retired.

"Hello, Emrys!" Jenny cried, winding down the window.

"Hello, Jen!" he called back. He wore a dark old jacket done up with a length of string and a checked tweed cap the color of mud. Like most of the farmers he had livid, wind-reddened cheeks; his seemed emblems of well-being and good humor. His eyes twinkled as he peered in at us.

"All right there, boys!" he shouted.

"Look at you with your string!" Jenny laughed. "You don't fool me! I said to the boys, there's the richest man in the valley, and his jacket's done up with string!"

"If only it were true!" Emrys retorted, and we pulled away, waving.

This did not seem at all strange to us: from an early age we were acquainted, as were all farmers' children, with the mysterious power of the European agricultural subsidies. "Some of these farmers are millionaires!" Jenny would exclaim, in scandalized exaggeration. "Forty quid a year for every ewe, and so they keep thousands—look at them all!" The fields on both sides of the valley were covered in sheep, and the hill was flecked with them.

"Look at these ewes, though. Don't they look well? He's a jolly good farmer, Emrys, a really hard worker."

We came to another combe, where the road descended into the shadow of an old copse. Jenny tapped the window, indicating a deep streambed, which wound away through darkly green foliage and rotting fallen trees.

"In the winter of '47 Jack's father lost a flock of sheep down here. They'd been to market, old Mr. Meredith and Mr. Watkins, and they'd bought forty hoggits each—ewe lambs for store, for breeding, you know—and then the blizzards came. From November to March it snowed. They had to keep digging them out of the drifts, and Jack says they were all buried under the snow together and they ate each other's wool, which I've heard they do, if they're desperate, 'ate each other naked,' he said, and then they froze. When the spring came Mr. Meredith only had eight left, and Mr. Watkins twelve. They died in that gully there."

"Wow," Alexander and I said as we tried to imagine the whole sunny valley black and white and filled with deadly snow.

"The winters were harder then," Jenny said. "Perhaps they'll come back."

"Hope so!" I said.

"Hope *not,*" Jenny emphasized.

Gwyn's farm was right at the head of the valley, straddling the stream. It was down below the level of the surrounding fields, as if hidden from marauders. The track led downhill from the farm gate toward the yard between barns and sheds of all kinds; henhouses, cow byres, hay barns, and something that looked like a railway car. As soon as we began the descent a rolling chorus of fierce barking went up and a wild tribe of dogs ambushed us from every side. They leaped out of windows, threshed and wriggled frantically under gates, hurled themselves over the tops of fences, and charged. Some were shut in: they furiously thrust their muzzles under the chewed bottoms of shed doors and barked and barked, saliva shaking in their whiskers. The noise was terrifying; when we had our own dogs with us it was unbearable. Jenny stopped the car in the yard and remarked how cleanly it had been swept, while the dogs circled us and we made no move to get out.

"Look at that one. Mean or what?" Alexander said, pointing at a yellow-eyed brute, a heavy-hackled animal whose barking seemed to carry a particular malice.

"Yes, I wonder if that's the biter?" Jenny mused.

"Vicious," Alexander muttered.

"Gwyn's got one he told me about; you don't want to turn your back on him, he said. I should think not! Oh good, here he is."

A tall man, broad and strong, with an aquiline look and dark black hair, thinning on top, Gwyn wore thick serge trousers tucked into fat Wellingtons, a checked shirt, and braces. Jenny wound down her window and waved as he came toward us, keeping her wrist high, wary of a jumping dog. The hounds redoubled their barking, to impress their master, and kept an eye on him, for cues. He told them to be quiet. Most of them obeyed.

"Hello, Jenny," he said, stooping to the window.

"Which one's your biter then, Gwyn?" Jenny began.

The conversation wound from dogs to sheep, weather to markets, to prices, to people. Jenny asked after his wife and sons. He reciprocated, stooping again, to peer past her into the car.

"How are you, boys?"

"Fine, thanks. How are you?"

"Not so bad. Are you going to be farmers like your mother?"

We shook our heads. We had no intention of becoming farmers. Jenny and Gwyn laughed sadly. Finally, Jenny broached the question of shearing, and after a bit of thought Gwyn said he'd be able to do us in two weeks. She would pay him, of course, but he was doing us a favor and we all knew it.

"Two weeks time, then, you promise?" Jenny wheedled.

"Aye, we'll see you then," he said, and she thanked him, and prompted us, and we thanked him, then we said our good-byes and carefully drove away, avoiding the barking dogs.

We wound down the valley and all the way back up our hill. Alexander and I went up to the attic to our toys, at last, while Jenny had tea and a cigarette before going down to the meadow to check on the lamb. He seemed fine. She took a longer route back, checking on ewes in the Lower Meadows and the animals in the Rough Field, finishing with a trudge up the Patch, the steep little field below the house where she kept the ill, the oldest and most decrepit sheep, her "old biddies." A little while later she contemplated supper and decided on cauliflower cheese and bacon. She cooked, listening closely to the shipping forecast, and called us down when the meal was ready. Afterward while she enjoyed another cigarette and listened with half an ear to the wireless, I mooched around and Alexander sat at the table, looking at a book. This was one of the times when we all talked; in the winter we would be in front of the fire. We had no television, but between our toys and games, the dogs, the radio, and the stories we told one another we were

seldom bored. Now, as the evening quietened beyond the windows—
a listening hush, into which a mistle thrush sang loudly, summoning
summer rain—we discussed this and that. We often talked about
Robert, our father. Alexander and I loved to hear about him, and particularly about the early years of our parents' relationship, the times
before we were born, when they were happy together, when they began
their great adventure with the farm. That night, not for the first time,
Jenny found herself describing how she had met him.

"I was staying with Max, in Scotland, at a place called the House of
Tongue," she said, staring at the floor, as if into the distant past. "When
I walked into the room Robert was the only man who stood up."

We listened closely, nodding along. We had heard the story before;
I had built up a vivid image of how it might have been. It was not an
entirely accurate picture but it was as close as I could get to the truth,
and to explaining how we three came to be here, on this mountain, so
high up and far away from the rest of the world.

I

In the Eye of the Sun

THEY MET AT THE HOUSE OF TONGUE, AT THE TIP OF Scotland, near the farthest point north. As she walked into the room he was the only man to stand up. They exchanged bright smiles, the kind that come from shyness: neither was comfortable in the grand drawing room, under the glassy stare of shot stags and the crossed swords of long-conquered Scots.

Like a spy in a boys' adventure story, the young man's manners were too polished, his unaccented speech too English. Robert was born in Shanghai and raised in Kenya and South Africa. He was not at home in the chattering party that surrounded him; he was too quiet, too watchful, terribly polite.

Jenny was also self-conscious but she flushed and bubbled with it, buried it under avalanches of enthusiasm and laughter until, in the middle of dinner, someone sneered something about a "bloody homosexual" in Parliament. In a trice she reacted.

"But what on earth does it matter? I don't think it makes the slightest difference! So what if he's queer? So what?"

There was an embarrassed silence—and for the first time Robert looked beyond the pretty, skittish surface of the girl on the other side of the table. He said nothing, but she caught his sudden, steady look, and beyond the agreement in his spreading smile, she saw something else: the assessment of another intelligence, another will.

After dinner they spread out around a great fire with cigarettes, cigars, and spirits. The host, Max, sat down with Robert to play chess. They were friends and rivals; similarly ambitious, agitating young journalists. They had been in Nigeria together, covering the Biafran War. Most of those at the House of Tongue that night were journalists of some sort: Jenny was the *Evening Standard*'s assistant literary editor.

Max was following Winston Churchill's *My Early Life* as a manual for grand success. He liked to win his games, and he had played Robert before. Jenny sat nearby and watched. Her presence added an edge to the contest. Robert thought for a time, sometimes a long time, before shifting a piece. Max bit his fingernails, the effort of each execution clipping across his face. The game slowed and intensified, the pieces clotting across the board in gently bloody confrontation. Jenny sat watching the men, following the game, and at some point (she remembered, decades later) realized that she wanted Robert to win. On his turn Max moved quickly, defiantly; he pressed, he attacked. His game was good, aggressive and alert, but, in the end, Robert won.

The next day was misty, the grass as wet as the sky and the loch deep green below the pelt of bracken. After breakfast Max handed out rods, guns, and bright cartridges. The women made jokes and mocked distaste and went along with it anyway. Jenny denounced it all and went for a walk. She may not have been as easily confident as the others, but she knew her own mind, and never concealed a conviction.

"I think it's disgusting! Foul!" she cried over her shoulder at Max and his laughing crew. She said of him later, "I could never love anyone who insists on killing things the whole time."

Robert walked too. He left before breakfast and went miles. He did not shoot or fish. He looked out to sea and put up grouse. There was nothing, not even a croft along the shore. He packed a meditative pipe and smoked, sitting on a cold rock.

Jenny went across the moor, slipping and sliding in high boots of inappropriate green leather which soon became blackened with peat slime. Every pop of the guns confirmed her resistance to Max.

Later, in a warm evening with no wind, the loch dreamily still and the old sandstone house glowing red, Max took her out in a rowing boat. The creak and drip of the slow oars seemed to amplify the glassy peace; Jenny felt that the herons and even the midges were listening. They moved out into the middle, drifting into the lacquer green reflection of the hill. Max seemed calmer than he had been, not chasing her anymore, thinking about other things. They eyed the water.

"My God, someone's coming in!"

Jenny stared at the pale figure, which was throwing itself forward in a shallow dive, a great fish flopping.

"Well, that is quite mad. It must be absolutely freezing."

"It's Robert," Max said, narrowing shooter's eyes.

Robert pulled toward them, breaststroke, gasping huge breaths. Ten yards away he took an extra deep one and plunged under, shimmering to the side of the boat and surfacing with a sputtered cloud of vapor. Jenny saw his shoulders were brown and flecked with sunspots and moles. Kicking beneath him, shrinking and growing, his feet were white.

"Isn't it freezing?" she cried, shivering.

"Very refreshing," he said, shuddering his voice. He turned, ducked under, set off.

"Loopy," said Max.

"I can't stand cold water! Ever since my mother used to make us swim in the freezing sea I just can't bear it. Being an adult is never having to get into the water," Jenny said, watching Robert swim.

Jenny noticed one of Max's friends, a girl called Anne, looking at Robert. As she followed Anne's gaze Robert glanced up, not at Anne, but at her.

"I think I've fallen in love with Robert," Anne announced.

"Have you? Golly. Do you know him then?"

"He's going to be my problem," said Anne thoughtfully.

Jenny decided she would go back to London when she looked out of a window and saw the lawn was covered with mackerel. Max was laying them out, dozens of bright silver-blue fish.

"What are you going to do with so many, Max?" she demanded.

"Oh, Lord, Jen. Don't tell me you don't like fishing either! This is Scotland, for God's sake!"

"I think it's fine to kill things for the table. But how on earth are you going to eat all of these beautiful mackerel?"

It was a long way to the station, so she called a taxi. She was waiting for it, saying good-byes, when Robert appeared, carrying his bag.

"I'm going to go back too," he announced. "I'll come as far as Newcastle with you."

For the first time they are alone together. Robert gives her to understand there is someone, a woman, in Newcastle. But when the great station arrives he does not get off. They cross the Tyne together. Each gazes across the compartment at the other. She looks at a beautiful young man. His hair is fair, his skin is browned, his face broad and handsome. The nose is straight, the jawline firm. His voice is authoritative, with that near-arrogant crispness that public schools and colonies breed, but he speaks softly, gently.

He has a habit of tilting his head back slightly as he listens, green eyes locked on hers, and nodding forward as he responds. His humor is quick and dry and never far away. He is not fixed; there is a fragility about his quickness, as if he believes in his own intelligence and is uncertain of all the rest.

He is familiar with the company of beautiful women but has never encountered anyone like Jenny. She leaps from her seat, crying out her delight at the dark magnificence of Durham Cathedral. She snorts with giggles when he is witty. She rolls her eyes at the other passengers, responds to the stolid ticket inspector like a naughty schoolgirl performing for her class; she seems to find authority provocative and ridiculous. Her hair is fine and dark, her eyes are bright and light brown. She has the elfin air, smile, and sass of the Chelsea girl she was not long ago. She smokes cigarettes carelessly and talks continuously, veering wildly among innocence, mischief, and insight. Their fingers touch as she hands back his matches, and he notices how cool hers are. They smile across the compartment, charmed and laughing with nothing to lose in that blissful conspiracy of ignorance and curiosity with which love affairs begin.

They begin to unfold their lives for each other. Robert talks of his childhood, of following his father's postings to Kenya and South Africa, of university in Cape Town, of his marriage at the age of twenty-three, of opposition to the regime, of friends imprisoned and murdered, of his flight to Britain with his young wife and Janey, their little daughter, of the failure of that marriage, of divorce.

Jenny listens, responds with sketches of her own upbringing in Shrewsbury, and her boarding school in Kent, where she was the only girl who was not the child of missionaries. She tells of her flight from what her mother always insisted was "upper middle class" Shropshire, of her happiness at Cambridge; she mentions adventures in America and Thailand, teaching in the East End of London, of how much she hated working in television.

When the train reached London they separated, but in helping her with her bags Robert somehow kept hold of the one containing her soiled green leather boots. On the following Monday evening he finished work earlier than usual and waited for her outside her office in Fleet Street. When she emerged, hurrying as usual, he gravely presented her with the boots. She barely recognized them. He had worked the leather for hours, with spit and rags and carefully chosen polish, and now they shone and gleamed.

"Heavens, Robert!" she cried. "They're beautiful! How sweet of you!" He gave her a watch not long after that, saying, "I notice you never seem to know the time," with one of the sidelong looks that always made her laugh, but nothing moved her like the polishing of the boots, which struck her as pure kindness.

❖ ❖ ❖

Robert was always working, and quiet in men's company. He shunned the wine-bar crowd in which she had many friends; he was never fond of the laughing Diary boys, the gossip and booze. They were well matched to their jobs. Jenny was pretty and bright and awkward and open all at once: the combination swept her past the wary fences of the writers and academics she interviewed. As assistant literary editor, she was responsible for book reviews, commissioning, and interviewing. Her subjects trusted her immediately and talked freely as her tape recorder turned; she missed nothing. At the office package after package of books arrived to be opened and considered. She sampled them, tested them against taste and instinct, read and reread them, and developed an expert eye.

In the din and dinge of old Fleet Street she was an unlikely presence. "You'll never make a journalist, dear girl, you're not nearly tough enough," said one.

"It's not what you write," grated her editor one day. "It's not even how slowly you type it. It's the pauses while you search your keys for the right letter!"

Robert blazed at his work. He was a news journalist, a good one, shifted rapidly by his bosses and his interests from story to story, from one specialty to another. He had a passion for it; he went for the heart of the issue as if angry headlines and cool paragraphs could slay the tormentors of the world.

They saw each other often, until one day his kettle appeared in her kitchen, and she knew that he had moved in.

Then one night they went to a restaurant in Notting Hill. Red tablecloths, dark walls. Robert listened while Jenny, inspired, laid out her dream.

"I don't want to be stuck in London," she declared. "I think we should buy a house in the country. Imagine a lovely old place somewhere away from all the wretched fumes."

"You're serious?"

"Yes, yes! Do you want to go to work on the Tube for the rest of your life? Wouldn't you love to have mountains to climb?"

"We can do that at the weekends."

"Yes, but we could have a house, too. We could have a house and fields. I miss the country. I miss nature. Come on, Robert, darling! Let's find somewhere beautiful."

She picked at her food and giggled as he couched his objections in jokes, but she was glowing with something else, something impatient. She was absolutely determined. She had made up her mind to do it. He loved her, and she had presented him with a decision she had already made.

So they began to hunt. They would hammer up the motorway on Friday nights to stay with Jenny's sister, Ursula, happily married to Geoff and living in the Forest of Dean, on the Welsh border. From there they launched themselves in every direction, and around and around they went, from real estate agents' windows to cottages and farms, to small houses and to large, up hillsides and down muddy tracks, back to real estate agents' windows.

They combed the windy edge of Wales, dropping off the ridges into hidden valleys, winding down to villages ignored by everything but the weather. Years later Jenny would see signposts and say, "I think we went there when we were looking for the farm. Yes, we did. Miserable place."

The journeys back down the motorway were long exercises in resignation for her. She thought she would never find the place she was looking for and mulled over what she had seen. Robert wondered how long they would have to keep looking. He loved the country and walking, was glad of the missions for the space and the exercise; the way people lived on the border with the past seduced his reporter's eye. He looked for their means, their crops and flocks. He looked at what their livelihoods had made of them and planned his next campaign at work.

✤ ✤ ✤

One rainy evening, following a fruitless day around Abergavenny, a small glum town, when they were just about to turn for London, Jenny remembered an estate agent they had missed. Robert waited while she ran back into town. Russell, Baldwin, and Bright were about to close.

"I don't suppose you've got a little farm somewhere beautiful?"

"Something came in today, actually."

The envelope contained an untidy summary of a place for sale, and detailed directions. Robert scanned it.

"Smallholding and outbuildings, seventy-two acres, hill rights. It's a working farm."

"Where?"

"The other side of the Black Mountains. Blooming miles."

"Oh! Real Wales!"

"Really far away Wales."

"We might as well look at it. It'll be an expedition."

The vendors would expect them at three o'clock. The departure from London was delayed by a hunt for the car keys.

"I moved them, I put them somewhere. I'm so sorry, darling, let me just think a minute. Oh! Here they are! How did they get in there? In the grill!"

Robert rolled his eyes. "Where else?"

As they crossed out of England, over the bridge, the sun drowned in veils of sky the same color as the estuary mud. Making the turn at Newport, the rain netted them, rattling on the car. Forty minutes north they climbed the rise into a little town.

"Oh, what a pretty place!" Jenny cried. "Isn't it charming!" Georgian lines proportioned the little high street, shops adjoined like ladies in their best, neatly lined up for tea. It seemed abandoned to the wind and rain.

Robert nodded, following Jenny's directions under the looming walls of an invisible manor, north up the tightening valley, right at a fork, into farther hills. To the right the mountains vanished into the murk; in every direction cloud hung sullen over rising ground.

"Right at the pub. Right. Right at house, steep pitch." It was very quiet beyond the car; when it slowed they could sense the peace, almost hear it.

The car paused, gathered itself, and assaulted the gradient in first gear. "Crikey!" Robert laughed as they were tilted back in their seats like fighter pilots, climbing straight up the side of the hill.

"My God, look at this. It's a pitch all right. Right at fork, through wood half mile."

"My God, look at *this*," Robert said calmly, hauling the car up and around a bend so steep it seemed to fill the windows on his side with wet road. The engine panted and gasped with relief at the top, flipping them over another rise into a soaking wood.

"My God, my vertigo!" Jenny cried. "It's an abyss!"

The right-side wheels spun over leaf litter banked against a straggle of rusted fence, which offered no protection from the cliffy drop into the trees. To the left the wood gathered in thick scribbles, tapping the roof above their heads and dropping water like sudden tears on the windscreen. The road proceeded on and up through a waving tunnel.

"Where is it taking us? We'll be swallowed in the mists like the ninth legion!"

"If we don't roll over backwards like a beetle. Hold on, it's another pitch." Robert swung the car around and up, as to the right flickered fields, more wood, cloud, and bracken.

They rose over the crest. Below the fields sloped more gently, and before them, across three meadows, the mountain, untamed and sudden, climbed into the sky. At its foot, nestling into the crook of a gully, was the house, sheltering under a stand of larch trees. They could see three descending roofs, white walls, and dark windows. It was a longhouse dug into the curved flank of the mountain, a little tumbledown manor at the head of its own valley.

The track was a double path of stones and red earth separated by a strip of grass which brushed the undercarriage menacingly, threatening to rear up and ground them. Robert took it slowly. Sheep stared with blank frankness from under the shelter of thorn trees, and thin gasps of smoke blew away from one of the chimneys.

As they neared the house half the track became a stream, pooling muddily at the yard gate. They stopped beside a high barn wall. The yard was a rough cobble of mud, muck, and protruding stones sloping steeply up to the front door. The tiled roofs were green with moss and rain. A huge midden slumped against the stable wall. Black cattle like buffalo hung around the lower end of the yard and the savage barking of dogs hesitated when Robert switched off the engine, then resumed with discouraging vigor. There were little orange cats running about in the mud.

"Ah-ha! The vendor."

A short round figure in a soaked black tweed jacket and mud-checked cap, with red cheeks and bright eyes, came down the yard to meet them. Robert shook his hand.

"How do you do? I'm Robert and this is Jenny."

"Emrys," said the vendor. "How do you do? You've come a long way."

"Yes, thank goodness," said Jenny. "Thank you for having us up your mountain."

"Well. It's a pity you can't see the view." Emrys shouted when he was shy. "There's a good view there, when it's visible."

"You're pretty high up, here?"

Emrys led them up the yard to the house.

"A thousand and something, I think it is. Geeyet outofit! Fly!" Emrys shouted at a white-whiskered dog's nose, poking under the barn door and barking. He was smiling, though.

"There'll be tea in a minute. We've been watching the television. You can't get much signal but when it rains."

The door opened to wet flagstones and a dim interior. The wall, Jenny noticed, was almost two feet thick. They went in. There was a tiny fire in a choked grate: the vast hearth Jenny looked for was blocked up. In front of it, in an angle formed by the foot of a narrow flight of stairs that went up behind where the huge fire should have been, there was one place out of the drafts where Emrys had his little daughter's cot. He led them through to the kitchen, which was stuck on at the back. It was a big step down to huge flagstones resting on earth; there was no flooring, and the smell of damp was incredible, like nothing they had ever experienced, a wet, dripping damp, wetter and darker than any cellar.

✦ ✦ ✦

Jenny fell passionately in love with it straight away. Someone had told her that you can fall in love with a place as much as a person, and now she knew it to be true.

They rattled away from the house along the track. It was bitterly cold at the far gate. Jenny opened and shut it and climbed back in, shivering.

"What an amazing place!"

"No bathroom. No water! Chemical lavatory in that shed in the yard . . ." Robert was thoughtful, but there was an excitement in the car.

"Think of the view, though. You'd do your business with a view across the whole valley!"

"Ye-es . . . dug into the hill at one end, terribly damp. We'd have to excavate it."

"God, it was damp! We'd have to have washes with the kettle in a tub. They've bricked it up but there must be the most enormous fireplace just waiting. We'd have to put a bathroom in. We could put a big bathroom in over the stable, and another bedroom."

"We'd have to put a water tank in first! Carrying those drums from the stream—you'd get pretty fit! And it needs a new roof."

"Golly. That wouldn't be cheap."

"I could get a book. It can't be that difficult."

"Wasn't Emrys sweet? What a nice man! And isn't it amazing? It hasn't been touched! It must be 1600s."

"You'd never manage these steep bits in the snow, even in a tractor."

"You'd have to leave the car at the bottom and walk, with your supplies on a dogsled."

"The fences are all falling down."

"And the sheep are wild!"

"Would we keep the sheep?"

"Oh, yes!" Jenny cried. "We'd have to have a few sheep!"

"So we'd be farmers at the weekends, would we?"

"Well, darling, I don't know. Let's come back and look at it again, when it's not raining."

❖　❖　❖

Jenny went to a lunch held by a small antiestablishment magazine. The entire establishment seemed to be present. She was seated next to an economist of high renown and low charm, a man with a bacon face who had always considered himself one of the best people. In a grand and public way, he was as sweet as possible to the girl sitting next to him, until she told him about her plans.

"Farming in Wales? What on earth do you want to do that for?"

"Oh, well! It's so beautiful and wild! And I don't want to spend the rest of my life on the Central Line, thank you very much. It just isn't me. And if I'm going to have children I don't want them to live on exhaust."

"And how are you going to make any money?"

"I'll have a few sheep, and I can carry on reviewing books."

"My dear girl, you'll never make any money out of sheep. I mean absolutely nothing. Farming's a dead duck."

"Is it? I thought there were pots of money coming from Brussels."

"Well, that's right. Without the subsidies the entire industry would collapse, certainly sheep farming, which is the lowest of the low in terms of yield; and as for hill farming in Wales, you'd be better off going down a coal mine!" He swept a popping eye around his listeners. "I mean it. In twenty years time there won't be any sheep farming left, and the hill farmers will be the first to go. I can show you the figures if you like."

"No, thank you!" Jenny cried, loud enough to turn heads. "You'll just have to come to the rescue. If it's all horrible, I hope someone will come and help me."

"We're going to see the view this time," Jenny said, to distract herself from the strain as the car wrenched itself around the cruel bend at the top of the first pitch. It was a clear August noon. London had been cool and still in anticipation of a hot day, and Wales was bright and windy. After the wood came the second pitch. Topping it, they saw the mountain for the first time, like a huge capsized sailing boat with its keel slicing the sky. The hillside was mauve and green and dark gray; great screes of stones in wild fields tumbled motionlessly down its high hull.

Jenny gasped and grabbed Robert's arm as he slowed the car, the engine noise shrinking away in the sudden vast space.

"Look at that," she breathed. "Just look at that."

The land dropped away from them, fell into woods, and leveled out far below in a patchwork valley of countless fields, ribboned with streams and hedges, scattered with stacked hay bales, barns, and here and there farms, little monarchies on the climbing slopes of the facing hills. Beyond them, rising out of the valley and into the farther bowl of the sky, were the mountains, great sweeping ridges, high crests, ice-cut shoulders and peaks, old dragons rolling across the horizon.

They found Emrys at the back of the house, scanning the mountain.

"What is it, Emrys?" Robert asked, hands on hips, chin lifted, searching the hillside.

"Fly—taking the sheep up."

"What's she doing?"

There was a disturbance in the bracken a hundred yards above them, and Jenny could see white bundles of sheep dashing suddenly through the dense fern.

"She's bringing them from there where it's steep. She'll push them along there then up over the tump, above the bracken, see."

Clouds marched along the skyline, and Jenny felt that she and Robert were foreigners—her old flares, his polished boots—up from London and proposing to buy all this, as though it could be bought, as though it could be owned.

Robert was thinking about walking up there, on an August day, pushing a few sheep ahead of him, with the whole of Wales below. He could see them there, his beautiful Jenny and him, on the mountain. He could just see them, far away but visible nonetheless.

The sale by auction was advertised in the *Express*; the Wellington Hotel, Brecon, custard yellow and pedimented, was the venue. The function room held a stout, curious crowd, elderly tweed jackets stretched across broad shoulders. Everyone wanted to know what the place would fetch, so high and far away from the road, cut off in the winter. Many had heard there were Londoners interested, and some didn't like the sound of that. Farms should go to farmers, young couples starting out. It wasn't the best land, but there were some tidy little fields up there, and plenty of water. It was a shame to think of it all being broken up and left empty most of the year. Mind, if that was how it was going to go, there were a few there who would rent the ground. And perhaps they'd sell? The speculators cawed and nodded, hands hooked in the belts of smart trousers, smiles on wind-red faces, winks and prices passed back and forth. There were a few with beer, but the notorious thrift of the hill farmers was not going to put a real smile on the Wellington manager's face. Most of these men were Chapel, as were their wives, and their money was not meant for drinking.

Everyone knew who was going to bid, and most had a fair idea of how far he would be able to go. Derwyn Norster had been born there. His parents had bought it during the war and he had grown up there. They had moved around the hill and down to the other side of the wood for better land and better access. Derwyn was Emrys's neighbor, and he and Ira had had their eye on the place ever since they married. Derwyn never really felt he had left it, living so close, with adjoining fields; as far as Ira was concerned they had a right to it. Their boys, Aled and Alwyn, knew nothing but farming. Aled was thirteen already and Alwyn was sixteen—they at least needed somewhere to live. If only they could have the farm back it would be like having the whole mountain. Derwyn had made Emrys an offer for it up by the hill gate only a couple of days after it went around that Emrys was planning to sell. Emrys had turned him down and there had been a row. Derwyn had a terrible temper. Emrys hadn't had reason to mention any of this to Robert and Jenny. When Robert asked him about the neighbors he'd merely said Derwyn wasn't such a bad old boy. It was what anyone would have said.

Robert found a place to park outside the Wellington. He had timed it to the minute, as usual, which never ceased to amaze Jenny, who had spent much of her life in desperate and doomed attempts not to be late.

"Right, then!" He grinned, collecting his pipe from the glove compartment and fitting it into the pocket of his jacket. He leaned over and gave Jenny a kiss.

She laughed. "Phew, I'm nervous."

He paused, reaching for her hand, as the rain rilled on the windscreen and the roof. "Oh, darling, you don't have to be nervous." He stroked the back of her hand slowly with his thumb.

"How far shall we go?" she said, slightly horrified at the uncertainty and the thought of money she did not have just rushing away with them, running out of them.

"I don't think we should worry about that too much. The question is, do you really want this farm?"

"Yes! Yes, I do!"

"Right, then."

He locked the car after them and took her arm. He was looking forward to it.

There were chairs set out in front of the auctioneer's table but most people were standing around the back and down the sides of the room. The auctioneer was talking to Emrys. Emrys, his wife, and their little daughter were all done up in their best and they had three seats in the very front. Little Anwyn's hair had been brushed so that it shone. Jenny smiled at everyone who looked at her. Robert kept his eyes down until he had found them somewhere to stand, in the middle, just to the right of center, then he took one very careful look around. Emrys gave him a nod and a smile. Robert smiled back.

"Ladies and gentlemen, thank you," called the auctioneer, an avuncular man with a shiny nose and tiepin, who looked at them all as though he had met each personally, not so very long ago, in slightly disreputable circumstances.

"Thank you all." He cast an eye around the room and it fell completely silent.

"Today, as you all know, we have a special sale for you, a very special sale indeed. Emrys Pryce has honored us with the commission to sell his beautiful farmhouse and seventy-two acres of prime farmland. The commission includes the barn and stable, other outbuildings, grazing rights, hill rights for over two hundred stock, and, as I said, seventy-two of the best acres you will find anywhere. The land is well drained and every field has access to one of two springs that have never been known to dry. The farm and land are of course within the protected area of the national park."

"The situation is as perfect as anything we at Russel, Baldwin, and Bright—"

"Russel, Baldwin, and Not So Bright!" Robert hissed in Jenny's ear.

"—have ever seen in many years of working in this area. The stunning views are quite unsurpassed in my experience, and I have no hesitation in describing what we are selling today as a piece of heaven on earth, a house in the eye of the sun. I know you would all hope to see a good price for this farm, the right price."

He paused. His assistant, a young man who aped his air, took the top off his fountain pen.

"And now, without further ado, I propose to get this sale under way. Please make your bids clear; I've got a pretty good view but I don't want to miss anyone!"

Emrys looked over his shoulder. Jenny thought she understood, and smiled comfortingly at him. He kept looking anxiously over his shoulder.

"So, ladies and gentlemen, for the house, the buildings, and seventy-two acres. Let's not dally around—for the house and land I'll start at five thousand pounds. Who'll give me five thousand pounds?

"Five thousand pounds on my right, five thousand I'm bid. Six thousand at the front? Six thousand, five hundred, sir."

Robert had not moved. Derwyn Norster was the man on the right, and he was looking at the backs of heads in the seating in front, for the man who was bidding against him. He nodded again.

"Seven thousand on my right, seven thousand and it's with you, sir. Do I have eight thousand?"

Robert nodded. The auctioneer was too smart to smile but there was a distinct thickening of his voice. "Eight thousand I'm bid, eight thousand to my left!" Heads turned. Robert's smooth face was almost expressionless, but his chin was tilted up, expectantly. Derwyn nodded, making a sign with his right hand. The auctioneer turned fractionally toward him. "Eight thousand, five hundred—" and Robert nodded sharply. "Nine thousand!" Robert nodded again.

"It's still with you, sir," the auctioneer told him, then looked at

Derwyn, who twitched his head. "Nine thousand, five hundred! Nine thousand, five hundred pounds. Do I see ten at the front?" Two heads, a man's, dark, and a woman's, gray, were leaning together in silent conference, then the man's head moved. "Ten!" But instantly, emphatically, Robert nodded. "Ten thousand, five hundred, and it's back with you sir, ten thousand, five hundred. Who'll give me eleven?"

The heads at the front were staring at the floor. Ira Norster was glaring about her with bulgy eyes. Derwyn made his sign, and the auctioneer, grave now, looked at Robert, announcing, "Ten seven fifty—" before he was interrupted by another eager nod. Jenny's heart was pounding. Robert seemed to be bidding faster than the auctioneer could call.

"Eleven thousand pounds! Eleven thousand pounds I'm bid, eleven thousand pounds, and it's with the gentleman on my left. Are we all finished at the front? Eleven thousand pounds?" He switched from the seated couple to Ira, who looked down. Derwyn was very red, and looking down, then at Ira.

"Are there any more bids?" the auctioneer demanded of the silent room. "Then I'm going to sell this farm. I'm going once, for eleven thousand pounds. I'm going twice, going three times, and *sold!* for eleven thousand pounds, sold to you, sir and madam."

Jenny screeched and flung her arms around Robert, and he hugged her. Emrys had one arm around his wife, who was crying over her smiles, and with the other he shook the auctioneer by the hand.

Jenny squeezed Robert's hands with all her strength. "Oh, well done, well done! So quick!"

He smiled, pushed his nose against hers. "You've got a farm on the mountain, Jenny."

Legend had it that even as the auctioneer was "going" once, Ira had been digging her husband in the ribs for another bid, and even as he had been going twice, Derwyn had decided to do it, and even as he had been going three times, Derwyn's hand had been going up—and then *sold!* to sir and madam. Legend had it that the auctioneer had wanted Jenny to have it.

And there was something else, too. Emrys had been looking over his shoulder for a reason. For Emrys had shown someone else around the farm, someone else who had fallen in love with it. She was an American lady, Emrys said, very classy, very rich. So rich she was going to buy the farm because she loved it, and visit when she could, and live on it in the summertime and at the end of her life. But the farm was sold on a Friday. On the preceding Monday, President Richard Nixon had devalued the U.S. dollar, and the American lady was never seen again.

Emrys took Robert around the land. The farm sat at the top of its own narrow valley; the fields sloped up steeply from a deep stream and rolled over into two wide arms of land that spread out, beneath the mountain, from the house. The acres fell into two rough halves. On each side their contours were similar: steep fields below the hill fence flattened into meadows, below which the ground fell sharply to the wooded stream. Each field was named. Emrys led Robert out behind the house, along a green lane to the Hill Fields. These ran for a quarter of a mile below the hill fence to a cluster of larch trees. From the larches the men worked their way down to thick woods, where there were badger setts and woodland birds, gray squirrels and fallen trees wrapped in moss thick as wool, growing fungus like great trolls' ears. Below one mighty drop, tangled in bracken and crowds of nettles, was the wreckage of a vehicle, rounded blue panels smashed into the earth.

"That's my old Austin," Emrys explained. "Ran her off the top there."

"Easier than the scrap heap?"

"Aye, and cheaper."

There was something shocking about the shattered carcass of the car, a frozen explosion gradually sinking into the wood. They crossed the stream and climbed up the other side, to the foot of steep fields. Emrys told him the names as they went. Below the Hill Fields, the Rough Field was all full of docks and burrs. Beside it, the L shape was in fact a stair shape, and dropped into Pritchard's Wood, which would be full of bluebells in the spring. Climbing up the other side, they had passed the badger setts in the Horse Fields, and the rabbit warren, and the mighty steep bank where anything that slipped would fall to its death, except foxes. Then, circling back toward the house, they had come to the Lower Meadows, where they were now, which were the steepest of all. They trudged up to the top of them, and there were the meadows, the best pasture. Of these there were three: the First Meadow, nearest to the house; the Middle Meadow; and, over toward the road where they had first seen the view, the Far Meadow. Along the top of them ran the track. Above the track, overlooking the meadows, were "the Quoikers," as Robert heard it, big sloping fields, southwest-facing, like the house, and wide open to the view. The Quoikers climbed up to the hill fence. The Far Quoiker had been divided across the middle into two; it had a line of oaks, alders, and ash trees halfway up. The top half of it and the Near Quoiker were prone to gorse. Emrys had plowed it a couple of years before but the bushes had come back. (Robert checked and found the sound came from two words, *coed caer*—"wood field.") Last, they came to the Patch, which was the nearest to the house, just below the yard, beyond the pens: it was flattish on the top, where the land rolled over to the track, and then it plunged down to the stream. Emrys kept a few old things in the Patch, and the old horse, and there was a bright green sludgy bit in the middle where the runoff from the yard accumulated.

When they got back, Robert went to Jenny and put his arm around her. "You have absolutely no idea what a wonderful farm you've bought."

Emrys understood but did not share their enthusiasm for the land; to a farmer it was "banky": too steep and too thin-soiled. After the walk he said, "Come with me, Robert," and they went off into the Big Barn, where Emrys had his cider.

As it got dark they stood underneath one bulb, which hung from a beam. The upper half of the barn was full of bales, the lower half was empty, the floor a bed of hay. In the middle was a race: great stone flags on their ends, staked and framed with posts to make a corridor four feet high across the width of the barn, where you could pack sheep in tight, or back a cow up, or make a pen for new lambs with a couple of bales. Emrys had the cider in glass bell jars; it was roan red and fizzy. With few words and many smiles he refilled their glasses.

They had a couple and then a couple more. By the time they emerged their cheeks were flaming and they had to drop their shoulders to change course. Robert went down to the bottom of the yard and pissed a steaming arc, as one car, like a firefly, spun along the road far below.

Emrys sold them more than a hundred sheep. It was always done, he explained. When a farm changed hands some of the sheep would stay behind. You needed a flock that knew the ground, that knew what was what, he informed them. Two thirds of their number were the Welsh Mountain breed; small, hardy, protected from the weather by their thick white fleeces, which would be shorn in the summer and sold. The remaining third were Suffolk crosses; larger, black-faced animals with thinner coats. They would deliver bigger, more profitable lambs, but they were more likely to die in bad weather. Scattered among the flock were a few Badger sheep, beautiful creatures that appeared to be wearing black makeup around their eyes and mouths; a few Radnors, which were russet-faced, and a few Speckles, their white faces flecked with gray. "Welsh, Suffolks, Badgers, Radnors, and Speckles," Robert repeated. Straightforward enough.

"That's right." Emrys smiled. "And you've got thirty yearling theaves, and you'll want to buy another tup when Tommy gets too old."

"Thirty what?"

Emrys was amazed and amused, but he was tactful about it. Ram lambs were tups, ewe lambs were theaves. A one-year-old was a yearling, and most yearlings would be theaves, as the tup lambs went to market in their first nine months, if possible before the winter, so they would not have to be fed. Yearlings were sold as "store" in their second autumn, to larger farms looking to replenish their stock.

"So what's a wether?"

"Castrated yearling tup that didn't go to market or didn't sell. That's a wether."

"I see!"

❖   ❖   ❖

Emrys was in no hurry to move out. His wife, Thursa, wasn't well. She had "farmer's lung," silicosis caused by the dead brown dust of old hay. The farm Emrys had bought up the valley was not as comfortable as it should be for a baby and mother: Emrys wondered if they could stay at the farm while he got the new place ready. He would keep an eye on it, and the sheep, for them until they were ready to move up from London.

2

First Lambing

Several of Jenny's boyfriends had tried to marry her. She ducked them, postponed them, pleaded uncertainty, and waited for a surge of conviction that never came. Now Robert stood in their place. Robert, with one divorce behind him, the mixed-up child of his own parents' disastrous marriage. Robert, who wanted security and believed that it was found in marriage. Who wanted to fit into Britain, to be connected to it. Who was charmed by this intelligent, complicated woman, and who charmed her in return. Who saw her indecision, her uncertainty, and felt it feed his determination. The weaker her conviction, the stronger his. One day he said, "Right, then, let's get married!" and went across the valley and up over the top to Ebbw Vale to fix it with the registry office.

Jenny wanted a service of blessing in the village church after the civil ceremony. The school for missionaries' daughters had failed to quell her rebelliousness in the face of authority but it had given her a strong sense of the sacred. She needed to bow before authority now, she had vows to make: to do Right and eschew Wrong. But authority would not have it. The rector of the church refused. Jenny fretted.

"I'm not going to feel married, Ursie!" she wailed to her sister, and telephoned the bishop.

"But the man you are going to marry has been divorced," the bishop intoned. "You cannot marry in church."

"But I just want a service of blessing," Jenny pleaded. "Lots of people have them: divorcées—"

"In England," the bishop emphasized. "But this is the Church in Wales."

But Jenny did not give up until at last the bishop relented and instructed the vicar to bless the marriage.

Before the wedding they stayed with Ursula and Geoff. Geoff had definite ideas about how these things were done. The night before the wedding he invited Robert to his local pub. He marched Robert up the hill, installed him at the bar, and confronted him with as much alcohol as Robert had ever faced.

The morning of the wedding found Robert pallid and Jenny shaky with nerves. Geoff drove Robert; Ursula drove her sister. As the little Morris Minor hummed the miles away Jenny could not settle in her seat; she shuffled around, fiddled with her seatbelt, wound the window down, smoked half a cigarette and threw the rest away, shaking her head.

"Are you OK, Jenny?"

Jenny gasped and clutched her stomach, as if gripped by pain. "Oh, Ursie! I don't think I want to get married! I don't know if I want to go through with it. I'm not sure about it at all! Perhaps we'd better stop."

Ursie looked at her sister. "Do you really want me to stop?"

"I don't know!" Jenny cried. "I just don't know. It's too late to change my mind, isn't it?"

"Well, it is pretty late, but it's up to you, luvvie."

"Oh, Lord! I'd better go through with it, hadn't I?"

"Yes, if you love him."

"I do love him."

"Well, then. It's just nerves. You'll be fine. He's a lovely man."

"Yes, he is. He is. OK, better now. Phew!"

"Hang on, dear girl. Nearly there."

They married at the registry office, and from there proceeded to the village church. Now it was the rector's turn to suffer an attack of nerves. Seeing the large crowd of friends Jenny had invited, he pulled her aside and said he could not go ahead with so many "members of the public" in attendance.

"What?" she cried. "But you promised! The bishop—"

"Direct family only," said the rector. "I will perform the service for you and your direct families only." Trying not to feel furious, resentful, and ashamed, Jenny explained the situation and asked the crowd to wait for them.

The window behind the altar was divided into diamonds of clear glass. Behind the fish-eyed rector, Jenny watched the deep green motion of yew trees against the shining sky. Kneeling beside his bride, it struck Robert that it was the second time he had been on his knees that day, having spent a good half hour vomiting into Geoff and Ursie's lavatory.

After the service came the celebration. The editor, the boys from the Diary, Max, friends from the BBC, the newspapers, theater, politics, and the Foreign Office had all made the trek. They bumped along the track fearing the worst for their cars. Jenny sat them all on hay bales, dwarfed by the mountain and dazzled by the view, and the party was a success. People walked and drank and gossiped and disappeared up the mountain and reappeared in the yard. It was a lovely time.

And that is important, because beyond the doubtful bishop and the flaky rector and the equivocating omens of Jenny's nerves and Robert's hangover, it was as if the farm and their friends blessed them unreservedly. Robert always noticed bad signs—his eye picked them out for him—but he refused to entertain superstition. Jenny always noticed good omens and kept a hopeful lookout for the world unseen.

She wished on new moons and evening stars; she kept horseshoes on their sides, in case it was true that they would be used as boats by witches if placed upright, or that the luck would run out of them if left with their mouths tilted down.

They awoke the next morning to a beautiful day and the sound of hooves on a hard surface.

"What's that?" Jenny poked her head out from under the covers.

"The pitter-patter of tiny feet?" Robert exclaimed. "That was quick!"

He jumped out of bed and went to the window. "Darling, there are sheep all over the roof of the shed. How have they managed that?"

She joined him at the window. "What are you doing there?" she cried.

They were yearlings, last season's lambs, grown big enough to follow their curiosity and their love of ash leaves over fences and up the little jump at the back of the shed where the roof met the bank behind. They slid and bleated.

"Hang on, we're coming!" Jenny trilled back. That was the end of the honeymoon.

Their neighbors were short-spoken, would nod uneasy greetings as they passed in the lanes. Derwyn Norster was shy of them and shouted nervously when they met. There were no hard feelings about the sale, he said. Sitting in the tractor cab behind him, Ira stared at Robert with popping eyes. Near the far gate, at the end of the track, stood an empty cottage belonging to someone who never came. Derwyn owned the land and the outbuildings, and made use of the pens and the barns. The yard was a holding and sorting area. Every time they came and went, Robert and Jenny were faced with a squalid parody of farming, the kind that takes place out of sight of the world. Horses with protruding ribs, chained dogs cringing in the muddy corners of sheds, gaunt sheep with hunched backs. When winter came, everything belled its hunger.

"Would you look at those poor benighted sheep!" Jenny exclaimed.

"Look! It's absolutely scandalous, they're so thin! What's he trying to do, starve them to death?"

Robert winced and went quiet. There was nothing they could do about the infuriating, depressing scenes.

Emrys became ever more taken up with his new farm, while Robert and Jenny still worked the weeks in London and sometimes could not come for a fortnight at a time. One or the other would appear, on the weekends. Emrys could see they needed a hand, so he introduced them to Jack Meredith.

The ways of the premodern world were embroidered into the lives of Jack and his brother Alfie. They had been born up the valley in one of two houses by the forge: they were never sure which, having lived in both. Alf was as old as the century, Jack a few years younger, and they had had seven more siblings. As children they had walked three miles to school, where they wrote on slates and had any tendency to speak Welsh beaten out of them. Their oldest brother went to France in the Great War, to work with the horses, hauling shells and stretchers. The family had been poor and sometimes hungry in a land that crawled with game, but their mother would tolerate nothing but exemplary behavior: when Jack found a nest of duck eggs and brought them triumphantly home she scolded him. The duck was not nesting on their land so those were not their eggs—Jack must take them back.

He noticed all the animals' doings. One warm day when he was young Jack successfully tickled a trout. It was basking in ice-bright water below the stone on which he lay. Stretched out, his body flush with the rock, Jack inched his arms into the stream and approached the fish with hands of loving, deathly slowness. As if lulling the creature into a common dream with him, he stroked its belly with the tip of a finger, slowly, slowly drifting more fingers under it, as it hovered, hypnotized. Then with an abrupt convulsion he jerked the animal up and out and into the air in an arc of spray, landing it on the bank. When I was told about this it seemed only a short step from sorcery, a miracle of a kind impossible to imagine now, something of a vanished time.

As young men Jack and Alf had signed on as laborers on the construction of a reservoir on the other side of the mountain. Leaving every morning in the dark, they plunged up through the bracken, over the ridge, across the moor, and down the other side. After a day building the dam they climbed back up over the top and down, walking nearly ten miles, chunks of it straight uphill.

One of Jack's favorite sayings was "Save a match and buy a farm," and he and Alf had done so: they bought a place higher up the valley and farmed it for decades, until, too old at last, they sold up to Emrys and retired. Now they lived in a cottage in the village. They had a round-shouldered yellow fridge, a kettle with a Bakelite handle, enameled tin mugs, and on the floor, beady mats woven from bright patterned plastic. They spoke little and watched television a lot, as if traveling, in their retirement, the world they had not seen.

They had pipes in their pockets and walking sticks with clefts for their thumbs: if they were at home the sticks leaned against the wall by their front door. They shaved with cutthroats every morning, and once a week took the bus to collect their pensions. On Friday nights they put on their smart clothes, polished their shoes, brushed their white hair, and went to the Farmer's Arms. The landlady, Millicent, was a fiercely partisan woman who often refused to serve strangers, according to an obscure system of whims. She adored the brothers; their chairs were the nearest to the fire. They were, as everyone said, proper gentlemen.

Jack had a diffident certainty about him; he was not a sage so much as a true witness, one who had seen and understood the century through its gradual encroachment into the valley; who had watched the coming of the tractors and the end of the horses; who had seen nitrogen fertilizers and pesticides turn the grass of certain valley fields an unnatural blue-green and empty their hedges of wildlife. He believed that people who were "too fond of the world," by which he meant farmers who overstocked their fields in pursuit of profit, came to a bad end.

To reach our farm Jack walked over the bridge, up past the campsite, and on up the lane to the bottom of Pritchard's Wood. Skirting along the edge of the trees, noting any fresh excavations around the badger setts (Jenny always asked for the latest news there), he then traversed the steep Lower Meadows before climbing up into the First Meadow and appearing in the yard. It would be a day's labor for most septuagenarians but it was nothing to Jack.

He was shy around Jenny at first, a bashfulness she assaulted with barrages of questions. "Come on, Jack!" she cried. "What's the gossip? Oh, go on, do tell!" Little by little it came out. This family hates that one, has done ever since they shared a boundary fence. So-and-so had it away with his sister under a bush—but her husband thinks the child's his. That man's a thief, always has been (or was once; it came to the same thing). This one is a tidy farmer—this was the highest praise. The area's traditions were not much changed since a day toward the end of the twelfth century when the traveling scholar and clergyman Giraldus Cambrensis, Gerald of Wales, arrived at the top of the valley and asked what was to be found farther down. He records his discovery thus:

"The natives of these parts, actuated by continual enmities and implacable hatred, are perpetually engaged in bloody contests. But we leave to others to describe the great and enormous excess which in our time have been here committed, with regard to marriages, divorces and many other circumstances of cruelty and oppression."

Jack and Robert found a quiet friendship that pleased them both. Jack showed Robert how to put in a fencepost. First the crowbar, four and a half feet of solid iron ending in a dumb point. It would sink into the turf by itself. You found a place where there were no rocks, drove the bar in, and stirred it, drilling a cone in the red earth. You did it again and again until most of the bar was buried and you could hardly stir it more. Then the post went in. You gave it a couple of taps with the sledgehammer and then stepped back, hefted the sledge, and swung it around and over in a great arc, smacking the post a mighty blow and driving it deep into the soil. Jack did it in four, if the ground was good. Then it was Robert's turn. He managed the crowbar, got the hole pretty much straight. The sledge was amazingly heavy, but he was strong and delivered a good blow. Jack stood impassively. The second shot wasn't quite so handy; Robert's shoulders and forearms ached and the post hardly moved. By the third his muscles were screaming and the hammerhead glanced its target; a crack appeared in the top of the post. The next splashed white chips out of it, leaving a long splinter of wood dangling by the bark. Jack shifted unhappily.

"Want to try not to split the post. Rain'll get in and rot it, otherwise."

"Right," said Robert, breathing hard. "I see." He looked at Jack. "Tricky."

"Aye," said Jack.

Now Jenny had her farm on the mountain the journeys to and fro were quite different. The opening of the M4 reduced the journey from Hammersmith to the farm to 163 miles, a figure that burned itself into my father's memory. (In the early years Jenny could not drive. She made the trip as his passenger, or as British Rail's.) On return journeys, when they reached the outskirts of London, she thrilled at the glitter and glower of the city, its rumbling complexity, its talk, turn, and change. On the way out, Newport, hull down, crooked low under the dark hunch of Wales, marked the beginning of something much older than men and their works; another kind of time survived there, primitive and silent, amid the humped shapes of the hills. When she went up by herself she took the train as far as Abergavenny and looked for Len Cole, her taxi driver, who did not mind going all that way into the mountains, then up the pitches, through the wood and along the track, to see her safe inside. On moonless nights the dark was sepulchral, and the house freezing.

"Thank you, dear Len, you've saved me again. Would you like something to drink?"

"Oh no, thank you, my dear. You'll be all right now?"

"Yes, yes, I'll be fine. Crumbs, it's cold! We really must get a stove or something."

Exploring the house in the months after the sale, she found rags, nests of hay, and scraps of newspaper wedged between boards in the ceilings and floors; tatty brown clumps stuffed over the lintels and lin-

ing the cracks. She went around with many grimaces, pulling them
out, unplugging, scrubbing, and scouring. "Euch! God, how disgusting! Incredible."

It was only after days of this cleaning, on a windy night, when
drafts emerged everywhere, torrents of small cold devils, that she realized she had undone generations of careful lagging, that everything
had its purpose, and that dirt was better than chill. As the wind grew
the house began to sing, whining and moaning at the corners. Things
sounded and shifted and she felt scared and safe at the same time,
remembering the great thick walls. The stand of larches and firs
behind the house rushed and gasped. She slept uneasily.

When Robert's car bumped up the track she was relieved and
pleased; as soon as he was ready she took him on a tour of her latest
discoveries. In the firs behind the house there were goldcrests: fearless,
tiny green birds with streaks like gold flames on their heads; they
made a minute piping sound. In the little gullies where the mountain
folded into the fields there were woodcock; long-beaked, shy, and
exquisitely camouflaged in black and bracken plumage, they jumped
up when you were almost upon them and fled on skirling wings.

Arm in arm they walked along a green lane—*their* green lane, they
reminded each other—where hazel and blackthorn met overhead and
the thinned autumn foliage clicked and shifted with the business of
birds. Robert pieced together half-remembered songs and hummed
them to her, and Jenny felt like running and jumping and kicking her
legs in the air, and would have done, had she not been wary of scaring
the sheep. The flock looked at them, bleated, and made off, streaming
through gateways and broken fences in panicky haste.

They went as far as the larch wood, a tousled clump on the skyline
marking the extent of their land. They hushed as they walked across
its silent floor of dead needles; trunks like slim silver pillars rose into
a dense canopy, thickened here and there by shaggy, chaotic nests big
enough to hold a man.

They were watched, then suddenly ambushed.

"Ravens! They're ravens!" Robert exclaimed as huge birds crashed
out of the treetops and flung off into the wind, croaking curses.

Back at the house he unpacked a box of food, wine, and books.
English-Welsh Welsh-English Dictionary, The South Wales Landscape, and

one other, a special present for Jenny. A huge book, tall and thick but narrow, decorated on the cover with a rich painting of a tawny owl: *The AA Guide to the Birds of Britain*. She was delighted.

That night, curled up in bed, Robert read to her. They started a new book, a collector's edition with a preface by the author, Graham Greene.

"Are you lying comfortably?"

"Yes, Robert."

"Good. So: *The Heart of the Matter*. Part one. . . ."

They arranged to take their holidays in March to coincide with the lambing, but the lambs came before their leave. Robert arrived a week before Jenny and threw himself at the work of feeding and preparing for lambing. He walked the flock, staring at the ewes. When the first few began to birth he consulted Emrys and Jack. When the lambs came thick and fast, he knew, it would be a fight against a tide of unknown foes. His approach to the unknown is unvarying: identify the problem, talk to anyone who can tell you anything, buy the book, understand the principles, practice and perfect the trick. By this method he taught himself everything from playing the flute to long-distance swimming to winning at chess. Decades later books such as *Sheep Farming for Profit* and *Quantitative Genetics in Sheep Breeding* stand dust-covered on my mother's shelves, unopened since the day my father finished them. They appear to be monuments to two different ways of living: hers founded on passion, instinct, and experiment; his on logic, realism, and method. They approached their first lambing, and their adventure, with contrasting styles but equal determination.

Jenny came to join the struggle, enthusiasm and excitement crackling out of her. They set off to look at the animals, sliding on the yellow-green grass, squelching through the red mud at the gateways.

The flock was strung out across the unfenced Hill Fields, sheltering under thorn trees. The new lambs were scraps of uncertainty in wet white coats, unsteady on long legs.

"The ewes are very big," Jenny observed as the animals set off, lumbering hurriedly, bleating over their shoulders. The new mothers circled their children anxiously, unable to abandon them. After a thorough search of the fields Robert and Jenny concluded that things seemed quiet for now and returned to the house.

"Well, that was a bit dismal. What shall we do now? If only we had a fire," Jenny chattered, wrestling her boots off. In the corners of the room, beyond the reach of dim lightbulbs, the damp gathered like unseen cobwebs.

"We could unblock the fireplace," she said suddenly. "How about that?"

"Sure. . . . Sure?"

"Well, I don't see why not."

"OK, then. I'll equip myself with an implement." Robert jerked the front door open (it stuck on the flags whenever it rained), strode out, and returned after a couple of minutes with the sledgehammer, the crowbar, and a small claw hammer. He laid them down with a clatter and stood with his hands on his hips, sizing up the white plaster.

"Right, then. Stand back!" He hoisted up the sledgehammer.

"Hold on, darling! I think take the plaster off first."

"Oh. I was just going to wallop it."

"Yes, sweetheart, I know. Just take the plaster off and then wallop it. We don't want to do any structural damage, if we can help it."

Chuckling, Robert swapped hammers and attacked the surface. Plaster came away in flat white cakes; damp slabs fell revealing dirty bricks. He worked upward swiftly, as high as his midriff, then up to his chest, and still there was no sign of anything but brick.

"It must be huge," he said, ripping and scraping, spattered with lime flakes and dust.

He reached shoulder height and suddenly there was wood, a horizontal line of wood, scored black where the hammer had scratched off the covering plaster.

"Bingo! There it is."

"Wow! It really is huge. Pray no one's cut the beam or anything awful."

Robert worked his way left for over a yard before the brick ran out, and then there was a thick smear of cement. He went back the other way for another yard.

"Have you ever seen anything like it? And the beam's fine, isn't it? Do you think they've filled in the whole space? Oh, I hope they haven't blocked up the chimney!"

"We'll find out." Robert tapped the brickwork. The hammer rapped flatly.

"Can't really tell. It feels as though it might be hollow, though."

He passed Jenny the hammer, and she tapped a line across the middle, her head tilted to one side.

"Yes, oh, yes. Are you going to wallop it, then?"

"Unless you think it'll bring the roof down."

"Go on, then. Just please be careful, darling." She stood back as Robert measured a practice swing.

The hammer went back, paused, and flipped forward. There was a crash. Plaster cracked, jumped, and crumbled. The hammer struck once, twice, and on the third blow a chunk of brickwork disappeared, leaving a black space. He swung repeatedly without pause, aiming at the edges of the widening hole. The wall crumbled away. They could see a curving stone buttress, a shelf, and in the wall, an iron door.

"It's a bread oven!" Jenny cried. "And what a great beam! Why would they cover all this?" When he had battered out the last bricks they were able to survey the whole hearth. It started six inches above the floor, with stone flags four feet deep. It was over two yards wide, high and huge, changing the aspect of the entire room. Robert peered up into the chimney, drew back, and smashed the hammer up, dislodging fragments of wet chipboard. He pulled it all out, wincing as soot and twigs tumbled down, and looked again. It was dark and there was no light at the top.

"There's a real draft. It can't be blocked. I reckon they've just stuck a tile or something over the top." He was filthy and sweating, and smiling.

"There you are, missus. A fireplace. The biggest in Wales."

"Whoopee!"

They carted all the rubble out the back, along with the remains of Emrys's small grate, then they got out the tin bath and boiled the kettle a dozen times. Jenny watched Robert wash. She loved the shapes of the muscles in his back.

"Do you think we should have had another look around them?"

Jenny asked as they made their way up the stone stairs and ducked through the low door into the bedroom.

"Oh, I don't know. They looked quiet. Fingers crossed."

The crows struck in the dawn, as Robert and Jenny were waking. By the time they had made their way out to the soft fields, ranging from hedge to hedge, checking, anxious in the quiet, the birds had taken their prizes and departed on black wings. Robert saw it first: a young ewe on her side in a patch of mud by a fence. He started to run. She had begun to give birth late in the night, perhaps as they were going up to bed. Now she was exhausted, unable to stand. She had kicked as she struggled, on her side, scoring the mud in arcs under each hoof. She looked at them and panted, covered in mud, and around her tail, blood. Jenny moved the tail aside. Hanging out of the ewe was her lamb's head and one foreleg. Blood covered the small face. Jenny realized that one of the eyes was missing. She took the leg and pulled; the small damp limb slipped out of her grasp. They changed places, Jenny talking to the ewe softly as Robert tried to free the lamb. He slipped, swore, and heaved. The ewe groaned; Jenny cried out in sympathy.

"OK, got it. It's out."

"Is it alive?"

"I don't think so."

They passed the little body up to the ewe and she nuzzled it, raising herself a little now. Jenny cleared out the mouth, found more blood.

"Christ, I think the tongue's gone. I think they've taken the tongue."

"It's dead, isn't it?"

"Yes, I'm afraid it is."

They stood and moved away from the ewe. She licked the corpse, nudging it. When it did not respond she bleated.

"What a bloody, bloody thing. It must have died of shock, do you think?" Jenny wiped her hands on the grass.

"Maybe, yes." Robert looked at his feet.

They went around the rest. A pair of twins had been born in the night. They were licked clean white and circled adoringly by their mother as they trembled and peered about. Their umbilical cords were short bright strings. Jenny and Robert watched them for a while.

"We'll deal with the dead one after feeding, shall we?"

"Yes, I'll bury it. We ought to find out about this business. We could have saved it if we'd been up."

She nodded. "Yes."

"So we'll have to go round them more often."

"Yes. We can take turns."

"We should talk to Emrys as soon as possible." Robert's voice was quiet with anger at their ignorance. "We need to know how you tell when they're going to do it, how you tell when they're doing it, what you do, what goes wrong. We're in the dark."

"Yes, OK, quite right. We'll go down to the valley and call Angela as soon as we've done the feeding. She's got hundreds of sheep." Angela ran a huge Herefordshire farm: she was one of the few friends from Jenny's previous life who could help her in this one.

"And we'll call the phone people and get them to put a line in."

They trudged back to the house, feeling their knees muddy and wet. A spatter of rain came over the hill and three crows rasped coarsely at the hurrying couple.

"And we'll have to do something about those buggers," Robert said.

The telephone box was on the main road, opposite the garage. Angela's voice was loud and firm down the line.

"Don't panic, Jen, it's just like people. They look broody. Sometimes they split off from the rest and find a place they like. Not always, though. First the water goes, and that's what you look for. The tail will be all wet and there's a bit of blood and stuff. Then you see them nesting. They turn round and round in the same place and they sit heavily and you can see they're trying to get comfortable. Then they start pushing. It takes a few hours, from beginning to end. Just like people."

"Right. Then what?"

"Well, if he hasn't fed them too much."

"I shouldn't think he has, frankly."

"Good. And if they've done it before the lamb should just slip out."

"And what if it doesn't?"

"Well, you want them coming nose first, with the front feet under the chin. They should look like they're diving. If they're having difficulty, getting tired, you can just give them a pull. But what you had this morning was a head."

"Yes . . . and one leg."

"Yes, a head is no good, you really want to watch for them. The shoulders are too wide to get out when the legs are back, so the head just hangs there and the ewe gets exhausted. When you get one don't panic, just push it back in, find the front legs, pull them under the chin, and try again."

"Crumbs."

"You'll get the hang of it. The trick is to spot them quickly because in the cold the head will swell up and then it's an absolute bugger."

"Right."

"And keep an eye out for twins, especially with first lambers. They can get into trouble with the second one. And make sure you get anything really weak into the shed and out of the weather. And you should get some penicillin and some syringes. And spray, purple Terramycin spray from the vet. Give the umbilical a squirt of that, stops infections."

"Oh, Lord, luvvie. This is all absolutely terrifying."

"Give me a ring soon. I've got to dash; we're having triplets all over the place."

"Oh, dear Angela, thank you. Go quickly! I'll ring you soon and say for God's sake help! what do I do with this!"

"Yes, do. Bye now, Jen."

"Bye, bye."

She went back to the car and studied the notes she had made while Robert went into the box and called the phone people. Filthy Land Rovers rattled slowly by, heads inside turning to look at her.

Spurred by the disaster, they patrolled almost ceaselessly.

"It's a great mistake having them all over the Hill Fields," Jenny panted. "Much too much walking!"

It was true, Robert agreed. They were working over thirty acres of sloping ground, quartered by thorn trees, banks, and woods. Ruined or incomplete fences left much of it open; haphazard lines of wire enclosed only patches. The land faced the north wind, which came straight across the gully from the far gate, hypothermia whistling in its teeth. When the sheep sought shelter they would hide behind the mounds of collapsed stone walling, under the thickest thorns, in the sunken heart of a copse: all had to be searched and searched again.

So they walked and watched from first light until after midnight. Sometimes, on dry nights, they would see another torch moving on the other side of the valley, someone else doing the rounds. Births could happen at any time. Ewes would look broody for hours, for days, and do nothing but charge for the hay that Robert and Jenny hauled each morning. Or it could all be over in half an hour: the small, wet baby would appear between patrols; they would shake their heads at each other and admit they had not noticed anything different about the mother, before or since the birth. Feeding was brutal work—without a Land Rover or tractor they wobbled overloaded wheelbarrows down muddy slopes, shoulders aching and the barrow pulling to get away.

In between feeding and lambing, there was hauling and chopping firewood, collecting and carrying water (in ten-gallon drums that threatened to pull arms out of their sockets), patrolling and repairing fences: it was exhausting. One night, having recuperated a little in front of the fire, Jenny found her legs so stiff she could not get up. Laughing weakly, she cried to Robert to come and help her. Sprawled in the other chair, he groaned, "Can't! Can't get up! Too tired . . . too weak . . . better leave me here with Jack's gun. I'll be all right." They got the giggles.

They agreed on a division of labor: Jenny would do most of the late rounds, as she did not mind staying up and loved her bed in the mornings. Robert, whose days naturally began at daybreak, would do the earlies.

Setting out into a March night with just the torch for company was a nervy business. Sometimes, depending on the currents of Jenny's imagination, it was terrifying. There were certain places she never liked much, eerie patches that she hurried past, her senses prickling. The patch of yard behind the Big Barn was the worst, a dark lump of shadow beyond the reach of the light. At the beginning and end of each round she had to pass this place, where the ground rose steeply through knotted darkness up to the mass of the fir trees that guarded the house from the north wind; they looked tall and wild as she hurried by.

She would try to go quietly down the track, but you cannot be silent in an anorak and Wellingtons; every movement sounds loud. Once out in the fields you cannot see anything without giving away your position: you are either blind or completely exposed. With a flick of your thumb the beam from the lambing torch leaps forty yards and picks up the reflections of pairs of eyes well beyond that. You turn, very slowly searching out and studying every sheep within range, fighting the urge to whirl and cover your back.

As the nights passed she learned to trust the sheep: if they were calm there was nothing to worry about. Only when she heard them calling, or found them jumpy or bunched together, on their feet and alarmed, would she admit fear.

There were absurd, darkly funny moments. Emrys told them about one foul morning, when, stumping out into the wind and rain, the first thing he found was a dead lamb, newborn and apparently perfect but dead, lifeless in the muddy bloody grass. He slapped it and pummeled it to no effect, and in a burst of temper hurled the little body into a tree. He came back an hour later, still angry. "And the bugger was bleating!"

There were calm periods, when the weather would smile and the patrols would yield nothing more than easy singles to attentive mothers, then with a shift of the wind the temperature would fall, ewes would inexplicably abandon their lambs, and everything would veer toward disaster. Any night in the lambing fields could turn into a battle.

One lamb came quietly on a drizzly late March afternoon. Later, when the sky had lowered and the light was quite gone, they found a ewe in trouble. She lay on her side, pushing, but she jumped up when they came close. After watching her lie down again and struggle, stagger up, lie down and struggle, they decided to catch her. They slipped and slid; three times she evaded them until finally they cornered her down by the stream and Robert's lunging dive took him within reach of her back leg. He held her while Jenny investigated. Robert moved around the ewe, angling the torch toward her tail.

"What have we got?"

"Only one leg. The other must be back . . . Steady!" The ewe struggled. Jenny lowered her voice, forcing herself to sound calmer. "Steady on, silly old thing, we're not going to hurt you . . . there, there . . . what's this? A foot, yes, I've got a right foot . . . but no left."

Jenny heaved, pushing the lamb back, then worked her hand inside the hot, contracting channel until she found the left foreleg. She pulled it forward, worked it gently, teasing and pulling carefully, fearful of damage, until it was aligned with the right leg. Now she worked at both together. The ewe groaned, her flanks flinching with contractions, and Jenny pulled and pulled and at last drew the lamb out into the cold night. She cleared yellow amniotic slime from its mouth and suddenly the lamb coughed and shook its head; the miraculous, unbelievable ignition of life.

"Wonderful!" Robert smiled and wiped the rain off his face.

"Hold her," Jenny panted, pushing her hand in again. "Yes, there's another one—it's twins."

"It'll be a while, won't it?"

"Yes. We'll let her get on with this one, shall we?"

They withdrew, leaving the ewe muttering over her lamb, licking it greedily.

"What's that over there? Oh, Lord, don't tell me."

Barely twenty yards away in the rain-sparked beam of the torch lay a black-faced Suffolk ewe, on her side and struggling. She would also have to be caught. Again they separated, circling in quietly from either side, and again the ewe fled; up the fence, down the fence, until they cornered her in the same place they had caught the first, where she and her lamb still were. The Suffolk made a final, hopeless charge. She blundered past the new mother, grunting and plunging in panic. The new lamb was barged mewling into the stream before Robert's hands came down on the runaway's back, his fingers clawing for a grip in her thin wet wool.

"Christ!" Jenny cried, and Robert half-laughed; a mirthless, tension-breaking sound, as Jenny rescued the lamb from the freezing water.

"Welcome to Wales," Robert said as Jenny rubbed it and pushed it toward its mother, then came back to kneel beside the second capture.

"Oh shit, Rob, darling."

"What is it?" He was incredulous that the fuss was justified, and a certain tone came into his voice, an edge of annoyance.

"A back leg. One back leg!"

She pushed it back in, groped for the other, and slowly began to work amid the hot, tight inches until she had its other leg. She pulled and rested, pulled and rested, encouraged the ewe and pulled again. She grunted with effort as she gripped the soft wet stubs of the lamb's feet and heaved: the lamb, its amniotic fluid, and its placenta emerged in a wallop of heat and liquid: reds, golds, and slimy whites bright under the torchlight. This time there was no cough, no bleat, no shudder of life.

"Nothing much happening," Jenny gasped. "Come on, lamb." She cleared its mouth with her finger.

"Give it a shake."

Jenny picked the body up and swung it from side to side. It was breathing, she thought, but very weakly. Robert jiggled it, rubbed it. "Oh, please, come on, lamb!" Jenny implored it. "Live!"

They backed away, leaving it to its mother, standing and watching as fingers of rain found ways into their collars. The ewe licked the little body eagerly but it did not respond, so Jenny went down again and worked on the lamb, rubbing it and talking to it until at last there was movement in the skinny frame. "It's going to live!" she announced, delighted, as the mother ran off, bleating despairingly.

Robert went after the ewe, driving her back toward her lamb, but she was now so flustered that she did not pause and went trotting on into the next field. He pursued her at a run across the sloping ground, his Wellingtons heavy and his balance precarious. He overtook her and turned her, dropping back as she approached the lamb so that the ewe slowed too, but again, calling desperately, she overshot it, ignoring the little white heap in the torchlight. He cursed. Twice more he turned her back, twice more she overshot.

Finally, after almost an hour, Robert caught her and carried, pulled, and dragged her out of the fields, up the track, across the yard, and into the barn. They penned her in the race with hay bales and presented her with her lamb. It was warm in the barn, out of the wind. They watched, speechless, as the lamb tottered around under the mother's tail. She encouraged it, nuzzled it, and its head tipped back, its back dipped, and its tail shivered. Jenny and Robert grinned tiredly at each other. It was suckling. That moment, a lamb's first drink, was already a benchmark. If it drinks it has a chance, they had learned. Suddenly they were aware of their wet clothes, runny noses, heavy limbs.

"Very good," Robert said. "Forty-eight from thirty-four!"

"It's not standing very well, though. I hope I didn't dislocate its poor legs when I swung it round like that—quite stupid!"

"It'll be fine. We ought to go and see about the twin."

They trudged back to the field, keeping the torch off until they were near the corner by the stream. Then Robert flicked it on, and there was the ewe, with her first lamb standing and now bleating, and there on the ground was the second twin: tiny, unlicked, abandoned.

"Forty-nine from thirty-four," Robert said levelly, "if it lives."

They caught the first lamb, which alarmed the ewe, and placed it near the second, which was alive but flopping helplessly in the mud. But the mother was concerned only with her elder child; she kept leading it away from the humans.

The humans shook their heads. "I know," Jenny chimed, "I'll hobble it."

She caught it again, loosely tied its front legs, and placed it beside its twin. It fell over. It bleated. The ewe bleated back and nuzzled it, steadfastly ignoring the feebly struggling sibling. Robert looked skeptical. "Trampled, soaked, and incapacitated, and barely been alive an hour!"

Jenny gave a frayed giggle. "Oh, well! We'll have to get them into the barn, then!"

"You heard the lady," Robert muttered to the sheep.

Jenny carried both lambs, one under each arm. She paused every few paces, using the torch to show the mother that she had them, while Robert steered the ewe, which followed her babies, calling lustily. In the barn they built a second pen and confiscated the favorite, leaving the mother with her unwanted second twin. The ewe eyed it. Bleated. The lamb bleated back. She nuzzled it.

"I'll stay, sweetheart, you go to bed."

"Sure?"

"Yes, yes—you've got to get up in a minute!"

It was after two. Jenny woke him at five, on her way to bed, to say she had called the vet about a prolapsed uterus, a thing like a pink balloon of flesh hanging underneath one of a hundred near-identical dirty white tails.

"It's the phantom!" Robert mumbled, his eyes tightly shut.

"What phantom?"

"I saw it too. A prolapsed uterus. Wasn't there when we went to look for it."

"Well, I saw it, and the vet's coming."

The vet did come but there was no sign of the phantom uterus.

Gwyn Dinas was a tall young man who farmed cattle and hundreds of sheep at the head of the valley. He had a young wife and a small son, and needed more ground than he owned. Jenny and Robert agreed to rent him a field; some of his sheep appeared one morning in the Far Quoiker. Jenny declared they were the tiniest, thinnest, most pathetic animals she had ever seen, with the exception of Derwyn's victims at the far gate. Robert frowned and nodded. Jack Meredith said nothing. Gwyn had little money, he knew. The animals were bound to struggle when the farm had no money. As the days passed and the rain stayed, Gwyn's animals looked worse and worse, standing on mud, bleating and belling at feeding time. Gwyn did not come and did not come and at last Jack was unable to stand for it.

"Going to chuck those buggers a bale," he said, and went down the track to them, lugging the biggest hay bale he could find across his chest.

"Something in their bellies, anyway," he said when he returned.

Jenny loathed the sight of the starving masses at the far gate, and returned the dirty looks of Derwyn's sons with glares of her own. But the plight of Gwyn's sheep was almost unbearable, so close to the house and on her land. Jack and Robert impressed on her that she was not to start feeding them regularly, since Gwyn might stop coming altogether, and it would do them no good. Then one of them died, became a pathetic, sodden smear of wool against the fence, and she watched out for Gwyn; when he came, she charged down the track to confront him.

He was standing over the body, looking over the rest as they ate furiously, silent, for once, gobbling hay.

"Gwyn!"

He turned.

"Hello there."

"Look, one of them's died now. Look! It's dead!"

She was almost shouting, and she felt tears rising in her eyes.

"Aye," Gwyn said. Then he crouched down over the little body and ran a large hand gently over the wet wool. "Poor little bugger," he said quietly.

Oh, God, thought Jenny, he's upset too. She went back to the house, not quite crying, and resolved to feed Gwyn's sheep whenever they needed it. Gwyn seemed to come more often after that, and no more of them starved to death.

And then, slowly, came the miracle. At first it seemed too frail for the weather: catkins shivered in late snowfall; buds were tiny green huddles; wind-flung birds barely held the sky. But one day at the end of the third week of April they noticed thicker colors in the air. The pale paintbox of the fields had darkened and the once-tired brown hill had turned a rich, wet mauve. Suddenly a warmer light surrounded them; it was, at last, the bright spring.

3

A Farming Year

THE WEATHER WARMS AND WEST WINDS TEAR DOWN TREES in Pritchard's Wood. Jenny goes walking there one day, marveling at the great glowing carpets of bluebells. Needing a pee, she squats down among the stalks. She is finishing when she feels with sudden and awful certainty that she is being watched. She jumps up, hauling up her trousers, and looks around for the spy. Nothing. Something draws her gaze upward, into the canopy, which is bright now, jeweled with many greens, young leaves, and soft yellow buds. And there, not fifteen feet away on a branch, are the watchers. Three tawny owls, hardly more than chicks, huge dark eyes staring, gravely amazed. "Hello, darlings!" she whispers, and backs slowly away, beaming her delight. The owlets blink.

After the hell and thrill of the first lambing they return to work and the year becomes a series of weekend trysts with their other life on the mountain. The farm's claims are held in check, thanks to Jack and the M4: Robert and Jenny travel up the new motorway for the flag days of the farming calendar: haymaking, putting the flock out on the mountain, the shearing, the sales. The daily tasks and crises are left to themselves and Jack. He keeps an eye on things, but there is work there for three men, and he is only one, and old. He is not expected to bury the dead, gather tons of apples, mend miles of fences, and rebuild walls. There is no one to dig channels, throw out stray sheep, repel marauding dogs, or repair hedges.

So apples and corpses rot into the ground, pecked over by birds. Bands of ragged strays raid the Hill Fields, coming and going over fences that rust and sag, pushing through rambling hedges in which the badgers have made wide runways. Streams riddle their own courses through the red earth, woods thicken with fallen trees, old walls slip and blush with lichens in gold and silver-green. Birds and animals consolidate their holds on the house and buildings: in the fire-place one morning Jack finds an astonished young kestrel, which had dived down the chimney after a mouse. As he approaches, the bird throws itself onto its back in the ash, talons out, hissing, ready to die fighting.

"So what did you do, Jack?"

"Put my cap over the bugger!"

Some of the tasks are ghastly, such as castrating the tup lambs. Each lamb is caught and lifted up and presented to the vet, who stretches a rubber ring across the jaws of sinister steel pliers, leans forward, and snaps it over the root of the woolly little bag of the lamb's testicles. The lamb kicks desperately, bleats. The grip of the ring will cut the circulation; after a time the scrotum and its contents will drop off. It will not hurt for long, the vet says. It will all just go numb.

"But it's just frightful! It's a horrible thing to do!" Jenny laments at the end of a long Saturday in the pens. The lambs that have been done look miserable. They sit down, pathetically trying not to move.

"Can you imagine what it must feel like?"

"Barely," Robert replies, wincing. "I'd rather not!"

"It's frightful," Jenny repeats, angrily.

"But farming is frightful. You can't deny it," Robert returns, briskly. She shakes her head, but not in dispute. It is a glum fact. The tup lambs are sold to the abattoirs to subsidize their mothers' next year of life. If they are not castrated they will not grow as much as they would otherwise, and the markets will not take them. At least their sisters survive, for a few years. They will be sold to other farmers to produce more lambs until they are deemed too old, when they will be slaughtered too and turned into dog food.

Jenny can barely reconcile these year-to-year truths with her moment-by-moment love of the animals. She vows they will all have happy lives, swears that nothing will die needlessly, if she can help it, and tries not to think about the abattoir. It is a barmy equation, Robert feels, all his logic affronted by her sentiment. He tries not to confront her with it, but cannot always conceal his irritation.

In May there is drenching. With the coming of the rich, fresh grass, the flock begin to "scour": glossy green splashes of manure appear under their tails. Drenching means gathering, catching, and forcing a squirt of antibiotics down every throat. This stops the diarrhea and reduces the chance that flies will lay their eggs in the soiled wool— reduces the chance, but does not remove it.

The flies swarm with the warm days. In a calendar rich with horrors, "fly strike," as the treatment bottles call it, is among the worst. The flies lay their eggs in tails, sores, dirty hooves. From each egg comes a maggot, a wriggly little yellow tube with a mouth at one end and an anus at the other. The mouth eats, the anus expels. The excrement stinks, which excites other maggots and draws more flies. Maggots and flies are wonderful things for clearing up corpses, but they are quite terrible when they find a purchase on the living. Undisturbed, maggots will eat a sheep alive. At first their little bites itch, so the sheep scratches, rubbing itself on tree trunks or fenceposts. This opens small cuts, widening the maggots' menu. The sheep jumps and twitches and rolls in the grass; it makes no difference. Eventually, the sheep withdraws to some quite place, and there, silently, the maggots eat it.

The solution is vigilant patrolling. Jenny and Robert go together, in the evening, as the sun catches the golden meadow grasses and draws intricate shadows out of the tall thistles. They stoop along the field boundaries, looking into the quiet spaces between the clumps of nettles and the dark shadows under the trees where the sheep go to hide when afflicted. When they find one alone, or scraping or lying hunched, they move in with great slowness, soothing the animal with soft words. Then in a dart one of them grabs it, and they examine the problem.

"Yes, look, maggots in her tail! God, how disgusting. . . . Look— the little bastards."

The maggots burrow furiously into the wool as Jenny squashes them, rakes them out with her fingernails, kills them in the grass. Robert is not sorry that she has taken the lead. Like a surgeon's assistant he passes her tools as she asks for them. First, the shears: she snips and clips until the tail is a thin white cord, the pink flesh showing through the shaved wool. Robert looks up through the mosaic of leaves to the dreaming blue sky, darkening now, over the hill.

"Terramycin, please, darling."

He passes her the aerosol and she sprays the injured area with bright blue antibacterial agent. The lamb bucks with pain. "All right, sweetheart, I know it stings, but it'll save you. Cream, please."

Robert removes the lid from the small plastic tub and holds it for her. Jenny scoops out a thick wedge of sour-smelling yellow paste and smears it generously over the tail, the rump, and down the back legs. It will kill any eggs and repel flies for a few days. "We mustn't forget to ask Jack to check her."

"All done?"

"Yes."

The lamb scrambles away from them.

Jenny wipes her hands in the grass. "Very good." She grins. "Probably saved his bacon. Suppertime soon, do you think?"

Robert makes a face. "Maybe a drink first, hmm?" They both look down at her hands, streaked with green shit, yellow paste, and blue spray. He starts to laugh. She snorts.

One of their friends had a cine camera, and he filmed Jenny and Jack at work in the pens. There is no sound, but it is a few minutes of proof, visible evidence of the proper summers I have half heard about, half imagined. It is 1973, but were it not for the purple swirls on the dress that covers the bulk of my mother's belly, which contains me, and the color film, it could be 1873. Jack is wearing an old fawn mac. He has it on backward, like a smock, the belt bowed across his middle. His old tweed cap is brown and he looks thin, a thin old man with his coat on backward, patiently, gently catching sheep, which my mother then injects. There are no concessions to her pregnancy. There is no taking it easy. She is absolutely absorbed.

It looks like June; the sheep are still in their coats, so it is before the shearing and the heat. It has been raining and now it is warm. The nettles are thick and gloomy green; you can sense the ferocious toxin in their dark stalks and tiny spines. The pens are in a dreadful state. The floor is a thick churn of mud and sheep shit; humans and animals stumble wherever they move. The pens are walled in drystone, but not cleanly. Where the walls meet the ground there are tumbles of rocks; the sheep slip and jump around them.

Then Jack and Jenny are inside, having a break in front of the fireplace. There are two high-backed wooden chairs, nothing else. It is not the room I remember, which was carpeted, with pictures on the walls and a sagging sofa on either side of the fire. This has bare stone flags, it is no more than a shelter, a place to rest between bouts. My God, I think as I watch, they had nothing.

My mother is smoking and sipping coffee from the blue-and-white mug she still drinks from, thirty years later. Jack puffs on his pipe. They are probably talking about the sheep; she asks him something, watches his face as he replies, then she nods slowly, thinking. He adds something and puffs his pipe. And it hits you, as you watch. This is not an image of Londoners trading the rat race for the quiet life; this is not about city people bringing their energy and money and drive to a haven away from the traffic and trivia. This is far simpler and much more frightening than that. It is a leap backward through centuries. It is an attempt to gather in the fraying threads of old ways and plait them into a lifeline. It is one woman and one old man in a bare room, and the essence of their discussion is survival. How he survived, by his flock's survival, and how she can survive by hers.

She drains the last of her coffee, throws her cigarette end into the ashes, and they both go back to the pens.

✦ ✦ ✦

Then it is shearing time. It will need more than a weekend. Robert and Jenny take a few days off and plan the movements of the flock like generals disposing their troops before battle. They prepare the barn under Jack's instructions: the stone floor in the middle is swept and swept again (the shorn fleeces must be kept clean and free of hay); a great hessian woolsack is tied in place (a stone in each top corner so that the strings will still grip when it bulges full); a door is lifted off its hinges and set up as a table on which Alf will roll the wool. They lay in quantities of bread, cheddar, and cider. On the evening before, Gwyn and another neighbor, Jessie, who will be shearing, come to inspect the facilities. Their approval is a great relief.

Early the next day they are back, roping their shearing machines to the beam, laying out bits of old carpet on the floor, oiling and tightening the blades of their clippers. Jack and Alf arrive. Jenny and Robert gather the first batch, collecting them from the dew-sparked field, pushing them in procession into the yard. Suddenly the sheep are not being gently herded by two amateurs. There are loud whistles, Gwyn's dogs slicing across their lines of escape, men waving their arms, shouts. The sheep pour into the barn in turmoil and the gate is closed smartly behind them. Jessie and Gwyn take off their jackets.

Jack and Robert will be the catchers. The first two ewes are hauled over the low side of the race and balanced on their rumps, straddled between the shearers' legs. By precise placing of their feet the shearers contrive to keep the animals immobile, while leaving the shearers' hands free: the left for turning and restraining the sheep, the right for the clippers. They tug on the start cords and the barn fills with the rattle of the shearing machines. First the clippers draw a line up the breastbone as far as the throat. Then the animal is tilted to one side; the shearer leans forward and begins to draw steady stripes along the length of the body, starting low in the belly, then moving in parallel up the flanks. The underside of the fleece is a creamy gold; it falls away from the blades like a blanket of foam. There is an oily, spicy smell of lanolin, which will cover everything for the next two days. After a minute and a half of careful work, during which the shearer is bent almost double, the complete fleece falls away from the ewe, leaving her smooth, hard to hold, and frisky. The shearer skims the last of the wool from her tail, switches off his machine, and shouts, "Pitch!"

Jenny, six months pregnant, darts in with their brand, an iron C on the end of a short shaft, thickly covered in oily black pitch. She carefully imprints the initial on the animal's shoulder before it is released. Then the ewe scrambles away, hooves skidding on the stone floor. As she reaches the sunlight she skips, leaping into the fresh air and the bright yard, kicking her heels with joy and life, while her coat is collected by the roller. Alf picks hay and dirt out of the fleece before folding it, rolling the sweet, slightly sticky wool into a fat bun. He twists and teases tufts from the neck, making a thread that he uses to wrap and tie the bundle before pushing it deep into the woolsack. Robert maneuvers the next ewe into place, Jenny dabs a nicked rump with yellow paste, Gwyn pulls his cord, and the machine chatter starts again.

The heat swells. The sunlight lancing in through the slit windows thickens with motes, clouds of hay dust kicked up by the penned and wheeling flock. The shearers never slacken their pace. Sweat slips down their foreheads and drips off their noses onto newly shorn flanks, which twitch as if fly-tickled. Each animal is as fresh and as fearful as the first; each must be held, turned, bent this way and that. The practiced certainty in the men's movements seems to calm the ewes; only a very few struggle for more than a moment.

By two o'clock the barn is empty and eighty sheep bell and skitter around the yard, fast and delighted in their near-nakedness. Work stops and Jenny serves lunch on top of the low wall in front of the house. The men eat bread and cheese, their thick, delicate fingers thoroughly washed but still reeking with the oily smell of the wool.

"Oh, no, thank you, Jen, no, no," they demur, refusing top-ups to their small mugs of cider as though the sips they have had are already a great decadence.

Robert and Jack drive the ewes back to the meadow, returning with the yearlings bleating in front of them, a river of bobbing heads, pricked ears, and baying tongues.

"They're looking well, Jen," Gwyn says. Robert notices her pleasure at the compliment. But it evaporates, moments later, when she feels there is too much aggression in the ring of men and dogs driving the fretful animals toward the great dark door of the barn.

"Quietly!" she demands. "Steady, please, Jack!" She lowers her voice, without sheathing its harder edge. "They will go quietly. There you are, good girls." Gwyn and Jessie are careful not to let their smiles show.

Then they are shearing again, stretching the afternoon across the backs of more than forty animals. The mood in the barn follows the rhythm of hard work: optimistic for a while, then turning quiet, as muscles tire, then dipping as someone struggles with a particularly resistant animal and swears, then lightening again in an exchange of laughter. The smell of wool and sweat blends with the sharp reek of fresh droppings and hot urea trampled into the hay floor of the pen. The only breaks come when one of the woolsacks can hold no more and the men pause to heave the bulging brown belly across the yard to one of the sheds. "Five bags full," Jenny sings, unable to help herself.

Tea is taken at four o'clock but not lingered over. Everyone is slower now.

"Saved these for last, have you, Jen?" Gwyn grins as the final batch is driven into the barn. There are only five of them but they are much bigger than the yearlings: three wethers and two rams, the latter stamping their feet and swinging their horns at Gwyn's dogs.

There is a stampede as Robert goes in to catch the largest. He takes him under the chin, straddles him, and half rides, half guides the animal toward Gwyn. They both struggle to turn the ram over as he grunts and pants, fear and adrenaline bulging in his wide eyes and heaving sides. There is something grimly telling about the overpowered ram. His great fleece rolls off him in a creamy wave and is borne away like a treasure. Shorn, the king of the flock looks scrawny and silly, with his too-large head and curling horns, like an old man in white thermals wearing an extravagant hat. While they have him down Jenny inspects his hooves and Gwyn peels back his lip to look at his teeth. They spray a dash of antibiotic on his forehead, which he has scraped raw, fighting the other ram, and then they let him go. He stands up, uncertain for a moment, before trotting out of the barn.

The sun has gone by the time the last animal bucks out into the yard and the machines stay silent behind him. The shearers straighten up and wink at each other. Jenny congratulates them, thanks Alf and Jack, briefly rubs her husband's back. He can feel the sweat suddenly, cold between his shoulder blades. Gwyn and Jessie pause, Jessie accepts a cigarette, and they let the achievement settle for a moment. Then they pull on their jackets and bend down again, opening toolboxes, unscrewing clippers, cleaning meticulously. Jack goes around the barn with an old feed bag, picking up the dags—lumps of wool from around the animals' hocks and tails, matted with manure. The Wool Board pays a penny or two for a sack of dags, so a farmer collects them.

The shearing machines are taken down from the beams and stowed in the back of Gwyn's Land Rover. The door is put back on its hinges and the last woolsack is lugged across the yard to the shed. Eight bags full, and barely room to close the door. Then everyone gathers around the bailey wall for a glass of cider and settling up. They fix a figure per sheep and Robert writes out two checks, adding a little to the agreed figures, for luck. After a couple more sips the men pile into the Land Rover, with a word to the dogs, which leap in the back, and in a splash of headlights and a spurt of smoke they are gone, rattling down the track. The barn and the yard seem very still after their departure: a satisfied calm pervades them, like the sweet green dew smell that rises from the meadows. They leave the barn doors open to let the air circulate and go inside to wash and eat and sleep. The water stings in small cuts and grazes, skin that looked brown becomes white, and no amount of scrubbing can remove all the purple spray from fingers or the dark rims from the ends of nails. The thick kiss of the sheets feels wonderful.

A few weeks later there is dipping, which the Ministry of Agriculture insists upon and which involves dropping every animal Jenny and Robert own into a deep concrete trench filled with toxins: organophosphates, which will one day be banned and blamed for farmers' illnesses, depressions, and suicides. Where the dip splashes on skin it burns. Inhaled, it gives headaches that last for days. But it kills every kind of tick, louse, and parasite, and brings the sheep a few weeks of relief from the flies.

Jenny's job took her back to London but Robert stayed on at the farm through the summer. He was between papers and the thought of returning to London depressed him. Perhaps he could make Wales work. He contacted the *Chronicle*. Did they need a reporter? They might, the editor hedged—did he have any experience?

At the age of twenty, Robert had been covering an area of South Africa the size of Britain for a radical newspaper. After his flight to England he had joined a provincial daily, from where he had gone to a London tabloid as a subeditor. He had risen rapidly, before moving to a national paper. He had covered foreign wars, made national headlines.

When could he start? the *Chronicle* inquired, and there, suddenly, was the problem. Actually, Robert realized, he could not start. He could not face becoming a journalist on a local paper; he could not imagine devoting his time to the affairs of Abergavenny.

Alone at the farm, he rose early every morning and climbed to the top of the mountain, timing himself, doing it quicker and quicker every day. His record stood at eighteen minutes, which meant going like hell up a viciously steep gully, followed by the conquest of a punishing series of ridges as the ground changed from bracken to hummocks of thick whinberry wires, rising at last into the whale head of the top, and a scramble up its scree of rocking stones. Behind him the view deepened and widened, dominated by the grand mass of the Brecon Beacons. Below their northern flank the hills and fields of Radnorshire undulated softly into mid Wales; to the south was the massed escarpment of the Heads of the Valleys, sunlight flickering on car windscreens as they slalomed down toward the Usk. Turning around on the top, he could see into England as far as the Malvern Hills, and on a clear day, from the far end of the ridge, a pewter sliver of the Severn Estuary at the mouth of the Bristol Channel.

He would lie on his back to recover his breath, gulping down cold drafts of the sky. Gazing up into slowly unfurling banners of cloud, he could almost feel the earth turning beneath him.

When he had recovered his breath he would descend and see what needed doing.

"I think I'm going to put a new roof on the stable and the Beast House. What do you reckon, Jack?"

"Get someone who knows how to do it, that'd be the best."

"Mmm. I thought I'd have a go at it myself, actually. Save money."

"Oh no, I don't know. It's not so easy."

"Well, I've got this book . . ."

Jack was not convinced. Robert set about acquiring roof tiles. One tile, he learned, is not the same as another. They are all ranked by size and position; they have names. He stripped the roof down, salvaged tiles that could be reused, replaced beams and battens that had rotted. He bought roofing felt and polyethylene to protect his progress from the rain. Soon a new stone skin began to grow across the skeleton, and Jack began to smile to see him up there, with his book, patiently measuring, fitting, pegging.

"Tidy job, looks like," he conceded at last. Robert could have hugged him.

One afternoon, as he was working quietly in warm May sunlight, Robert heard, coming across the meadows, the high cry of a horse. The cry came again, and again, and it was unnatural—not a whinny but a sort of whickering scream, repeated at irregular intervals. Robert climbed down his ladder and began to jog, then run along the track. As he neared the far gate and Derwyn's sheds he could hear a man's voice shouting, blending into the screams. He vaulted over the gate into the yard. There was a commotion in one of the pens, and there was Derwyn, bright red, a thick stick in his right fist, and there was the horse, terrified, plunging away from him but unable to escape, her back scored by blows that Derwyn continued to deliver, oblivious to Robert's arrival. Derwyn was shouting, "You bloody bugger, you bloody bugger, you . . ."

"Derwyn!" Robert jumped into the pen. "Derwyn! What the hell d'you think you're doing?"

Derwyn ranted and lunged for the horse again. Robert went for him. Seizing the club, he drove Derwyn hard against the wall of the pens. Derwyn cried out and sagged, panting, as Robert released him. The fury died out of Derwyn as he saw its match in Robert's eyes. There was a fight there, if he wanted it, and in a moment they both knew that Derwyn did not. He looked confused now, and frightened. He began to say something, a plaintive, whining sound, but Robert cut him off.

"Enough! That's enough." He picked up the club and hurled it as far as he could. He opened the gate and stood back; the horse saw her chance and ran. He waited for Derwyn to come through, closed the gate behind him, and turned away without a word. He walked slowly back to the house. He was halfway up a mountain, money was short, and his nearest neighbor was bonkers.

Robert finished the roof, patrolled the sheep, and conquered the mountain every morning. Sometimes he walked down to the valley to drink at the Farmer's Arms in the evening, and climbed back up again later, a bit drunk, very tired, aching for bed. But still he woke in the dead hours, afraid that they were making a mistake. Outside, the night was a dark and silent maw. The yard light, one bulb high up on the end of the Big Barn, burned like a solitary certainty: there is a farm here, high on the mountain, and there is someone at home.

At ten to four in the morning, wrapped tight in the covers, he stared, with his eyes closed, at the trap he felt he was in. He did sums and knew, absolutely knew, that there was never going to be any money in this. He lined up the tasks to be done, measured guaranteed expenditure against uncertain income. He wrung himself for having no job, wondering how he was going to get back into the world, imagined his colleagues and rivals, their London lives, their progress, their families, knowing that everything there was moving, while here nothing moved, nothing had ever moved. The house was sunk in deep, oblivious peace, except for the few feet around him, in which the air was unquiet, tense with his frustration. He clenched his teeth in anger, at himself, at Jenny. What on earth were they doing there?

He rode out the anger and waited out the fear. He felt better in the morning, as the view and the mountains greeted him, and his spirits rose in answer.

Robert found a new job with a superb, if low-paying, national newspaper in London. The farm was a challenge again, not a life. It was another world at the weekend. It was a privilege and a steward-ship for which the price, as he saw it, was farming. Jenny would not countenance any retreat from it.

Robert watched her, one afternoon, talking to the vet. Her intu-ition was sharpening all the time. She had a gift for seeing, sometimes sensing signs and symptoms, and she was accruing a knowledge of treatments. She was synthesizing Jack's ways and sayings with the vet's diagnoses: the latter never concluded a visit to the farm without submitting to a detailed interview. He was in the middle of one now. Jenny listened intently, her head tilted to one side, while he explained something. As they talked, standing quietly in the pens, a ewe approached Jenny and nudged her leg. Unthinking, Jenny reached into a pocket and came out with a couple of nuts, little cakes of beet pulp, which the sheep adore. The ewe guzzled them and stood for a moment while Jenny scratched between her ears, quizzing the vet about the powers of vitamin B_{12} and when you should administer it. Robert loaded his pipe and lit it, watching the exchange as he puffed.

It was not merely that she had found something that interested her, something that she wanted to do: she had already left want and interest far behind. Sometimes it was as if everything here—the red earth of the yard, the dull stones showing through the dirty white-wash of the big barn, and the young nettles crowding its corners—required that she be there, in the pen, with a sheep at her knee. As if the land and the heartbreaking view needed her to complete it.

In early August they wean the lambs: dividing them from their mothers and splitting theaves from tups. It is hard, heartless work. The animals are separated by hand into different pens before each group is driven away to new fields at opposite ends of the land. They must be out of one another's sight or they will spend hours trying to break through the fences. Moving them is fraught with frustrations, as animals desperately hurtle back the way they have come. When it is done the groups cannot see one another, but they can hear. They cry to one another for three days and nights. Jenny lies awake, listening to them, guilty. The night rings with the bleats of sheep and lambs, but she hears mothers and children. A month later she will give birth to her first child.

They took the first batch of lambs to market in the back of Der-wyn's van.

Robert kept a diary of sorts, a kind of ledger. His energy and determination are bold in its pages; he may never have meant to be a farmer, but here he is, farming, and he means to win its battles. He writes at speed in a broad, forward-leaning hand, the words often lifting off the pale blue lines. There are no corrections. It is like a ship's log, a record of weather conditions, incidents, and figures; only once or twice does he write narrative.

The first lambs to market were a mixture of four Suffolks, which, he records, went for £10.70 each, and seven Welsh, which went for £9.55.

"Seemed reasonable to me," he comments, "but quite a rebellion by many farmers who had brought big lambs for which they wanted £12 plus but were offered little over £11. They refused in quite large numbers to sell."

At the end of August the hay is brought in, having been left lying in the field for ten days. The whole process, from cutting to baling and hauling, should take four days, as Robert notes. It will have lost its freshness and much of its nutrition. But it has been a lousy summer, and he has not been there to plead with and chivvy his neighbors, who have had their own problems with their own harvests. Trying to cheer him up, Jack says the bales are not so bad, considering.

One hot night in early September, Jenny knew her child was on its way. Perhaps because she was familiar with the agonized heaving and groaning of ewes giving birth, Jenny was in no hurry to hand herself over to the hospital. She sat with Robert on a bench in Holland Park, not far from their flat.

"I'm not looking forward to this much," she muttered.

Robert squeezed her hand. "It'll be fine."

"I wish I could just have it here."

"You want me to draw it?" Robert grinned.

"Sure! I could just go and curl up under the hedge over there."

"Hmm. I haven't got my Terramycin spray."

"Oh, Lord, Rob. I think it's on its way—it feels like it is, anyway. I think it's coming."

"Right. Come on."

By the next morning she was exhausted, had experienced the worst pain of her life, and had given birth to me. She stayed at home in the flat and nursed me while Robert kept the farm going at the weekends.

Later in that month, he recorded in his diary, a neighbor was killed. Mr. Jones was making a turn at the top of a steep field in his tractor when the machine toppled over, crushing him. The field in which it happened ran up alongside our first pitch. (Whenever we struggle up it in the future, in various underpowered and overloaded vehicles, having been told this story, I will think of Mr. Jones on his game little gray machine, with no cab or roll bar, jaunty until the last second, when its wheels became unglued from the earth.)

At the market, prices fell. The best fetched £9.50, the worst £7.20.

"Pitiful," Robert commented. He tried again in early October but it got worse. They arrived at market with thirteen lambs in a borrowed trailer to find a huge crowd and thousands of sheep. Sheep in the pigpens, sheep in the cattle pens. Their best went for £7, the worst for £5, "and wouldn't have made that if one of the auctioneer's relatives hadn't done some illicit bidding on our behalf. Most depressing."

A week later, "our yearlings reached £11.90, with a little help from the auctioneer's assistant, which was the top price of the day by a good £3. But I refused to sell then and we loaded them in again and took them home. I'm sure everyone thought I was mad. But we had decided that they should fetch £14 at least, although as Jack says, correctly up to a point, you can't make your market at home."

There were always rumors that somewhere, in one of the local markets, the prices had suddenly bobbed up, the other day—that some dealers who no one recognized were there, paying good money—but Robert and Jenny's financial position was weak, and worsening. In an effort to improve lamb weights and therefore the profit they might make, they decide to buy a larger ram. They had started with two rams purchased from Emrys: Tommy, a big, yellow-eyed old man with magnificent horns, and Beacons, so called because his humped back reminded Jenny of the view of the Brecon Beacons. The new animal, Ron Vaughan, was purchased at the market. Jenny wrote an account of his arrival.

I had admired Emrys' Suffolk lambs with their chocolate faces and black-stockinged legs, but I was doubtful about an Othello jumping about on our little white ewes. After much debate, Robert and Jack went to market. I waited with some trepidation for their return. The trailer pulled into the yard, Robert got out, grinned, and then Jack emerged, towing their purchase on a piece of rope. They stood, waiting for the verdict. The ram was young, but large. He had beautiful ears, long and black, adorably tipped up at the ends. His legs were strong and black, his eyes a liquid dark. Jack was looking at him like an immensely proud parent. "The best ram in the market," he said. We named him Ron Vaughan, after his previous owner, and waited for October 25th. October 25th was one of Jack's most important dates.

"There's nothing to beat a March lamb," he said, so October 25th was the day selected, ewes' pregnancies lasting five months. The day dawned gloriously, golden sun and a crisp frosty wind. We got up early. "A perfect day for tupping," we said, as Jack arrived, keen to see his child perform. Our twitching little ewes were waiting obediently in the pens, and then, panic. Ron Vaughan was *gone*. We pounded about—how could he have disappeared—he had been in the back patch—just outside the kitchen . . . And then Robert spotted him. He'd somehow escaped out onto the hill, no doubt tempted by Derwyn's mountain gypsy flock who had been patrolling beguilingly along the hill fence. Ron Vaughan was glimpsed surrounded by bracken and two or three gypsies, wasting his talents. As we approached the gypsies ran away and he panted after them. We started climbing and running, Derwyn's ewes climbed higher and dodged lower and soon Ron Vaughan was collecting more and more amorous females as he waded his way through the bracken, trying to do his best. Up and down we rushed. "Bugger it, bugger it," we gasped. At last Robert caught him. We dragged him back. Jack could only say "Well well well." Ron Vaughan looked as if he needed someone to mop his brow.

So they prepare for next year's market, while this year's is glutted with sheep, demand is falling weekly, and there is nothing anyone can do about it, beyond the auctioneers' feebly sly attempts to run up the prices. But they have to get rid of the rest of the tup lambs, or they will end up feeding them through the winter, to no purpose, so at the end of October they try once more.

It becomes clear even before they reach the market that it is going to be no better: the streets are full of Land Rovers and trailers. The market is a sea of gray chaos; vehicles maneuvering in all directions, frustration and tension on every face, the rain slanting down, thousands of sodden and crying ewes and lambs packed into every pen, jammed into trailers, wet wool bulging through the slatted sides, overflowing the sheep pens, the pigpens, the cattle pens; the gutters run black with their manure. Farmers grip the hurdles that barely divide their animals from all the rest, staring across the churning lake of soaked white backs and wailing tongues at the little knot of caps around the auctioneer, whose chants are all too short, and on every face is the knowledge that this is all loss. And among them, one of the very few sellers who has another way of making a living, perhaps the only one who does not have farming anywhere in his history or his blood, Robert is trying to get rid of four old ewes and the last dozen tup lambs.

The ewes are up first: two go for £2 each, but nobody wants the other two so he gives them away. It gets him a few looks but it is not unheard of. Then the auctioneer moves on to the lambs. The ring of bidders and watchers, mostly watchers, moves with him. The odd hand reaches into the pen to squeeze a rump: experienced fingers can tell how much meat there is under the wet wool. Heads shake. These have had orf—a disease that blistered their gums and stopped them eating much for weeks—and are underweight. And they had not been castrated, which meant, as Robert explains in his diary, "we couldn't keep them on, as we could have done if they were wethers, and for the past few weeks they have been losing weight, instead of putting it on because their minds were on other things." They fetched £3.80 each, making a total of £49.60 for the day. "Not too clever, as Jack would say," Robert writes.

While most people with any sense would be trying to get out of this doomed, archaic business, Robert, who has a great deal of sense, seems to be doing everything he can to get in. In the months that follow he buys hundreds of stakes for new fencing, hires a builder to reroof the back of the house, dips and drenches the ewes, digs a drain across the paddock, accumulates a stock of "cake," nuts and oats for the winter—bag by bag, driving loads up from town each time he comes— and hires and harangues a man he refers to as "Davis the Drainage," who eventually installs a 1,500-gallon catch tank at the top of the Quoiker, which, coupled with a pipe down to the house, one fine winter day, finally brings running water to the farm.

At first it is only a temporary tap by the back door: "Wonderful!" Robert writes in his diary, and it must have been, after collecting ten-gallon drums of freezing mountain stream water, in all weathers, and hauling them up a hundred yards of rising ground. It is the first significant improvement to the house in three hundred years. Soon afterward he has the north end dug out of the red embrace of the mountain, and the damp wall that emerges reinforced with cinder blocks. Then he puts in for planning permission for a bathroom, the beginning of a process that takes months.

He visits more frequently than Jenny does, now, and there is a sense that they are managing separate spheres: she is often in London, with my nanny and me, while Robert comes down at the weekends to work on the farm. During the week, the feeding and day-to-day tasks are in Jack's hands. His sayings tend toward the negative, but they are faithfully recorded.

"At least it's not so cold today."

"Not so bad, no."

"Apparently it's been the warmest December for a hundred years."

"Ah—a green Christmas means a full churchyard!"

"Does it really?"

"They do say."

Despite the relatively warm winter they are short of grass: they have too many sheep for the space and much of the hay has gone moldy. In these circumstances every square foot is valuable, and the great many moles that live under the fields are looked upon as a menace. Their red-mauve hillocks are everywhere, Robert records.

"The moles have made an awful mess of the second meadow. Jack
has trapped a few but says there are some educated buggers there. He
reckons to trap them in the end so long as the wind doesn't move to
the east—for you'll never get them then, he claims."

Jack campaigned against the moles over the years. Educated they
may not have been, wary they certainly were. Long snouts testified to
their superb sense of smell. Jack, who smelled of must, pipe tobacco,
and rain, tried not to handle the traps at all, cocking and placing them
with sticks. He approached the chosen ambush point from downwind
and carefully positioned the trap astride the mole's tunnel, steel jaws
gaping, handles sticking out of the ground. Often he caught nothing
and could be seen in the meadows, moodily flattening molehills with
a spade. When he was successful the velvet-coated corpse would be
brought back to the house in triumph and passed to Jenny or Robert
for inspection: they marveled at the incredible softness of its coat and
the great shovels of its front feet, like the hands of an ogre, long-nailed
and long-fingered, angled backward, for breaststroking through the
earth.

4

Two Wishes

R OBERT SWINGS THE CAR UP THE YARD, STOPS AT THE top, and switches off the engine. Three hours solid driving and he aches, yet he hesitates in his seat. When he climbs out into the yard the warmth that has been with him since London will be sucked away by the cold clean air and another lambing will begin. It will be a week at least until Jenny joins him, and there is much to do.

The diary has become part of his routine; now he writes more than notes. One snowy night he notices a sheep looking odd, broody. At quarter to ten he goes out to check on her.

The snow was now quite thick on the ground and the moon, though behind the clouds, was full. The torch seemed to flood-light the whole field. She was still in the same place but now a big black head glistened under her tail and she was very wild. As I followed her doggedly, still undecided what to do, across the fields, hide and seek round the hedge, scattering the ewes in every direction, it started to snow again, quite heavily and driven by the wind. She turned back and as she headed for the bottom corner I decided that was the only place I had a chance of catching her. She seemed to have the same thought and rushed wildly from side to side but I finally got her down the bank and then the problem was that she had two exits with a ten-foot stretch of hedge between us. In a flash of inspiration I stuck the torch in the hedge and crept round the other side. She watched me but seemed baffled by the light coming from the other direction and by the time she had decided which way to run I had her. It was just the head and I could feel no hint of a leg so I turned her up, balancing the torch on her bottom, and tried to push the head back but she fought like mad and I nearly lost hold of her. It took about 20 minutes to drag her up to the house and get her in the barn and then I went to get Jack. It was about 10:45 and luckily he and Alf were still watching telly in front of a very hot fire. It had stopped snowing and we managed to get back up the hill without the car skidding too badly. A nightmare performance, but Jack eventually managed to push the head back, the lamb bleeding from the mouth and its tongue hanging out and deep purple. Then we got one leg forward but couldn't get the head back through the hole and though he tried the wire loop he's never used it before and couldn't get it to hold. So I rang the vet, we loaded the ewe into the boot and I got to Abergavenny at midnight to find Mr. Jones waiting. He got the loop in very quickly and the second leg, which he said was across the lamb's chest. Still, he had to pull very hard indeed. Miraculously, the lamb, which was an enormous Suffolk, was still alive. And then Mr. Jones pulled out a second. I had all three back in the barn by 12:45 and after another quick round went to bed.

When Jenny arrives they use Robert's diary to pass news and messages. When I first opened it, thirty years later, their exchanges struck me like the confirmation of a rumor I had long wished to believe: a time when they were happy together, committed to their great adventure. His writing: "Beautiful badger girl born overnight, #58 from 45. Jack drew a single before lunch. Derwyn came up with a lamb with a torn throat to show what the fox had done. Can't think why."

Here her smaller, vertical script interrupts: "Jenny thinks him absolutely mad to rush around displaying a dying lamb when he should be caring for it for heaven's sake. 10pm SNOW. Saw fox again in the Horse Fields—lying flat to the ground with bright red eyes then streaked off. Saw fat rabbit under the holly by the road. Young ewe doing it under top hollies. Sheep v. nervous of me—migrate when I get close. Wish I could wear my waterproof trousers but would probably cause a stampede."

She has a busy night, delivering lambs, moving newborn twins and their mother to a less-exposed part of the field, and going back to the house for a milk bottle. (They have learned a lot in their first years: lambs can be jump-started with a suck of milk drawn from another ewe and stored in the fridge. The first pints a ewe makes are thick and golden colostrum, rich with protein and antibodies: a few gulps stands anything on its feet. The word *colostrum* and the yellow syringe had the ring of manna about them.) She concludes the entry: "Ewe below hollies by the gate delivered one. Have no idea whether it's the first of twins—too cold to stay and find out. Confused by ewe and lamb of Derwyn's whose wretched bull is non-stop belling plus a bereaved ewe. It's bloody cold. Everything b. cold me bloody cold and FED UP! Finish 2 a.m (2 broody)."

The next morning Robert begins, dryly: "Jenny must have really stirred them up. Overnight: three sets of twins and two singles, one v small. #68 from 52."

The division of labor keeps them to different halves of the clock, but by their tones they are happy; Jenny's protests about being fed up are designed to provoke his smile. Their relationship is almost as absent from the diary as I am: I appear occasionally, as my initials, normally around 1:30 a.m., when I demand attention between Jenny's late rounds of the sheep. But it seems a good partnership and close: Jenny is now carrying their second child.

The weather yaws from snow to sun and back again: Jack was right: a freezing, killing spring followed the green Christmas. But in the diary the even, flowing lines of Robert's strong script record an orderly progress: "April 5th, snow and snowing. 88 from 68. Thaw at lunchtime. Four weakening sets of twins inside, also two other sets, cripple in one, rejected twin in the other. Suffolk single in the bottom of the badger wood. 89 from 69. Lovely evening."

The fringe work at lambing is just as draining as what goes on in the fields, the main theater. Those weakening sets of twins and the cripple will need feeding, as will the weeping rejected twin. When a surrogate mother can be found, it will need hours of being pushed to her udder.

Robert is still up at midnight, helping another birth halfway down the badger wood, which is perilously steep, dark-crowded with the shapes of hunching trees, and slippery in the thaw.

More snow comes the next day. Jenny and Jack spend the afternoon "unplugging" and marking lambs. The remains of the colostrum squitters out of the lambs as a thick yellow paste, a waxy cream that hardens and crusts, causing life-threatening constipation. Unplugging it requires unsqueamish fingers and a brave nose: the vile smell is something between feces and rancid butter.

"Heavy snow, blizzards, drifts," Robert reports the next day. "The crippled Suffolk twin died (its mother mercifully lay on it) bringing the number of lamb deaths to five."

Considering the conditions, it is an excellent score. The day after that they have a lamb born dead, but the story of the rejected twin ends happily. An old ewe has a single in the night "which she licked and left to die. Jack skinned the lamb and put the skin on the reject for whom it was some sizes too small, but the ewe didn't seem to mind."

It is a common trick among sheep farmers: the corpse is skinned, yielding a perfect little jacket, with holes for the head and legs of the orphan you want to foster. You dress it and pen it with the bereaved mother, nice and tight, so they cannot get away from each other. The ewe, smelling her own lamb, her beloved, though she knows something is not right, will, in the end, stand for a suckling. After a day or so they bond and the adoption is complete. You throw the shrunken little skin away, somewhere out of the reach of dogs and foxes.

A week later the end is in sight, Robert scores 144 from 115 and allows himself to calculate the distance to the finishing line (44 to go). They share a page only once more, when a tame lamb called Rudi, which they are feeding, disappears. At the same time an abandoned lamb is discovered, in Robert's words, "twitching in the rain in the middle of the Quoiker. Jenny administered whisky and milk and the lamb recovered—revealing himself to be Rudi." Jenny continues:

> Who is now (11:55 p.m.) fully recovered from what must have been a monumental hangover from whisky and penicillin and is avid for more. Failing that he has curled himself up in his mother's bowl much to her obvious irritation. A warm night! Worms out and would you believe it zipping in and out of their holes. All seemed quiet in our fields but as for the cacophony issuing from wretched Derwyn's wretched animals . . . last time it was miserable cows. This time it's horses screaming and what sounds like an expiring ewe and two lost lambs on the hill. Wind from the west. Cloudy.
>
> 12:30 Have fed Rudi and Reluctant Drinker again—I think he has sucked but please check him first thing because he's very hungry.

The last pages in Robert's diary record a small outbreak of orf, which they treat and contain; a successful operation by Jenny to induce the birth of twins by opening their mother's cervix; a visit by my grandmother and a friend, and a trouble-free end to the lambing. They go back to London on April 19, and return the following weekend to drench 75 yearlings and calculate that they have had 175 lambs from 144 ewes, with 15 still to go. That week, on April 21, 1975, in their basement flat in London, Robert writes a letter. The salutation, "Dear Jenny," and the sign-off, "Yours, as ever, Robert," are handwritten. The rest is typed.

The letter is ostensibly all about money, "the gravity of our financial plight," as he describes it. But in its lines and tones there is a picture, clear as a lightning flash in a dark night, of a relationship in dire trouble. He begins by saying that because his recent attempts to make her understand or engage with their situation have failed, and caused tension and ill-feeling between them, he has decided to write down the facts as he sees them.

There follow lists of expenditure and earnings. First, his personal costs and earnings, then the farm's, then hers. Everything is included, from feeding the cats (£3 per week) to tobacco (his pipe, her cigarettes) to capital expenditure on the farm. He takes account of inflation, notes the absence in his budget of things such as presents, pensions, life insurance, or entertainment; lists all the different costs and incomes of the sheep in the last year—from £200 gained from the Wool Marketing Board to £3 per ewe for the sale of ten old ewes—and uses the figures to forecast the sums they can expect to make next year.

They do seem to be in trouble. He is spending more than he is earning. The car, which has done 32,000 miles in the last twenty months, is the largest contributor to his debt, which is increasing by £30 per week. The farm is £1,247 in debt, and losing, with the cost of traveling to and from it included, another £40 per week. The rosiest projection he can make for the following year, if they have a good lambing and sell two hundred lambs, leads him to forecast a further loss of £1,200 when the cost of the car is included. And they are expecting another child, which means, he thinks, that they will have to move out of their small, cheap London flat, into somewhere bigger and more expensive.

He notes that she has two thousand pounds in an account that she insists is her own, and outside their marriage, and that she is proposing to borrow another three thousand pounds to install a bathroom at the farm. Even if they could find a loan provider, how can they go into debt to cover living expenses, he demands, when they have no way of paying off any interest, never mind the loan itself?

The situation, he says, is not merely unsustainable, but mad. Her reaction, he claims, has been "Oh, we shall just have to go further into debt," which he says he finds "baffling and infuriating."

He notes, in a tone of amazement, that her solution is that she should take the children and go to live at the farm.

He has three objections. First, he works in London from Tuesday morning to Saturday night: he does not want her and their children to live 160 miles away; he does not want to live alone at the flat or share it with a lodger who would help pay its rent; he wants to live with her and the children in London, where he works. Second, he says, he cannot afford the farm. And third, he does not believe she could cope alone with the farm and two young children.

He says she has proposed three alternative solutions:

1. They should keep the farm and buy a bigger flat, so that she and the children might divide their time between Wales and London. Fine, he says, except that he cannot afford the farm or a bigger flat.

2. They should get divorced, he should sign over farm, flat, and child to her, and pay maintenance. But he does not want to get divorced, he says. She has no grounds for seeking it, except that he cannot afford what she wants. "I love you and the child. I want us to stay married," he writes. And he cannot see why he should sign over flat or farm.

3. He should earn more money. He points out that his paper is not a wealthy one, but that he likes the job and the paper, and has recently been given a pay raise: hardly grounds for divorce.

His solution, he says, is simple. They should sell the farm, pay their debts, sell the flat, and use the proceeds to buy a "respectable" house in London. She has already rejected this, but now he begs her to see that it is the "only possible" course. He says he will sell their car—a Volvo—and use the money to make repairs to their decrepit Volkswagen beetle, in which he will make the necessary trips to Wales to do whatever needs to be done to prepare the farm and the stock for sale. From next weekend, he says, he will not be responsible for any more bills incurred by the farm, other than those relating to preparation for its sale, which would certainly not include any further building. Unless he has her agreement, he says he will have to take steps to give the disclaimer legal validity.

He finishes with a sincere apology: he is, he says, "truly sorry that you will undoubtedly have found this letter rough, unloving, offensive and pompous. But I am deeply disturbed about the possible legal consequences of the mess we are in, and there must be no misunderstandings. Yours, as ever, Robert."

The letter came as a jarring shock to me, as I traced the chronology of their marriage, and it throws a different light on the diary entries that led up to it. Now it seems that their partnership was not merely absent from their exchanges on paper, but crumbling beyond the pages. Now it seems that it was not just practicality that made them keep different hours, and kept them to different shifts, each plodding the muddy fields alone. As they went their separate ways, up and down the track, they must have been thinking in different terms, and wrestling with the other's.

"Why won't he join in with me anymore?"

"Why can't she look at this realistically?"

My first reading of the letter confirmed my childhood impression of their relationship and its fate: an idea that my mother the mad romantic and my father the icy rationalist were pulled apart by her recalcitrance and his caution; a mutual refusal to compromise or defer. But now I am not so sure. Nowhere else, in no letter, diary, or exchange of notes is love ever mentioned. But here, in a letter purporting to be unloving and rough, is something like love, and love's desperation. And, depicted only in the echo of its plea, but clearly nevertheless, is an image of a woman prepared to ditch a man who loves her because he cannot afford to keep up with her, a woman with an airy ruthlessness in her romanticism, who seems to have already chosen, or at least threatened to choose, the mountain over the man.

Before her reply, three weeks later, Jenny writes a feature for the Friday, May 9, edition of the *Evening Standard*—"on being a midwife to a flock of sheep." In places she quotes Robert's diary, and reports him using a torch to dazzle another sheep before catching her. She quotes Jack on infection, "the worst enemy of a sheep is another sheep," and signs off:

"The cuckoo came on April 22 and we now have 179 lambs with ten ewes still to go. We have lost weight. I need a new pair of Wellingtons and the feed bill is enormous.

"But the ewes, however elderly, have done us proud and their lambs run races, as they should."

On the following Wednesday, May 14, 1975, on *Evening Standard* notepaper, she types a letter to her brother-in-law, and legal consultant, Geoff.

She has four questions:

1. Is it legal for Robert to refuse to pay all farm bills? He is joint owner; they arrive addressed to him.
2. Would the legal disclaimer he threatens be granted?
3. Can she, as his wife, be forced to live where he decrees?
4. Even if she lived at the farm against his wishes, married or not, is he not obliged to support his children?

She notes, "Since his BLAST of the Trumpet Robert has been incredibly nice, and much relieved." And she concludes, "I have absolutely no doubt AT ALL that were I to sell now—when the prices are bad, when the house is still not right, and without trying to give the children a country childhood, the resentment and boredom and frustration I would feel in suburbia would ruin our marriage in any case. If my effort—if I decide to do it—does not work, THEN I will consider selling; and that is still the safety net."

I was not oblivious to their differences, though I was only a little over two years old. I have an image of a happy family, a mother and father with their arms around each other, gazing lovingly at their child, but it is not the image of my family. I do not remember ever seeing my parents kissing or hugging. I do not remember them as a unit, but as two distinct individuals, who often referred to each other, but never to "us" or "we": they were my mother, Jenny, and my father, Robert, but they were barely, if at all, a couple. But I had nothing to compare them with, and they were very loving toward me, and so my life at this time was, I think, happy. Lindsey, my lovely young nanny, would tickle me to make me behave; my mother came home after work; I remember the farm when the bathroom went in (Jenny borrowed the three thousand pounds from her mother) and I can hardly have been two then. I knew there were tensions between my parents, but I also knew and shared their contentment and collaboration.

I remember their happiness and excitement the night Alexander was born. I was uncertain about the whole business and spent the hospital visit stuffing myself with crisps from a bowl beside another mother's bed. When they asked me, in that traditional consolation for the put-out eldest, what I would like to call him, I replied, heavily, entering rather grudgingly into the spirit of greeting and celebration, "Twinkle. Twinkle, twinkle, little star." (I had already been saddled with the pet-name Pim because I was a fussy and tearful child, "nimsy-pimsy" in my mother's rather horrible phrase. So it was thanks to my pedestrian taste in nursery rhymes and tremulous response to the world that Jenny's heroic children, Horatio and Alexander, became known as Pim and Twinks.)

1976. I remember Alexander and me being bathed together, and read to. The four of us went to the park, the seaside, and the zoo. There are photographs of the famously hot summer; everyone wears floppy white sunhats, sits around on burnt yellow grass, and smiles redly at the camera. My father has long fair hair. In the photos he looks straight into the lens, evenly. The camera never seems to catch him unawares. My mother sits around, feeds children, plays with us, watches Robert. She is often talking when the shutter clicks; he is quieter. There were long drives down the motorway. Jenny told the tale of the Pobble Who Had No Toes as we crossed the Severn Bridge, and her family listened; I remember my father laughing on one nighttime journey as I bestowed magical powers on my mother and she cast a spell: "Abracadabra, turn this tatty Volkswagen into . . . a magnificent chariot!"

There was a Christmas dinner at the farm, when Robert cooked the goose with its neck and head still on (the beak looked like crackling). I can still hear Jenny's horrified squawks and his peals of laughter.

I watched Alexander closely. I vaguely remember the incident that my mother described to my aunt involving a hammer I had found. I was hefting it. My mother had just finished feeding my brother. "Oh, well done, darling, you've found Robert's hammer. Better be careful . . ."

Aunt Ursie's reaction, "Watch out, Jenny, it only takes a moment," seems an uncharitable assessment of what was going on in my mind, but like all older brothers, I certainly considered my sibling's demise in the years to come, though never with such apparent coolness. He was quick to start crawling, then walking. He did not say much.

The fireplace at the farm was our first adventure. Left one afternoon in front of the cold hearth, I contrived, by a series of mimes, to persuade Alexander to join me among the ashes and cinders. He did not look too happy with their taste but he joined in readily with the daubing and delving. When my mother discovered us she screeched in impotent vexation. She marched us to the bathroom, stripped and scolded us. I remember the reproach in Alexander's eyes as she scrubbed him over the basin. I like to think we were allies from then on. It was obviously fortunate that with his development of speech Alexander became able to give his side, and to say who started what.

I do not remember Robert and Jenny arguing—they concealed their disputes—but they were quietly pulling apart. Robert built a shed in the garden of the London flat which he furnished as a study and retreated into: it seems utterly reasonable now, but then it was Robert's Shed, a symbol of separateness.

Then there was the way they referred to each other by name when talking to us, a habit that my brother and I adopted: it was not until we reached double figures that we dropped Jenny and Robert and started calling them Mum and Dad.

They read to us a great deal. We were relentless in requesting the same favorites, night after night. My father found himself reading the same stories in exactly the same way, turning the pages, using almost the same intonations, like a traveling player, methodically re-creating a narrative brio. His core repertoire included at least ten books but we normally chose from the same two or three. The canon included *Cannonball Simp,* about a small black dog whose owner abandons her (she becomes a cannonball at a circus); *Shady Glade* (the machines tear up the animals' forest, so they ride a boxcar through mysterious cities to another, safer Shady Glade); and I went through a craze for Richard Scarry, which was certainly partly visual. I was very keen on the adventures of Lowly Worm, who has an apple-shaped car that he drives fast and sometimes badly. "Where did you learn to drive?" someone shouts at him.

"Where did you learn to drive?" I echoed.

"Cape Town!" my father answered.

"Why?"

"Because we lived there."

"Why?"

"Well, we lived abroad. I was born in Shanghai."

I learned to read with Peter and Jane and their dog, Pat. We read the lot, every evening after my bath, as far as the adventure that features a large yellow helicopter and a quite mature Peter and Jane. They lived in an eternal summer, as did most of the human characters of our children's books: it was left to animals and pink monsters to experience fear, shame, and confusion. I was given a toy that made a great impression on me: a small plastic R2-D2 from the film *Star Wars*. I loved it from the miraculous moment it appeared at the head of my bed. My mother left me notes in the same place, folded pieces of paper with the message written in tiny script. They were stories, fragments of fairytale and role-play. I dictated replies to her, which she wrote out in the same way. I clearly remember one of them referring to a "him," obviously my father, and the feelings I recall, as one of the notes was written, read, or delivered are all conspiracy. It is such a clear and strong sensation, as vivid as remembered love or guilt, and I think that moment became part of a secret subconscious album, like a collection of dark documents, assembled to explain their divorce. Part of my guilt. For the child of divorce is guilty, or feels himself to be, of a kind of original sin, the deeds of which I have always felt I could almost remember, even when I was very young.

Soon outings were conducted by one or the other and there was a growing sense of their individual existences: they ceased to share the same frame. Robert went running in the evenings after work. There were long silences when they were together; their division became the norm. Now working night shifts at the BBC, Robert was fatigued and depressed at home. Jenny took it personally: he switched to nights so that he didn't have to see me, she said.

They still hummed up the motorway at weekends. They still lambed together, in 1976 and 1977. At Christmas and during beach holidays with Ursie and Geoff and their three children they appeared together, like a husband and wife, but they faced different ways. Robert looked to his work and London, Jenny to the farm and the children. Now his logic seemed cold, her passion selfish; with the evaporation of love and excitement it became hard to remember how their contradictions had ever been submerged. And as he sank into that mystery, bitterly embracing his own miseries, Jenny proclaimed herself and her certainties ever more loudly, and more desperately. Her heart was no mystery at all. It beat for her children and her farm.

Farming had nothing more to offer Robert, and he was an outstanding journalist. He was making his name, destined for promotions, plum jobs, Baftas, and Sony awards—successes and satisfactions he would never find at home. For all his wife's domination and determination (and hadn't he deferred to her over Wales, over the farm, over the sheep?), she could not change that fact. He did not abandon his family, but he never looked like coming back. His career and his future were in London.

Jenny took stock on December 17, 1977. Her diary is also a kind of ship's log, but she is a very different kind of captain.

We have decided that while Robert makes good at the BBC during the next year the children and I should come and live at the farm. It makes sense. I can help Jack feed, Pim will go to the village school—a dear little place where he will be one of only 27, in a class of 12. I shall have to leap up in the mornings for a change which will be good for me. I am anxious about two aspects.

a) That we'll only see Robert at weekends, and b) that the evenings will seem long and scary. Ever since that wretched burglar broke in I've lost confidence at night. We seem such a long way away from the neighbours. I don't know which is more scary. A quiet night, when I can hear the cat swallowing, and the embers clink-clinking, or a wild one when the barn door bangs and the wind rushes through the attics. I am taking three precautionary measures. A telephone extension in the bedroom, a dog

from the RSPCA in Newport or somewhere, and a television set
so that I can watch the reassuring puffy features of Richard Baker
reading the 9 o'clock news! And without a daily paper I won't feel
so cut off. We will be here for at least 9 months. It will all depend
on Pim's progress at the village school. Jack will be 75 on January 25th.

The life she has left sounds miserable. Staying in bed as long as possible while Robert goes off to work and "makes good." The London
papers—sections of them written by friends and familiar names—
sharpening her sense of being out of the loop. Wishing she had not
given up work: she had a nanny for her first child and stayed on at the
Standard; should she have done the same with her second? It makes no
difference. Now she is sitting with her back to the fat embers of the
great wood fire, her pen steadily crossing the pages.

Robert, the children, and I came in convoy to the farm. Two cars
were necessary. Robert took the children and 2 TV sets (one for
Jack) in the car the BBC have lent him, and I followed after with
everything else including the kettle. Toys, teddies, books, Christmas presents, pictures, sponge, clothes clothes clothes. It was a
yellow dank cold day, with a wind. Grey and bleak it looked from
Hammersmith fly-over, but if someone had suggested we wait
another day or so I would have felt almost relieved. We stopped
once or twice. The bonnet on the Morris is tied down with string
because the catch is broken.
    We eventually came up the track to the farm. It always looks
so bleak and unwelcoming. The white wash looks flaky, the stones
dripping, and to get out of a warm car to open up a cold house
and to be brisk and cheerful and pleased to be here is always an
effort. I keep my coat on, try to see the children keep theirs on
too, and make for the kettle in the kitchen which is an ice house.
Then upstairs, make the beds and put in electric blankets. Pim
and Twinkle rediscover their toys, the cats appear to be fed, and I
light the fire Jack has laid. It is dark, we are warmer, the children
are in bed after cold washes, Robert lights the cooker, and after
London the wind outside and the smell of fresh air and the feel of

the hills around us in the dark make me wonderfully peaceful. We go to bed. After a while the mattress grows warm.

Sunday December 18. Spent the day organising, unpacking, discussing sheep and feeding with Jack. Robert left at 7:30 for his last stint in London before his fortnight's holiday. Twinky cried when he left, and Pim was miserable. We watched his car lights bobbing and retreating down the track. They felt bereft. I felt, because I'm not settled in yet, I suppose, apprehensive. We talked in low voices. I was listening to the sounds in the yard and wishing I'd asked Jack to stay the night just to tide us over.

"Are you absolutely sure, Jenny," said Pim as I kissed him goodnight, "that there is nothing here to harm us?"

"Absolutely sure," I said. And came down to check the bolt on the front door and sit with my back to the fire imagining prowlers and peeping toms in the yard. Later I painted the wall behind the shelves in the kitchen a pinky brown colour which looked, I thought, quite horrid. Went to bed quite happily nevertheless.

Monday night. Still painting, I was sure someone was outside watching me through the kitchen window!

That Christmas we bought a huge tree for one pound, and with the firelight, the shining baubles, snow, carols on the gramophone, and the certainty of reindeer galloping across the stars and a man coming down the chimney, which was wide enough for the fattest Laplander, our Christmases glowed with delights. There was no television, then or ever. I remember Robert plugging one in, and fiddling with it while it snowed and fuzzed, and eventually giving up. It was hauled upstairs and abandoned in the Beast House bedroom. "We don't have television," ran our standard line, "because there's a mountain in the way of the signal."

All the myths and traditions of the season made perfect sense at the farm. The lanes were full of dark holly, which we hauled in by the feed bag full; there was mistletoe in the hedges, the fire roared with great Yule logs, and on Christmas night it seemed perfectly obvious that all the animals would talk. And it snowed. One extraordinary night, after the snow clouds had cleared, we went tobogganing under the moon. It was an unearthly scene: the valley a twinkling masterpiece, as if the starlight had thickened and fallen on the world, covering everything in soft, cold perfection, leaving only the outlines of hedges and woods, dark-etched shadows against the glowing snow. The world tilted as we slid and sped, down the field under the bright heavens.

Alexander and I loved the whole season and over the years we gorged on it. There would be school Christmas, and the farm Christmas, and Christmas with our cousins, and then—in the years when he no longer came to the farm—for a week after Boxing Day, Christmas in London with Robert. We made the most of everything: when the decorations came down it was winter followed by lambing, and no one has cause to dread this pair like hill farmers and their families.

I began my time at the village school. The "dear little place" appeared to me a frowning presence by the main road; its moody stones and high windows might have been designed to shut out the view, the valley, and the world. The shadowy schoolroom seemed to yearn for ranks of Victorian children, scribbling on slates, chanting in time, kept in order by the teacher's bark and the cane. Now there were two dozen of us, more likely to be drawing pictures than learning anything by heart, all itching for break time and the chance to charge up and down the field outside playing British Bulldogs. My mother said that if we yelled loud enough and she was feeding in our lowest field she could sometimes hear us, which was a comfort. The other children were all neighbors in the village; I was a peculiar oddball, articulate with adults, uneasy with other children. I longed for the weekends and for really bad weather, for anything that would keep me at home. I was lucky: in January the quarter-pint milk bottles that waited outside the school door sprouted columns of glistening golden ice, and the temperature continued to drop. February in particular, in Jack's phrase, was a little bugger of a month. With Robert gone, the weather closing in, and nothing ahead but months of feeding and lambing, we were suddenly embarked, as if in an old stone ship, on the adventure Jenny had both dreaded and longed for. It was the winter of 1978.

Feb. 13th. For the last week we have been in the grip of icy winter. Everything looks dead—the fields, hills and sky have lost their colour. Hard, pale deadly cold. The hardest frost for nine years they say—snow half-hearted, but small flakes and vicious. Northeasterlies drive it in bitter puffs. My old sheep with their thin coats must feel it over their backbones. The fields are harder than London pavements, crossed by dusty tracks where the animals walk at feeding time. Their hooves drum on it and several fall over. Walking as sheep do on tip-toe, with ruts and molehills hard—it is no weather for high heels. The cauldron has grown a wide crystal rim, the trough in the Quoiker is embalmed and curtained in icicles. Pim and Twinky stood on the ice in the yard trough without making a single crack and even the bucket of water I left in the Beast House for two of Gwyn's sick lambs had frozen by the morning. It is a worry to me. Taps are frozen. The children are running out of clean dry clothes because of the lack of hot water—I make dashes to town for food whenever I can but the pitches are either covered with a skin of ice or snow and I frightened myself three days ago when the car barely made it.

Jack is in a bitter mood also. He caught our bug—diarrhoea and vomiting. Like ours it was short-lived and he looked better today. And having wrestled with the bales in separate fields and guilty silence I told him so when we met briefly at the meadow gate. "You look better, Jack."

"Think so? I don't feel it. Feel bloody weakened." A pause. "How are you then?"

Me, retaliating with immense irony and a bright smile, "Thank you so much for asking, Jack. Not really so bad. Our water has all frozen since yesterday. I'm carrying it from the stream."

"Aw." With that he marched off, once again abandoning his stick. Never asked about the children and at any other time he would have offered to help me carry the wretchedly heavy oil drums in which I lug the water. But I expect he reckons we're plague-ridden. Pim has a terrible cough but otherwise we're better now, and although it worries me how to keep fed, warm, clean and mobile, this sudden winter is strangely exciting. The evenings are eerily still now that the wind has dropped. The evening sky is an angry orange with growling clouds and the distant hills are bleached. The veins of the Beacons are black against the thin snow. Even the buds and the tight catkins on the alders which were a purplish pink 10 days ago have blackened and shrunk. You can almost hear the frost cracking its fingers. I use the car to carry bales to the meadows, jolting over the frozen mud, rattling and jarring the undercarriage. Every time I bring it back I wrap up the bonnet with an old mac and a sack, put stones under its wheels and release the hand brake. I wonder if there is ice banging in its water tank. Then before we come in we stand and listen, looking over our view. The sheep yellow, one or two bleats from distant lambs, cars changing gear in the valley, the roar of the stream heavy with snow, the evening wide. We saw a new moon three nights ago. I bowed three times, Jack showed it 10 p and lent it to Pim and I to do the same. Even Twinky waved it aloft. So sharp and clear was that little moon it looked as if it could cut. I made two wishes, sliding them into one.

Two wishes, sliding them into one! How characteristic that is. Greedy and selfless; pointless and urgent, romantic and fearless, too: as if she has never heard of the danger of wishes, of the possibility that they might come cunningly and cruelly true. Perhaps there is some essence here, encapsulated in this moon-dreamed moment. My father fixing on someone beautiful, willful, and unusual, whom he also hoped would be conventionally subservient and devoted. My mother taking a man with brains, looks, and cutting ambition, who stood outside all the clubs she aspired to, who stood, in fact, outside himself. The purchase of a mountainside, the application of passion and curiosity to the dispassionate and primitive business of hill farming; the disregarding, by her, of its flaws and ills, by him, finally, of its wonder and blessings—underneath everything there was this impulse: two wishes, sliding them into one.

Feb. 14th. Sunny but cold. Jack arrived. He looked sour, and was. Seems unable to make one cheerful or pleasant remark. Complaining now of cold and sore throat. At least we can't be blamed for that. I took him home as soon as possible and, joy oh joy, at 1:30 there was a clanking in the pipes and the loo filled up with water, the taps spouted. Did a great wash of clothes before it freezes again and gave the children hair-washes in a really hot bath for once. Watched an oil tanker attempt to reach us across the Far Meadow, but having circled the fields once or twice sliding on a skin of thawed earth, it retreated. In the evening we went to look at Gwyn's puppies. They are ten days old and the remaining three are fat as toads. The little girl we have chosen has a white tip to her tail and growled a tiny growl when I picked her up. Children very excited about the idea of having a dog. Thinking of names. I have thought of Floss or Tess. "What do you think of Tess as a name, Jack?"

"Doesn't matter what its bloody name is, so long as the bugger comes when it's called."

Feb. 15th. I had a bath! And was getting dressed in the bathroom when noticed the oil tanker had reappeared and its dauntless driver, Mr. Ferguson, was preparing to unwind its fat pipe and discharge some 300 gallons into our tank. Fantastic Mr. Ferguson. He is a man among men. He drives that tanker like a knight charging into battle and there it was sliding and skidding all over the yard as he backed it, only just missing my car and almost flattening the pen wall. He lost the air in his brakes, waited a few minutes, said, "I'm crossing my fingers now," and then, taking one hand off the wheel to wave his arm out of the cab window, he drove like a man possessed and thundered off down the track.

"He would have routed the German panzer divisions!" I shouted to Pim and we waved and waved as he crashed away.

Jack reappeared later. Less said, as they say, soonest forgotten. I told him to stay at home until he felt better.

Bitterly cold. The winter now upon us is a malevolent yellow. Robert was coming then didn't.

In the absence of the husband, father, man-of-the-house, we were often at the mercy of men, many of whom were coming then didn't. Jenny spent hours, days, on the telephone and in neighbors' farmyards, trying to persuade them to come up the mountain with their cargoes of oil, sheep feed, hay-making machinery, snowplows, trailers, tools. She flirted with them, cajoled them, pleaded and demanded, swore when she failed, cursed when they let her down or ripped her off.

"They'd never dare if I was a man!" she stormed, regularly. "They always say they'll come and then they just bloody don't! They'd never try it on like that with Robert."

They knew there would be good money in it: a single woman, apparently desperate for whatever they had, would be charged the top price. Even so, many preferred excuses to the fearsome drive up the mountain, the dizzy pitches and the chassis-gutting track. That winding drive up into isolation, and the lone woman at the end of it, revealed many characters.

Among them were "good men and true," in Jenny's phrase, without whose kindness life would have become untenable. Foremost among them was Jack, of course, though they gave each other hell when they lost their tempers.

"You're like Mrs. Thatcher!" he shouted at her once, and she could be, too, hectoring, relentless, utterly uncompromising. The comparison really got her, though.

"Jack! No! You can't mean it!"

But there were men like Dai the Garage and Gwyn and Pat, who, because she asked it of them, gave their time and strength and skill again and again, and never vented any frustration.

Dai became accustomed to the early-morning call—"Dai, I'm so sorry, the bloody car won't start, I'm so sorry, could you possibly . . . ?"—and to the mysterious "pinking" sound in the engine, and the snapped fan belts and expired starter motors: our succession of little vehicles performed as tractors, taxis, and Land Rovers. Lined with hay, dog hair, mud, and sheep shit, they hauled bales, children, animals, and feed bags up and down the pitches until they collapsed in heaps of stinking scrap. Dai was their nurse. His smile of greeting, as we pulled onto his forecourt, held a mixture of incredulity and amusement.

"Hello, Mrs. Clare, all right?" He always opened hopefully.

"Hello, dear Dai. Well, the thing is the wretched dog has chewed through the seat belt again."

"Oh, right." He nodded, eyeing the moss growing around the rim of the back window, a rapid grin flitting across his features as he added it to a mental inventory that included the mushrooms which appeared in the boot and the pair of sheep's ears now poking up over the backseat.

He was patient, forever dashing back into the office to produce VAT receipts for petrol, and generous, charging the bare minimum for maintenance and commiserating with Jenny when the price of a new part caused her to cry out in pain.

"A hundred! It can't be! It can't be!"

"Oh, they are, they are. Terrible, I know. I'm sorry . . ."

There followed a moment of silence while she stared at him, forlorn, then he laughed helplessly, and she threw up her hands and grabbed her head in dramatic distress. "Oh well! That's that then!"

Gwyn, with his expertise, his Land Rover and trailer, his shearing machines, his strong sons and intelligence network of friends and associates, was Jenny's link to the market, and her best hope at shearing, and a prized consultant on all kinds of questions: where to sell, when to sell, which rams to keep back for breeding, how to keep foxes away from the lambing fields:

"I've seen him, Gwyn, twice, he's a big dog fox—I don't mind him eating the afterbirth, but I'm worried he might take a lamb, if it's in trouble."

"You know where he's coming and going, do you, Jenny?"

"Oh yes, I've seen his run, there's a gap in the wire, and you can smell him."

"Get some pitch or some spray, if I were you, Jen, dab it all around there. Something strong—chemical. He won't like it. That'll be the best, since you won't shoot him."

When she missed the bank, or there was a cash-flow question, Jenny relied on Pat in town. Pat's grocery shop was on the corner near the ruined walls of the castle, a position that allowed Pat, who spent most of his time on the pavement, a view up and down the high street. He was a large, sandy-haired man with a red face behind glinting glasses. His voice was very loud; his shop seemed to me the center of the little town, and Pat its embodiment. He hailed everyone by name—"Mrs. Clare and the boys!" he shouted as we approached—and, apparently without prying, knew everyone's business.

"Oh, Lord, I've run out of money. Perhaps Pat will help," she muttered, through her smile, as she brought the car to a stop.

"Don't stop it here, Jenny!" Pat boomed. He often directed the traffic.

"Dear Pat, I've stupidly missed the bank. . . . Could you possibly cash a check?"

He regarded her for a short moment, and smiled. With the cash came two oranges, posted through the window into our hands. "There you are, boys!" he bellowed.

An excellent actress, Jenny did a most affecting damsel in distress, but for men like these she did not have to perform. And when the car broke down and she had to get us to school, or the oil burned low in the middle of winter, or when the sheep simply had to go to market, she was as needy as she appeared to be, and "good men and true" responded. When they had done, and accepted her huge, grateful thanks and small checks, how many different men must have driven away down the hill, shaking their heads at her strangeness, her prettiness, pigheadedness, and determination to survive without one of them at her side.

From the house we watched and waited for them to come, over the brow of the top pitch, along the lane, up the track; and later watched them go, in their tractors, Land Rovers, vans, and cars.

Tankers were particularly prized: in the happy expectation that North Sea oil would fuel a warm, cheap future, Robert and Jenny had installed a Raeburn stove—a poor man's Aga—at the heart of the house, in the kitchen. As well as rendering that room habitable during the winter, it heated the water. The arrival of Mr. Ferguson's bright red face, large voice, and small Shell tanker was always as exciting as she describes. For his part, Mr. Ferguson, though he delivered to many hill farms, must have dreaded his missions to ours. He was brave, but he became more cautious over the years. He often aborted attempts and never encountered the disaster he feared. In later years, when tankers were bigger, he stopped coming. Jenny lamented it bitterly and worked the phone again. His successor, Mr. White, nearly died trying to reach us.

It was a low, wet winter evening, tipping toward a dirty night, when the bright headlights of the oil tanker appeared suddenly over the top of the pitch. Mr. White had never been before, and as he steered through the twisting wood he hoped the worst was over: surely there could not be anything as bad or as steep as the horrible turn at the top of that first pitch. He gunned up the second pitch and felt great relief as the road leveled out gently at the top. Across the fields he caught sight of the yard light and a small farm with its back to the looming mountain. Jenny had instructed him not to try the track at the top of the lane but to go across the meadows. He climbed out and opened the gate, noticing how cold it was up there. The valley was a long way below. The grass was dark with rain, but he could make out a faint double line that led diagonally across the fields toward the house. He hauled himself back into the cab and set out.

"Oil tanker!" we cried, and from the window on the landing outside the bathroom, which had the best view, we watched him come.

He crossed the Far Meadow without difficulty. The tracks took him through a gap in a hedge then turned gently uphill, to his left, toward the gate in the top corner of the Middle Meadow. From there an easy track led to the farm. Halfway across the meadow, Mr. White felt the wheels lose their grip. The tanker paused, lost forward speed, and stopped. He revved the engine and reengaged the gears for another go, but the wheels spun impotently. Then, slowly at first, the tanker began to slip sideways. As it slid down the gentle slope it leaned, the oil tilted to the downhill side, and the slide gathered speed. Peering out, Mr. White could see that the field ended in a rusty fence, beyond which there was nothing but space and dark treetops. That fence ran along the top of a ten-foot bank above an extremely steep field, one of the Lower Meadows: ripping through the wire, falling, toppling over and over, the tanker's bounding roll down the Lower Meadows would end far below, in the stream and a spectacular explosion. Thirty yards, twenty, fifteen, the tanker turned a slow, balletic semicircle as it slid toward its destruction.

It was a shaken man who eventually settled in front of the fire with a cigarette. He had telephoned his firm and his wife to explain the near disaster. He was grateful for supper—some cauliflower, a lot of cheese sauce, and a rasher of bacon—and refused Jenny's offers to top it up with bread and more cheese. He tried to refuse to join her in a whiskey but she was insistent, and poured him a bigger measure than he would have asked for. He was sweet to Alexander, accepting without comment our extravagant names, posh English accents, and identical bowl haircuts. We watched him carefully. At Jenny's suggestion we produced a pack of cards: he showed us the basics of poker, explained his nickname, Chalky, which came from his time in the Merchant Navy, and told us a few stories about that.

He went to bed, after telephoning his wife again and wishing her good night, in the Beast House bedroom (named after the shed below it, we explained), in a pair of Robert's old pajamas. The Beast House was cold under its pitched roof, and accommodated guests, like the princess of the pea fame, atop three double mattresses piled on an old iron bed frame. The room smelled of wool. Burrowing into clammy covers and lying very still, Chalky White listened to the wind skimming over the ridge of the roof, and felt a draft, like a cold finger, brushing his cheek. He dreamed strange dreams.

We were sorry to see him go the next day, after they'd pumped his oil into another tanker and Derwyn's tractor had towed his vehicle back to the road. The field was scored and churned to within yards of the fence, everyone had shaken their heads over the near disaster, there was a small slick in the middle of the meadow (which would kill a patch of grass for years), and we would be lucky to get another tanker, ever, but our oil was resupplied and we had all enjoyed putting Chalky up: the more we waved at departing men the more we wished they would stay.

Feb. 16th. Feeding almost impossible. Snow and ice. Robert came at tea. Snow after dark.

Feb. 17th. Very cold but sun blazing by 10:30. Snow thin and very crisp—a bitter east wind but Robert and the children tobogganed in the First Meadow. Fed all day it seemed. No help. Robert had a sleep during the day and went to bed at 9:00. He doesn't want to talk to me. I have been trying but am giving up because I sound banal even to my ears. It was a lovely day though—warm in the sun and then ice crystals clinked in the snow as we walked over it. A woodcock rose from the stream by the cauldron. Marsh tit by Ty Newydd and fox and badger tracks crossing the lane on the pitch and rashly heading for Derwyn's fields.

*

Feb. 18th. The worst day of this winter—from every point of view. I have walked around all day with a heart which really does feel as heavy as lead—with dread and apprehension and responsibility so heavy that I found myself turning to Jack of all people for comfort. "The spring will come?"

"Oh aye," he said. "It will." I long for just one kind word. But ashes. And I'm smoking too much again. A terrible east wind. Almost gale force. The children are frightened by the noise of it in the attic. Dire warnings of "considerable snow and drifting in S. Wales." I thought desperately today of shifting us all out of here—perhaps sending the children back to Robert, to somewhere where you can be sure of heating and food. Thinking again about selling the sheep. Must do what's best for the children, no matter what. As for my personal happiness it truly doesn't matter. The poor sheep with their thin wool are crouching round the yard and in the woodshed. Methuselah's water bucket in the Beast House has frozen twice. We'll lose our water tomorrow I expect. The ground is rock hard. How do moles fare? And rare birds hop around the kitchen door despite the cats—a yellowhammer, nuthatches, fieldfares, redwings. No sun, anywhere, at all.

Sun. 19th. Blizzard.
    Mon. 20th. Worse. Deadly wind. No water. Dwindling hay.
    Tues. 21st. Ice on snow. Couldn't use wheelbarrow. Flat tyre on car.
    Weds. 22nd. Very tired. Wind dropped. Worst weather in south Wales for 30 years.
    Thurs. 23rd. Dug out. Back to normal. Pim back to school—shopping.
    Fri. 24th. Car tyre mended.
    Sat. 25th. Rain rain rain. I feel tired—the week spent surviving. No time to write this.

This desperate record seems to contain the final fracture: the day she spent feeding while he tobogganed with us was the first of all the rest. Henceforth he regarded the sheep as her business. When he came to stay he slept in the Beast House bedroom. He went to bed in the middle of the day, burying his head under the pillow. Now I know what it was: wretched depression. But then it was a mystery. "What's wrong with Daddy?" we asked.

"He's just very tired," Jenny said, thinking she was lying.

"What have I done?" Jenny pleaded with him, missing the point. This was about him, not her. He would not allow any illusions: he was out of it, she was on her own.

"What will happen to us?" she asked him once.

"You'll manage," he said.

She repeated that story bitterly, but in its cold way it was a compliment.

His resignation from their adventure crushed them both: his depression dried his tongue; through guilt or anger or self-disgust, he could not talk to her. It drove her wild—there was a pale splash on one of the sitting room walls where she missed him with a coffee cup—and she made my brother and me promise that whatever we felt, however angry or upset we were, we would never "go silent": she made it taboo. We kept our promises throughout our childhoods, teens, and twenties: shouting, wailing, swearing, and ranting with abandon, but never going silent.

I failed to keep this going and now today is March 20th, Monday. Spring did come, most wonderfully, for six warm balmy days and with Robert here at the weekend to look after the children, Jack and I drenched and injected and took our time in the warm sun and enjoyed it. We—Pim, Twinks, Robert, and I—were out and about without our coats and I even persuaded Jack to take off his jacket though he insisted on piling another old mac on to protect himself from possible dampness in the fleeces. I tried not to talk to the sheep too much which I know Jack finds soppy. "Come on, darling," I say if I'm not careful, "stand easy." Jack confines himself to "Stand still, you bugger" and hisses a lot like an angry snake, or perhaps old ostler with a troublesome horse. If things are really bad—if the animal is wildly frightened or finding being held unbearable and rears and struggles—Jack's ultimate anger and impatience becomes "Well. Well. Well." It is wisest then for both sheep and I to keep absolutely quiet. I like handling sheep. I like the opportunity to look at them closely and stroke their heads. Their eyelashes are long—their wool comes in many textures—short and tough like Elizabeth's—hempy and long like the old ewe with shadows under her eyes—wavy and silky which looks like its been to the hairdresser. I am better at injecting than I was, though to get these short fat needles under the skin and not between the skin layers nor into the ribs is tricky. And sometimes in pinching the skin up you go in and out the other side and only notice when the stuff drips down the wool to the ground. Now and again we paused for Jack to rest, for me to have a cigarette and open another 200 mls of the drench. It protects them against horrible ills and hopefully their lambs. From across the valley we heard foxhounds in full cry and through the warm afternoon saw the pin figures of the horses and riders as they rode along the tops above Pen Lan. "Got an earth in that spinney there," said Jack, pointing to a dim cluster of trees. The voices of the hounds had stopped. "The vixen will be in cub by now," I said, and hoped they would leave her alone.

We were pleased with ourselves when we'd done. Jack said his legs ached, so I did too. He said he felt buggered up, so I not to be outdone said I was too. I have become allergic to his endless complaints and to forestall them I'd been saying things like "Catching them here isn't hard, is it, Jack, just awkward." But it *is* hard, no matter how tamely they stand, and Jack had caught and held, with only two upsets, over 200 sheep. A grinding task done with marvellous patience and stoicism. His touch is quite wonderful—we could so easily have miscarriages after crowding them and bumping them, but moving between them as we do nothing is rough so we didn't get miscarriages.

What we did get was a shock. The sheep were all released and there they were grazing away in the evening sun when one by one they all sat down. This seemed odd because we took them some more hay, which they should have been famished for, but what was odder were their ears. They were all hanging like dish-cloths. "Look at their ears, Jack, for heaven's sake, look at their

ears! What on earth's happened to them?" He didn't say anything for a moment, just gazed. The flock looked like rabbits in
the rain, with their ears dangling straight down. Some had one
ear still standing up, though on the way down, and the effect was
appalling, rakish. In the eyes of the animals was a resignation
and gloom. They looked ill. And very funny. "I've poisoned
them. That's it. Poisoned them. That drench was recommended
by the vet but just *wait* til I telephone him."

"Never seen the like of that in my life," said Jack. We
wagged our heads, I vowed vengeance on the vet, we prophesied
dead ewes, dead lambs, and all the time they just looked at us
with their tea-towel ears and reproach. It was a golden evening,
still and warm, birds busy in the hedges. Tired and rather gig-
gly, I drove Jack home. Next morning most of the ears were up
again.

We went up the valley to Gwyn's farm and collected our new pup.
The little dog was eventually named Lark. She was bouncy and intelligent and she loved men. She was very fond of Jack, who showed her
more tolerance than affection, and she adored Robert. Her favorite
thing was walking up the mountain with him, or any of the male students who came to stay with us and work during the lambing—the
"lambers"—or, when we grew older, despite our shouts and sticks,
which scared her, my brother and me. Lark could have been a good
little sheepdog, but she was lazy and poorly trained—Jack was not
expert in teaching and handling dogs, nor was Jenny. To get Lark to
work well took a lot of coaxing and shouting and some luck; if anything went wrong, or anyone lost their temper, she would look at her
feet, lick her lips in a pained way, and skulk into the nearest hedge,
out of reach of retribution, withdrawing from the game. Neither
furious shouts nor pleading through gritted teeth would coax her
back then, and her cocked ears and light brown, slightly raised eyebrows could be a very galling sight as you ran to and fro, chasing
bloody sheep, while she watched. Squirrels and moles drove her wild
with hunt lust. She would chase anything, from a bee to a car, and
spent hours and hours sitting neatly at the feet of trees, like a black

question mark, her head tilted back, eyes fixed on a squirrel. Even for a young dog she had superb hearing and would give you advance notice of any interesting sound. When she came and sat on your feet it would be a few minutes before you heard the first grumble of thunder, which terrified her. I think she would have liked a more varied life than the farm offered her. The approach of walkers would be signaled with great excitement, and you had to watch her then, or when the little figures appeared on the skyline Lark would be off to join them. If she gave us the slip she would have to be recovered, hours later, in the best case, from the campsite in the village, where, having befriended everybody, charming them with her prettiness and self-possession, she would be in the process of relieving them of bacon and any other tidbits she could get. Recovery missions could be entertaining.

She had been missing all day, having disappeared, deliberately, exactly when she was needed for work, and finally we piled into the car and went down the hill to look for her. Sure enough, at the bottom of the campsite, chained to a post, there she was. A young German woman was feeding and petting her.

"There she is, the creep! They've chained her up. Christ, she's feeding her bacon. Would you please get her!"

We were in a hurry, anxious not to encounter the owners of the campsite, who were as sick of this as we were. As Lark saw the car she flinched. I leaped out, charged over, and unclipped the chain. From the car, Jenny and Alexander scolded over my shoulder.

"Wretched animal! Come here!"

"Bad dog!"

The young camper was distressed, and protested on Lark's behalf in poor English and, incomprehensible to us, German.

"She's very"—cuff!—"very"—cuff!—"naughty!" I huffed at the woman, slapping and dragging the cringing, reluctant hound toward our beaten-up and filthy car.

"Get in the back, you bloody thing!" shouted my mother.

"Bad!" my brother and I yelled, and we rattled off in a flurry of foul looks and curses, which changed as we went to hysterical laughter at the camper's expression.

Lark was a funny, lovely dog, a welcome fourth resident of the farm. But perhaps her greatest contribution to my life, and certainly to that of my brother, was her son, Toss, a dog who once saved our lives and also almost killed himself, laughing. Before Toss, though, was the first spring of Lark's life, that of 1978.

> Celandines, crisp leaves of the Lords and Ladies (wild arum) warm blue skies, two blackbirds nesting in the garden hedge, a pair of nuthatches in the ash tree—a frog and frogspawn in the pond, ravens flying high with large twigs in their beaks, heading for the larch wood. In the warm sun the ewes weren't so hungry for bales.

The snow came back later in March, thick and wet, driven by northwest winds and southwest gales. Every day Jack and Jenny fed the pregnant ewes and the hungry rams, dragging the heavy bags, lugging the buckets, run off their feet sometimes by the charging, ravenous sheep.

> Robert arrived on Thursday evening in the sun. So we were prepared, waiting, excited. Huge are the ewes; one or two quite alarming. I pray I haven't overfed them to bring gigantic lambs they can't get out.
>
> But like watched pots they do not boil. The old green biddy brought a tiny, perfectly dead premature lamb yesterday (Friday), and today (Easter Saturday) two lovely Suffolk twins and a small Welsh tup, but that's all. They boil and boil but do not come. I'm glad in a way because the weather is dreadful today. Hail pinging down the chimney, northwest wind slicing through the meadows and rain with drops as large as peas thudding on the roofs. Not a good day to be born. Later, dark curtains of snow and sleet swept across the meadows with a rushing sound. You could hear it coming. The wind veered in the evening—went warmer to the west. The sky was wild and lemon, black snow clouds herding over our mountain to the east—large stars in islands of duck egg blue. Just before dark—to confirm my worst fears—I drew a truly enormous lamb from one of our calmest yellow tickets. She had tried and tried and lay with her head on the ground watching me—

almost asking for help. Since then, to Marigold, a stocky little tup whiter than snow, on Easter Sunday at dawn.

Easter Monday—The lambs came.

Easter Tuesday—Pat crossed the street to say, quietly, "They found my father, yesterday, drowned in the river near Glangrwyney."

5

Battles

Oᴜʀ ᴠᴀʟʟᴇʏ'ꜱ ʀᴇᴄᴏʀᴅᴇᴅ ʜɪꜱᴛᴏʀʏ ʙᴇɢɪɴꜱ ɪɴ ᴠɪᴏʟᴇɴᴛ conflict. One of its earliest stories concerns Twrch Trwyth, who had between his ears a comb, a pair of shears, and a razor. King Arthur, so the story goes, learned that these objects were vital to the fortunes of his kingdom, and sent word to Trwyth, an Irish king who had been cursed, along with his seven sons, into wild boars. Twrch responded, hotly, that the lot of his band was already as terrible as it could be and that nothing would persuade them to surrender their implements. Arthur's messenger replied that Arthur was resolved to have the kit, and would not be deterred. Hearing this, the herd put the people of Ireland to the slaughter, swept eastward, crossed the Irish Sea, and landed in Wales, goring, tusking, raging, and rampaging after Arthur and his people. These animals were so terrible that a brush with their sharp and septic hair was enough to kill a man. So began a dozen wild scraps through west and mid Wales. Many people died, but the boars took casualties too. One boar, Llwydawg, became separated from his kin and was pursued to the Ystrad Yw—the country of the Yw, a little local stream—in the county that is now Powys. The men of the Ystrad Yw were farmers in peacetime, who cooked meat and drank milk (but ate little bread, as was common in Wales). They passed their time in the hills and brakes, wore their hair short so that it did not catch in thorns and brambles, and were not strangers to the arts of war. They shot short, immensely powerful bows made from young elm.

The boar made his stand somewhere in our valley, almost certainly near a stream, and I would guess high up, where he would have had the mountain at his back. The Red Book of Hergest, circa 1375, recording events which would have taken place hundreds of years before, says that Llwydawg killed a great many men and animals in the fight. I imagine it took place at dusk, under a flying sky, the thorns all laden with cold rain and the grass slippery as ice. Fat streams babbled over their red banks. I have often charged through the bracken and scrub in similar conditions; I have chased animals along the hill fence, and cornered them, and can imagine what it must be like to try to kill one then. But not a great boar, the size of a small car, though both heavier and quicker over this terrain, on his trotters, their split nails sharper than razors, the rotting flesh of his previous kills lacing their edges with poison. You are close to him now, your brothers beside you, panting, and he's watching you, looking specifically at you. He squeals, something like a scream, and comes. Imagine the speed of his charge as he comes, head down, tusks like great bloody teeth and his red eyes steady on your groin and lower belly. It is awful to think of running for your life over the stones and slanting stumps of the gloomy hillside, so perhaps you would fight. Or perhaps, at that instant, you heard your brother's bow loose, and his perfect killing shaft, exploding through its heart or brain, dropped the monster at your feet.

The men of the Ystrad Yw killed the boar Llwydawg, after losing scores of their own. What they did with the body is not recorded. They would have dragged it away from the stream, but I cannot imagine they ate it. Perhaps they torched it on the mountain. Nothing but the myth remains.

Human invaders left permanent marks on the valley. The remains of Roman forts and roads are still there: a squadron of Spanish cavalry was based on a small tump where three valleys meet, and perhaps their genes linger in the population, many of whom are small, dark-haired, and bright-eyed. Centuries after their withdrawal, the Normans arrived, sweeping into the mountains from the northeast. They built fortifications and churches, and their descendants formed a nobility whose allegiances lay with the English kings. Centuries of struggle between natives and invaders were fought out in the fields around their castles; Jack used to say that certain of the flat valley meadows were rich and fertile thanks to gallons of Welsh and English blood.

My brother and I began fighting as soon as he was able to challenge me, and we continued, occasionally in anger, but overwhelmingly in play, for years. I was bigger and stronger, with more reach, but he was brave and passionate, and crafty. He could throw and kick better than I could; though he took a while to speak, he walked early, and when he could run he was very quick. I'm pretty fast over short distances, and if I have to I can run for a while, but Alexander could keep out of reach. He was capable of ripping my jacket, kicking out, socking me in the head with a well-flung stone, and then sprinting off.

Once, when he did exactly this, I returned to the house in tears. Jenny was unsympathetic—I had punched him. "You didn't have to slug him, Pim," she said.

Another fight in the wood led me to deal him another, this time clearly unjust blow. He was outraged, and I admitted he owed me one.

"You can do what you like, I won't hit back," I said. I turned and began walking away. Alexander came up behind me and smashed me one over the ear and the back of my neck. It really hurt. I spun around, fists bunched, to see him regarding me with suspicion and reproach. I hissed and unclenched my fists.

"Well done," he said, with feeling.

We battled with one another, and against the elements, and against the lurking presence of death; the confrontations with horror, day-to-day victories, and the underlying fear of final forced retreat were often with us. As the first snows, pale outriders of winter, occupied the crests of the highest hills, Jenny pulled on her tattered lambing coat, her boots, and her hat with a blend of resignation and anticipation, the very image of a seasoned soldier going out once more, and when the weather finally relented, months later, she took them off with the tired relief of one whose bloodiest work was done.

May 23rd 1978. After a long cold spring, the first day I could cast my clouts. Yesterday, amid trauma and swearing from Jack, we drenched the lambs in humid sun. We also sawed off the tip of a ram's horns. The most beautiful morning—wonderful to be alive and here—sparkling dew, the air cold and clear—the sun jumping up over the hill behind us, the hedges, the young green leaves, the swallows' backs, Lark's new coat, glowing in the sun.

Lazy afternoon. The children ran home across the meadows, then they played in the trough and tipped buckets of water into the yard, making a stream down to the pens. Jack *fanatical* about waste told them to stop. I lay in the hedge underneath his garden and pretended to be asleep until Lark came and told me she loved me by walking over my FACE. I listened to the sounds in the hot afternoon—the hiss of the water in the trough as the ball-cock bobbed—the children talking and chasing Lark—a flock of rooks on the mountain, on the skyline tumbling, lambs bleating now and again—northwest wind sighing through the firs behind Jack's garden, and absolute silence from him planting leek seeds one by one.

The first day of summer. I thought back to the winter as I looked back into the yard; the children at the trough, Lark, the swallows.

The snow and blizzards, ice and the struggle to get the bales across the yard in wheelbarrow and toboggan—the *bitter* wind—and now young leaves uncurling on the sycamore, starlings, great tits, nuthatches, stonechats, and redstarts, wagtails nesting around the house and the cuckoo calling furiously for its mate and with its greedy marigold eye spying out nests of smaller birds and deciding which to disrupt. A thief in daylight but bringing a dangerous gift.

I found Pim a strange flower and saved it to show him. A wild arum with its single sinister green petal; and when we opened it to examine the pistol and stamens and the premature seeds which grow into fruity scarlet berries in the autumn, he was delighted.

Jack's garden seemed an almost secret place, mysterious and abundant. Out of bounds unless Jack was there, it both allured and forbade; enticing in the same way that Mr. McGregor's garden drew in Peter Rabbit of Beatrix Potter's tale. The garden was on a crown of ground overlooking the yard gate, screened from the track by tall hedge trees. The garden gate stood at the top of a tottering path of stones cut into the steep bank behind the Big Barn; beyond it the garden was a castle keep of growth and life. Among the beanpoles and their bright red flowers, like scraps of a pirate's kerchief, were butterflies; skippers and cabbage whites, kissing and shimmering between the stalks. In the far corner was a rhubarb like a vast sea anemone; around the edges were more butterflies, meadow browns and red admirals, stumbling about above the thick perimeter of nettles. In the middle was the earth, the rich, dark red earth, a deep cake of color and worms. Jack cut it and turned it with endless slow care, and miraculously, it seemed to me, it gave him bright startling carrots, twisted like witches' noses; parsnips and potatoes; onions and cabbages; peas sweeter than sugar. While he worked we scrambled up and down the bank below the gate, plucking at the pennywort that grew between the stones. The waxy little dishes of the plant's leaves intrigued me; I reduced them to a sticky paste. "It's an antiseptic," Jenny said. "Ask Jack. When he nearly sliced his sister's leg off with his scythe his mother filled the wound with pennywort, and it healed. Poor Beat! Imagine! She came too close when you were hay-making, didn't she, Jack?"

Jack nodded, and I looked at his strong, thick-veined hands on the smooth shaft of the spade. I had seen him swing his scythe. I looked at Alexander's legs and imagined it, imagined being the perpetrator of something like that. Jack smiled.

Thursday. Another glorious day—cold to start with N.E. wind but by lunchtime HOT—T-shirt-only weather. Sorted the Patch out after drenching, tailing, and marking the lambs. Spot does seem to be cured. Her udder is soft again. She and Arabella and

Loppy (who worries me a little because I love her so much and she is so small these days) have gone back to the flock. Spot's lamb—Arabella—is quite beautiful. The pride and joy of this year's flock. She always trots up for a talk and nibbles the tops of wellies to get attention. Jack said, "I will miss her—she do always come to me." I went to collect Pim and then on to town to buy dog meal (Lark must now be vegetarian, I've decided) and cold cream and 2 pairs of daps.

Children got out at Far Meadow gate. They set off across the field to talk to Jack, who was "tidying up the meadow" in preparation for the hay. Pim and Twinky stopped halfway and took down their trousers. Watching each other in a wide field of daisies with the view below them, they weed. The level of lead in the air in cities has become alarmingly high according to some expert on *The World at One* today. We watched Snowdrop and Simon as it got dark; they were playing by the old machine. Hot weather forecast. We need rain *soon* for the grass. Owls carolling tonight.

May 27th–June 4th. To Pembrokeshire with Ursie and the children [our three cousins] for 8 days of hot hot sun. Pimmy got sunburnt. I *sat* most of the time and watched the green surf and the silhouettes of the family running and playing across the sand, and did *nothing*. It was lovely.

Despite a screeching aversion to cold water, Jenny loves the seaside, and she loved taking us to it. Once a year, usually in late summer, we went to the west coast, sometimes with family and friends. They were magical weeks, in one of the most quietly wild and beautiful regions of Wales. There is one near-endless beach with tiny stones glinting like gems in its rock pools; there is the red beach, which has a stack of boulders like a dinosaur that you can swim through, and where once after a great storm we watched the largest waves I had ever seen lining up to swallow the rocks and torment the cliffs in sets of seven. In the infinite splashes of blue and white above the coast there were choughs and ravens, peregrines, kestrels, and squadrons of gulls, still-winged on perpetual patrol, line astern across the updrafts.

We always stayed in the same cottage in the same village, rented to my mother for a nominal fee by her old headmistress. It is the only place where I have been able to wake up at exactly the end of the night, and it became a tradition with me to dress and go down through the quiet to the front, then up to the point, and out along the cliffs, wide-eyed and suddenly awake, watching the sky gently extracting itself from the dark arms of the sea. Oystercatchers in their dinner jackets pipe the reveille, jackdaws chatter, boasting about their dreams, and out beyond the islands the gulf sky to the far southwest is a particular pale white-blue, the tone of pure air, washed, rinsed, and scoured by last night's squalls, catching the sun rays now, as the swells of cloud billow with light and the first warmth of the morning reaches for the cliff tops, where the thick and sodden turf rolls over, like God's green shoulder, down to the gasp and grasp of the sea.

These weeks awakened and fueled my fascination for birds. I do not know which I learned to identify first, probably one of our very own carrion crows (always referred to as "the bloody crows," "those buggers," or "those bastards"), but I remember the thrills of my first close encounters with buzzards, like magnificent little Welsh eagles, and ravens, kings of the crow family: fast, maneuverable, and powerful as hell, with their beards and great knife bills. I looked them all up in books, poring over their stats and pictures—I preferred paintings to photographs of birds; within a love of birds, as in a love of fungi or flowers, is a love of art and art-rich books, where most of us get our best views of the rarest species.

I liked the jackdaws that hung around the playground at school, clearing up after break times, but on a dawn walk along the cliffs, though I adored their chatter, from a distance they had the drawback of behaving, looking, and almost sounding like choughs.

Choughs are the Spitfires of the bird world. They fly better, look better, sound better, and in fact behave better than all their crow cousins. Their plumage is blue-black, with the same iridescence as the handsome rook. Their legs are bright red; their matching scarlet beaks are elegant and businesslike: down-curved, sharp. They fly like stunt pilots, hurling themselves into the swirling currents below the cliff edge with casual élan before rocketing up above you, flaps down while they take a look around and make sure you're watching when they break, peeling around, gathering speed for a quick climb and a near-stall into a dramatic stoop, a wings-closed, vertical plummet toward the sea. "Chow!" they shout, and "Chaw!"

They pull out whenever they feel like it, broad black wings, long fingerlike primary feathers extended, catching all their velocity and turning it to pure control; horizontal, diagonal, or vertical speed, whichever the bird fancies. You lose him for a second and the next instant he's sitting on a rock, looking at you, and keeping an eye out for ants. Choughs would make excellent pirates—they have it all, even the battle cries—but they have not developed tastes for robbery or murder. They prefer to catch their own ants. Piracy they leave to skuas.

The wonder of birds lay partly in their liberation from the land, and partly, paradoxically, in their miraculous conformity. It always amazed and delighted me to find birds where the books said I would find them, looking just like their pictures, and behaving as their descriptions said they would. So the bird book says of the redstart "widespread summer visitor, found in old woodlands," and sure enough, in the succulent sunlight of May, there in the ancient wood on the way up to the house, flitting between the hedges and lower branches of the oak, there would be the beautiful bird, with its handsome black mask and flashing scarlet tail.

Birds in their freedom, in their wills and ways, define a relationship with the land and sky that I crave, hopelessly, in the same way I used to wish for wings. A man in a field is an intruder, a visitor, at best a custodian. A bird in the same field is a focal point, a finishing touch, a vivid, living, acting detail, a flourish of pure existence. I woke up once at the farm, pulled back the curtains, looked out at the mountain, the limpid morning light, and saw, forty feet beyond my window, making its way slowly up the grassy bank, a big and utterly beautiful red grouse, his plumage a mottle of russets and chestnuts, his little wattles like scarlet exclamations. He was delicious, in his pride and beauty, as he picked his way up the bank, looking for shoots; he bewitched me. I wanted to touch him, to eat him, to be him; I wanted to watch him all day. I can see him still.

A component of this powerful attraction to birds is the hunting instinct. A man with a gun in a field is a hunter. When the beasts and birds flee you then, they do not do so, as normal, because you are other, weird and dangerous by nature, but because, like the fox and the falcon, you are a predator looking for prey. And like the fox and the falcon, you succeed in the hunt only if you enter the landscape, learn the rhythms and habits of its inhabitants, shake off your "civilization," and return to the world our species has been abandoning for centuries. I never hunted for food or sport; my outings were more like sallies of war. Much as I love choughs, ravens, and rooks, I would happily gun down squawking ranks of their crow and magpie cousins; indeed, I have spent weeks attempting to engineer their slaughter. Daily I looked out the window and scanned the trees in case one had turned up in the orchard. I regarded them as ministers of the devil, and, thanks to their infernal cleverness, and no doubt promiscuity, the entire valley was overrun with them.

Jack and my father went after them with the shotgun, using the old blue Morris as a hide—it eventually broke down near the Middle Meadow gate, and they would huddle in it, the cold double barrel at the ready—but they killed, as I remember, no crows. Crows know when you are carrying, and they understand the approximate range of a gun. I reckon they can accurately assess the different threat presented by air rifles, and they are infinitely suspicious. Their taste for a sheep's eyes and tongue is shared by magpies, which also go for the udders and anus of the victim, and we have known both species to drill directly into the flank of a stricken but still living sheep, plucking out a ribbon of bloody guts like so much pasta. I have shot at dozens of crows, mostly from extreme range and with little success, except once. One leafy summer day in the wood I surprised a raucous family, two inky parents and a flock of kaarking kids. They could not see me as I crouched directly below them, peering through the foliage. I shot one, trembling like an alcoholic in a flood of adrenaline, and they all yelled and swore and jumped around in the canopy, but they still could not see me, and an air gun is very quiet, no louder than clapped hands. My victim lay cooling in the leaf litter while his brothers and sisters shouted and squawked and I inched silently forward. Then, there, unbelievably, twenty-five yards above me and dead ahead, was one of the crows, high in a tree, beak wide open, in mid squawk. I shot him, too, and took the brace home in my game bag. It is an unforgettable feeling, triumphant, vindicated, but also humbled by the dealing of death: grateful for the chances, guilty for taking them.

June 4th, Sunday. The rain came at noon. The earth, baked hard, and the house, warmed all through, but particularly the bedrooms being under the hot stone tiles—seemed hardly to feel it. Two days later after cooler wind and further showers the fields still need more rain. Yet the grass does grow—not much in the butt—but it *looks* fresh and the "bents" are high in the Horse Fields, the buttercups and daisies high in the meadows. The cuckoo loud in the ash. Hope she's not thinking of invading the nuthatch's snug little hole which is halfway up the tree. But probably the cuckoo is too large to push her egg into the hole.

Sheep farmers look at grass as the Inuit do snow. "Bents" are long-stemmed grasses with a sheaf of seeds at the head. "Feg" and "sheep's feskew" are the best kinds of growth, the thick stuff you get on high moorland, the diet of those lively mountain sheep you see if you drive across the Brecon Beacons or any high pasture. At the other end of the scale there is "bare," which is self-explanatory, no grazing, and short of this there is "a bit to pick"—a city dweller looking at a field of this will see acres of short greenish grass, but a farmer will frown and say, "There's a bit to pick, but the animals will have to be moved soon." There is generally grass under the bracken, but it must be bitter and short of goodness, because sheep are not fond of it. "Ronk," Jack called it—a corruption of "rank." They would rather not eat the growth under the hedges either, though if left long enough on a bare field they will. The "butt" is the very lowest level of grass against the ground, and thus a measure of its potential crop—a field of short grass that is "thick in the butt" will sustain a flock for a while. Hay fields, with their many grasses, clovers, daisies, and buttercups, are the zenith of the farmer's achievement with his (or her) grass. By being careful with the amount of time the sheep spent in the meadows, we gained a luxurious, diverse growth every year, ready for harvesting in late summer. One year, in an effort to improve the yield, Jenny invested in bags of organic fertilizer: sacks of dried seaweeds, sands, and tiny little shells. The three of us trudged up and down the fields for days, scattering the stuff by hand. It felt slightly absurd. Then Jenny released a few sheep onto it.

"Oh look, they like the fertilizer. . . . Crumbs, they really go a bundle on it, it must be the salt. . . . Oh, really! Look! They're guzzling it all up, the pigs!"

And that was the end of the fertilizer.

June 7th. My 40th birthday! And I remember so well thinking 13 was old. A dull drizzle on and off all day. Spent the morning walking the flock with Jack and maggoting. We found three with grubs—he got soaked and when I went on alone I found Tommy Tiptoes also twitching. Managed to trim her easily—shears sharper and she very quiet. I talked to her while I did it and when I found the nest in her tail and they began their frenzied wriggling she ground her teeth and seemed almost grateful and cooperative as I got them out. Later I fetched Betty from her farm who came to tea bearing a birthday cake—not the most tactful of coffee sponges, having "40" emblazoned across it in small red balls!—but absolutely delicious and so very kind of her and I haven't had a birthday cake since I was 25. Jack and I and Betty drank Fine Fare champagne and we lit a fire and it was very pleasant. My husband sent a card but did not telephone. At 10:15 dogs were hunting in the L-Shape and the Rough Field and the sheep over there stampeded to the race at the bottom of the Patch, very distressed and baying to their lambs. Got to bed late and suddenly realised I hadn't seen Annie for days. Worried about her for about an hour—seems so odd she hadn't trotted up for nuts—before being joined by Pim, who warmed me up, and we went to sleep at last. The end of my birthday.

Betty was a white-haired widow, and the only other woman farming in the valley. She often spoke of her husband, "my dear Bryn," she said tenderly, seeming to recall a life of complete happiness, which death had stolen from her; "my Bryn," she repeated, refusing to let him go. She lived in a mournful, shadowed farmhouse, with a wild tribe of cats, dozens of them, and a sheepdog, with whom she shared beautifully cooked dinners, served on china. Her eyes were as quick as a bird's. She was like a grandmother and she dealt straight with us. "How many sheep in there?" she asked, shrewdly, after I had crossed her orchard. "You don't know? A farmer's son should *always* count." She was an inspiration to Jenny.

"How Betty manages I will never know," she would pant, struggling with a feed block. "But she does . . . she can even bang in posts!"

On another occasion, when she was babysitting us, we discussed one of our neighbors, Idris, who I said "should be in the loony bin."

"The what?" Betty demanded.

"The loony bin in Talgarth."

"You mean the mental hospital, do you? Who calls it that?"

"Mum does!"

"Will she call it that when she's in there?"

I did not have to think long: "Yes!"

"Well, it's very disrespectful. While you're here, you'll call it the mental hospital."

Around this time, in the first hot yawns of full summer, we went badger watching. The conditions had to be just right: a warm, still evening after a sunny day, with no wind to carry our scent.

"Would you like to go badger watching, boys?" my mother asked, knowing the answer.

"Oh yeah!" we chorused.

"Don't say 'yeah,' say 'yes.' We'll need to be camouflaged. Go and put on something dark green or brown, nothing pale, and meet me in the yard."

We assembled and set off down the track, remarking on the rosehip bushes, their vermilion berries like clusters of balloons, stuffed, as my brother and I knew, with feathered seeds that made the most vicious itching powder. We stuck to the track and ignored the sheep, Jenny ducking their greetings like a film star trying to go incognito. Down the lanes, under the hazels we went, watching our step, avoiding prematurely fallen nuts. At the bottom of the first pitch we paused by the gate to the Horse Fields.

"From now on no talking," Jenny whispered. "Tread where I tread, and go very slowly. When we get close do what I do. We'll crouch down and keep very still, like statues. We'll have to wait a bit but it will be worth it if they come out. The cubs will be big enough to ramble about, but they'll start off playing around the setts, I should think. We might be lucky. Are you ready?"

We nodded.

One after the other we followed her, cautiously climbing the gate at the hinge end and holding it steady for each other. Jenny stuck to the line of the fence, pointing out fallen ash twigs to be avoided. The sun had turned well over the skyline, and the blackbirds were pink-pinking in the hedges, confirming their claims on the world. The cooling land sent up the first twinges of breeze to nudge the tree tops, but Jenny had anticipated it and correctly guessed its currents; we were downwind of the badger setts.

The wood was a dimming, brooding thing. The different heights of the trees formed spires and aerial alleyways above the narrow gully that divided the land. The drop was so steep that we were level with the crown of the canopy; the curly whispering of the stream was barely audible, two hundred feet below.

As we drew nearer the setts Jenny bent double, trying to keep her silhouette below a badger's horizon, and we went slowly after her, copying every move. We inched up a swell in the ground, then crept down, just over the lip of the bank. Twenty yards from the setts we stopped. Our mother placed us just in front of her and we all sat, settled, and tried to keep completely still. There were more than a dozen holes ahead of us, each with its raised stoop where grass had covered mounds of excavated earth, but Jenny pointed wordlessly to two where the earth was fresh and scattered with the dried grass of badger bedding. We fixed our eyes on these.

As all our human motion drained away we became as still as stumps, and sank slowly into a kind of trance. Our ears brought us every tiny rustle and scuff of the world in its lengthening moments; the distant exchanges of a mountain ewe and lamb; the buzz of a motorcycle from the valley; the pillow talk of wood pigeons. As the light lowered to nocturne blues and lacquering greens all our senses stretched; we felt the dusk's harmony like concertgoers—its mystery, melancholy, and promise seemed to spread outward from the wood. It was as though we were almost invisible, our bodies forgotten, leaving nothing but a set of senses, like a family of ghosts, until a sudden flurry of loud chiming cries burst out of a bush nearby, as brash and outraged as a burglar alarm.

"Blackbird," Jenny mouthed in our ears. "He'll leave us alone; don't turn a hair."

We willed him away, defying him with our stillness. After a series of ringing accusations, during which I sent him a stream of psychic abuse, he relented and dived away to investigate something else. The first rabbit appeared, conjuring himself from a patch of nettles, motionless at first, as if engaging us in a keep-still competition. A minute passed before he lopped forward and sniffed the grass, where-upon the rest of his tribe began appearing, bobbing and hopping, their white scuts amazingly bright against the shadow-gathering field.

And then, materializing as suddenly as the rabbit, a large gray shape appeared at the mouth of one of the setts. A long face, with a beautiful silky white nose, black eye mask, and white cheeks contem-plated us with what seemed like great solemnity.

We barely breathed. The badger's snout lifted as she tested the air. She seemed to gather more than scent; she seemed to sniff the atmo-sphere of the quiet evening, the spirit in it, as though she knew there was something about, but could not detect threat in it. After a few moments of peering at us she emerged, followed by first one, then another, then a third snuffling cub. She nuzzled and sniffed them, grunting softly as if reminding them of dos and don'ts. They were adorable, like fat little bears, full of play and trepidation. Soon they were tumbling around, venturing out and dashing back in, pratfalling and beetling about. We watched with disbelieving, delighted smiles. The cubs squeaked and wrestled and rolled, until their mother mar-shaled them and for one moment paused, looking straight at us, as if cautioning us not to move. For a few seconds two families regarded each other, then the badger turned, her cubs went with her, and they vanished into the wood.

We gave them a couple of minutes, then stood, stiffly, and backed away as quietly as we had come. We joined hands as we went back up the pitch, and tried to keep our thrill to whispers.

"Magical!"

"Amazing!"

"Did you see them! Did you see those cubs!"

We had, for a few moments, experienced the world as our wild neighbors did. The dew smell rose in the meadows. We sped back to the farm, vigorous with happiness. For that twilight time we had slipped the separation between us and the world. We were of the mountain, and of the wood, and it was as though the animals, the wild creatures, had allowed it. It was bewitching.

Our mother impressed on us that we were custodians, privileged and responsible, tenants, like the badgers, of a tiny portion of this crumpled, timeless land. By the Horse Fields gate was an oak, older than anything but the mountain itself, a mighty tree, hollowed and bowed, sprung from an acorn, I imagined, when the only lights in the valley at night were the campfires of the armies of Owain Glyndwr, the last true prince of Wales, who led a rebellion against the English in 1400.

"Do you think it saw the Romans?" we asked Jenny.

"Probably its grandfather did," she said. "How I do love this tree!"

We stopped beneath it often. In its monumental age, in the generations of living things that had passed by it, was the assurance of our place in a sequence that had no imaginable beginning or end. To pause under its prodigious sinews and stare at the valley was to stand for a moment with the great parade of its witnessed history, to sense the vast procession that was still passing, from spiders and blue tits to kings on their chargers, and I felt time bending in the face of so much life.

Inside the Big Barn, stamped on the door with the brands each used to mark his sheep, were the initials of the two previous tenants, Emrys and Derwyn. We added our own, and looking at them gave us a feeling of great pride. It was the right place to make your mark, the Big Barn; it seemed to be the last thing about the farm that would ever change.

Friday June 23rd. While the children slept Jack and I worked to make the Big Barn fit for shearing. Moved all the old hay to top bay—swept, and laid bracken over two thirds of the barn floor to protect the fleeces from hay. He worried about the shearing and the weather—also "very doubtful" about my abilities as lifter and catcher. I am too. Later (9:30) Mervyn [a neighbor who lived near the foot of the hill] drove up bringing his bedroom carpet. "They will lie easier if they've something under them," he said. The carpet—black and quite lushly piled—had been damaged when the roof blew off his house in the winter. Nevertheless a thoughtful and generous gesture, I thought.

"Who's the catcher?" said he.

"I am."

"Oh. I see."

"You don't think I'll manage it then?"

"No," he said, straight and quietly. Then, "But we'll do the best we can."

I like him. Competent, contained, authoritative.

Saturday. The shearing of 90 yearlings.

Catching sheep is exhausting, even for a strong man. The animals are quick on their feet; yearlings particularly are lithe and strong. They can turn faster than a human, and they feint this way and that. When they are packed tightly and cannot escape it is merely a backbreaking question of stooping, grabbing, and heaving, but as you get through them the remainder have room to duck and space to get up speed. As you tire and your concentration flags your first grab is often in vain; you follow up, but the animal you have missed once is now panicking, hurling itself over its fellows to avoid you. Doing it herself saves Jenny the cost of another helper, and allows her to catch as she prefers to, as gently as possible, with her arms around the animals, rather than digging her fingers into their wool. She hates to see sheep held like that, imagining it is like being dragged by the hair. She tries to swallow her distress, but sometimes it blurts out: "Under the chin, arms around her!" she cries. "Careful—you'll hurt her!" And the men muzzle their frustration, and try to do as she asks. She works all day in the narrow race, talking to the beasts, trying to soothe them, straddling them, guiding them toward the shearers. She sticks at it, and as her strength wanes the shearers take pity, reaching over into the race as she presents each captive, and hauling it up and over the barrier. The first day is tiring but the next is a marathon: 193 ewes caught, lifted, and shorn, as well as the rams, Tommy and Ron Vaughan.

Tuesday. Earwig walking across my nightie. Cold and dull. Rain is coming.

Wednesday. Jack nettling in the afternoon. Visited Derwyn to ask him to cut our hay. Cow parsley and poppies in the hedges. Tonight thick warm mist—total silence. Not even an owl or an aeroplane. Very spooky. Druid weather.

Sunday July 2nd. Northwest wind dropped at last—warm, wet wind from the west—very strange: cobwebs and raindrops, hanging motionless on the gate—raindrops transforming the wire fences into rectangles of diamonds. Sheep bleating now and again but they must feel as if they walk through a warm bath so soft is the rain. Wraiths of fog rising from the valley floor—white plumes of it against the dark woods. We went to the Iron Age fort. Windy up there though—cloud hurling along the tops: Twinky and Pim soaking and cold. Came back to hot baths, beans, sausages, and bacon. Picked some spinach and served it up, complete with caterpillar. Must be more careful next time. Slugs invading kitchen—bloated disgusting leathery black one on mat outside the kitchen door. What *use* are slugs anyway? Silent, muffled night. Cloud in the yard.

July 5th. David Hughes came and we found unseasonable mushrooms in the Horse Fields, and gathered elderflowers for wine and elderflower fritters! He went too quickly, everyone thought.

David Hughes was a treasured friend of my mother's, a decade older than she, an Anglo-Welshman with slow, kind eyes, an author of novels and nonfiction, a critic and journalist, divorced from a Swedish film star. He seemed to me to have lived several lives. He had a laugh like someone rolling down a hill, and he hugged wonderfully. He was looking for somewhere quiet and cheap to live while he wrote his next book, *The Imperial German Dinner Service*. Whenever David came it meant good food, a dinner, candles on the kitchen table, strong cheeses, hard biscuits, and bottles of dark red wine. Jenny and David would sit around at ease, and my brother and I would play with corks and swords of uncooked pasta, dab the wax and maul the dog. If he decided to lodge at the farm, Jenny knew, his presence and strength would transform the prospects for the winter, and partially answer Robert's arguments: you cannot afford it, you cannot keep it going, you cannot live half in Wales, half in London.

> July 6th, Sat./Sunday. Another cross-roads. For *ever* in green pastures do I ask our ways to be: the countryside seems to be the only true and right place to bring up children. But I have condemned them to the city again. Decided to return to London in September: but I must hold my tongue.

My brother had joined me at the village school, but our progress was not sufficient. Jenny, a former teacher, reckoned we were two years behind our age group in London. Robert maintained that the farm was detrimental to our education and fatal to their marriage—though the last part, by now, was almost a retrospective argument. Yet Jenny agonized. Would moving to London save the marriage, which seemed dead in all but name? She does not seem to have thought it likely: did either of them have any hope for it, really? Would her children's lives be better served by London's teachers, pavements, and traffic, or by fields, hills, and village schools? Could she stand a return to the office, after the freedom of the farm? She despaired at the prospect of leaving, but decided we would return to London, with the farm as her safety net; she would still not relinquish it. It was the most serious decision she had made since marrying Robert, and it was the last one she made without consulting my brother and me: at five and three years old we were just too young.

> Monday evening. Walked the Hill Fields to talk to the ewes. The cats came too. It was evening—heavy and still and thick. Dark under the leaves. The ewes came to me and I stroked their shorn coats, and they gazed up: their faces and eyes the more gentle and

fine for being free of all their wool. The two swallows sat on the
wire together looking quite forlorn. Why aren't they hatching
babies? Are they both males?

Tuesday. Our last lamb born under hot sun, among nettles. Betty
and Jack came to dinner—a beautiful gleaming sunset: Turner—
gold flash through dark clouds—a warm night: loud rain falling
on the barn roof. How I do love this place.

Now the valley muttered with the sound of tractors: it was hay-
making time. Jenny set out on what became an annual round of begging to find someone who would make ours. The narrow windows of
fair weather, and the call of their own fields, made it an especially large
favor for any of our neighbors to grant. First Derwyn refused to do it,
as he and everyone else cut their meadows in the penultimate week of
July. We went to see Mrs. Billy Williams to see if her husband would
do it. Billy vacillated: he gave a yes, then a no, then a yes again, as the
weather broke. We went to an adjacent valley and asked Peter Evans,
who said he would do it. The rain came. The hay was on hold: we went
to Pembrokeshire, where we had ten days of hot sun. We returned to
find the hay still not cut.

Monday August 1st. Telephoned Peter. Standing by.
Long-range forecast: unsettled, sunny intervals. Drenching
driving rain all day. Very noisy tonight. Whisper of autumn?
(Leaves—hazels turning olive and nuts growing—hawthorn
berries turning brown—driving winds scudding the rain.) Like
the seaside. Met Pat. "Don't wish for money," he said. "Just health
and happiness, and you *so* happy with your farm and work and
lovely children far from the crowds and the rat race. Don't wish
for money."
I haven't told him that I am soon to give it all up, and my
heart so aches.
Extraordinary. Back from holiday having taken them miles
away by myself in the car to furthest Pembrokeshire and no telephone call or any money yet this week or sign of interest from

their father. I wonder if it's too late to change my mind. Jack is not well but bought him three oranges. A wild night, curtains of mist and rain hurtling down on us from the northeast and sweeping away over Brown's plantation. Met him and his dogs on the hill driving sheep our way. We turned them. Helped Lark and the children over the fence.

Tuesday August 2nd. Pim drew the curtains and said it would be a lovely day. Was too, in spells, and very warm: rain turning to mist in the sun and rising. There seem so many mouths to fill at breakfast time—after the children the animals line up. Lark—the cats on the wall, the three lambs out the back, wailing for their bottles. Milk, tins, and milk again! That's satisfying and I love it; but getting us three dressed, into our shoes/wellies and macs and finding my purse and shopping bag and shopping list is a night MARE. Called on Jack. He came to his gate in a thundery shower. Looking grey and "sunk." I am very apprehensive about this winter and how he will cope. Hope and pray David Hughes *will* come. Went to see Betty with the children in the evening. Sunlight at last and a thunderhead in the south. We walked across her meadows to look at a field of uncut hay and sucked clover flowers in an attempt to take the nectar. Twinky brought "tea" to me— handfuls of dock seeds now ripening on their tall stems. It was a lovely evening.

Wednesday August 3rd. Dull and drizzly. Took the children to the swimming baths in Brecon. Lunched in the Wellington Hotel—thought of the day we bought the farm—August 18th 1970. (Was it *really*?!)—and I bought the children orange juices in the cocktail bar where Emrys bought us celebratory beers. Everything seemed so bright then.

We had a lovely lunch for £2.50 each. Twinky slept on the floor throughout. The carpets are quite thick. Came home and they had a rain bath under the water butt. Then another hot one upstairs. They went to bed early as the sun came out. I walked down to the Horse Fields and came back via our Quoiker, where I saw nothing amiss. Collected a few mushrooms for a feast with

bacon. A glorious evening. Then Noel came with two hitch-
hikers. Germans.

Noel was a young doctor, with thick dark hair, a beard, and a
bewitching motorcycle. He was the first of the "lambers"—medical or
agricultural students, recruited by notices placed in college newspapers, who were given pocket money, board, and lodging (the Beast
House bedroom) in return for their help with the lambing. Noel was
kind, clever, and patient, and could turn his hand to anything, from
lambing and roofing to mechanics. Perhaps because of his beard, and
our relief and delight at his arrivals, I secretly associated him with
Jesus. I think it came from a blend of my tousled image of John the
Baptist and the parable of the Good Samaritan, stopping to help when
others passed by. Noel's girlfriend, Lesley, was a dark-haired beauty,
moody, funny and fun, whom I once saw naked through a chink in the
bathroom door. I treasured this mysterious and gorgeous image, a first
innocent encounter with the erotic. Noel and Lesley went through difficult patches, exacerbated by the isolation of the farm. They separated
once, and Noel was in despair, but then Lesley came back and it was
all right again. It confirmed my impression that love was tentative
and episodic, a kind of pain.

The lambers sometimes brought their friends and acquaintances to
see the view and relax in what must have seemed a bohemian atmo-
sphere. We all watched Noel's successor, Tim, christened Tree-Tree by
Alexander (Tim was very tall and had bright red hair, so it seemed to
fit), as he fell in love with Jill, a nurse. They lay about in the long grass
out the back, Tim's considerable length outstretched, his head
propped on his hand, visibly, to Jenny anyway, in love.

When lambers left, unless they wanted to return the following
year, Jenny asked them to find their replacements. She trusted them
to conduct interviews and select the next year's helper. In this way we
met Nicola, who single-handedly convinced my mother that north-
erners are very good news; Kevin, who was studying Old Norse at
Durham, and introduced me to Frankie Goes to Hollywood; and
Richard, a former soldier, a Green Jacket, who had the manner of a
man who could command troops in action, and who put a Herculean

effort into sustaining the life of a very pathetic lamb called Dishcloth. There was a hippyish fellow called Martin who was known to his friends as Marty Marty Shitman Hallworth R.O., U.S. Chaplain—a phrase that my brother and I adored. He claimed it came from a book called *Catch-22*. Martin was hilarious. He had one particular look, a sidelong, critically appraising pout, which made us scream. Alexander and I relished the presence of lambers—the house always felt more complete with someone in the Beast House bedroom—but we were not always a joy to them. I got a clout around the head from another Tim for repeatedly ambushing Richard and him as they tried to feed the lambs: Alexander and I popped up at their every turn, flinging handfuls of nuts and cackling.

They arranged a neat revenge—one spring Saturday, my brother and I were woken at eight and informed that our teacher had telephoned, requesting that we attend a special spelling lesson. We moaned, mourning the destruction of our beloved lie-in, dressed, stoically, and went downstairs to find the lambers laughing. It was April the first.

They arrived at the railway station, where we met them, craning to get a first look at the new arrival. One was told, by his predecessor, to look for "an eccentric-looking woman in muddy Wellingtons with two small boys." Some did not last much longer than the first encounter—including one young man who had been institutionalized, and whose father came to collect him after twenty-four hours, during which time he had masturbated into the pages of several of our children's books. (We were not told about it, of course. Only now do I understand all those stains and glued pages.)

Another was sent away when he fretted overmuch about a cut on his hand. He was, quite reasonably it seems now, reluctant to cook the lunch with blood coming out of his finger, but when a plaster failed to persuade him, he was told to pack his bags. Too wet, we snorted.

For those that made the grade, there was a fierce learning curve, with some unexpected challenges.

"It's like bloody Tom and Jerry," puffed Tree-Tree on the first afternoon of his third stay as he skidded backward down a muddy slope, clutching a sledgehammer, as Lark jumped up his legs, and we watched closely, and the post he was trying to bang in swayed precariously on the top of the bank above him.

When the old cat Barty died, Noel was asked to perform an autopsy and establish a cause of death. Noel laid Barty on the floor of the barn and undid his corpse with a scalpel. I watched as he carefully extracted Barty's parts.

"These are his guts—as long as a football pitch, if you stretched them out."

I was impressed.

"This is the liver, these are the kidneys, this is a lung . . . and . . . this . . . is his . . . heart!"

It was a bluish lozenge.

"It's not red!"

"No. . . . And nor is it heart-shaped. All those love hearts you've seen are wrong."

Whenever I think of a heart, I think of Barty's.

As he had for my mother and father, Jack provided the lambers with example and instruction. He personified the expression "a tidy farmer." Though he worked slowly, when he did a job it was a labor of love and skill. When Jack put in a gatepost, for example, he began by felling a tree. We still have the ax he used, a fearsome instrument he swung as lightly as a golf club, and the stump of at least one tree he used is still there. The top is deeply scored; after they had chopped it down, Jack, a lamber called Robert, and Tim-not-Tree-Tree held a coin-splitting competition.

They placed twopence pieces on the stump and took turns swinging at them, mighty blows, the ax heaved up and over their heads. At first the boys could both hit the coins, but when they moved on to fivepence pieces only Jack was striking the middle, and only he could split pennies. I hoarded the debris, particularly pleased by the twos, their dark copper slashed to a winking edge.

Jack would next strip the branches off the trunk, then dig a deep pit. Sinking half the log into it, he left five and a half feet protruding, on which would be hung the gate. Those gateposts are all still there, and good for another twenty years.

Thursday August 3rd. Noel and Pim went to town to buy rafters and nails and flooring for the attic. Showers and sunny intervals all day. Coming back from town (in the sun) with Twinky the road was clouded with flights and flights of white butterflies. Everywhere we looked! Must have simultaneously hatched in the bracken above the road. Twinky and I both enchanted. In the afternoon I walked the sheep. Saw a hare in the distance. Saw a stray dog running over the Far Quoiker and nosing about in ours. Since it wasn't actually chasing the sheep did nothing. Shots heard in the evening.

Friday August 4th. Dull and dreary. Mervyn drove his tractor across our uncut hayfield bringing scaffolding. As he and Noel were sticking it up and I was doing three weeks' washing and also getting lunch at the same time—two friends of Noel's turned up—Di and Ruth. Chaos. Not enough food. I *spun* out some fish. In the afternoon, in the sun, Jack and I and Pim set off to walk the sheep. I went with Lark to the top of the Quoiker, and felt very happy in the wind with the view and Lark behaving herself for once. Then, under the ash trees, was the gutted fleece, skull, and backbone of a tup sheep. Looked almost too big to be a lamb, but it was—all that was left of him was a brown hind leg, a bit of rusty forehead and a horn. He must have died/been killed in the night. Curious and worrying. No ewe bleats for him. She would know already. Lambs never bleat when their mothers die.

Sunday August 6th. Rain again. Called by to see Gwyn, who says the market's good again—so I suppose I must send some little Welsh tups this time, God forgive me. . . .

    A wonderful angry sunset. Wind from the N.W.

    11:30. Screams tonight—strange and eerie. Is a dog killing another lamb?

Friday August 11th. Wonderful morning—sun jumping over the hill. Took 17 lambs—5 Suffolk crosses to market. Kept back two Welsh: one with orf, another with his face all blown up by a sting. His life saved by a wasp. Too many people staying. Whitewashing. Took children on picnic up through the bracken. Shafts of gold through rain clouds from the west—sun and cold wind. The bracken smelt warm though. Green apples. Green plums. Greenish white hazelnuts. One or two fronds of bracken are gold among the leafy green. The council ditcher came to saw down the verges and layer the hedgerows. He seemed surprised anyone lived up here.

Sunday August 13th. Wonderful morning. The first of the lakes of mist in the valley. Dew on cobwebs. Wind rattling through the gold of the witch tree. Rams curled in hollows in the early sun. Where are the swallows? Have they left so early? Must ask Jack if he's seen them. The garden giving forth potatoes, carrots with white worms in them, lettuce, and soon peas. Town for newspaper and swings. Dug up the remains of spinach. Sheep still crying for their lambs, under the dark hedge in the Hill Fields I saw two ewes sitting alone as it got dark (9:30), they looked utterly lonely and their voices are thin and cracked. Soon they'll forget—it's just at night when there are no lambs to snuggle up to. I watch Catkin and her lamb sometimes. Their love for each other would seem quite ridiculous to people who don't watch sheep.

The lake of mist in the valley was one of our touchstones. Following Jenny out through the front door, we saw her take a pace into the yard, stop, and gasp: "Look, children!"

The tops of the browning hills rode like islands above creeks of cloud. The sunlight was dazzling, thrown back by the white below; it was like being in an airplane as we dropped down the lane to school. But it was in ascent that I came closest to the miracle of the mist. It was a dull, muffled day when I began to climb the mountain; a moody shroud hugged the ground. The bracken was a red-mauve tangle, every stem loaded with water, and the grass was a silvered green slick. It was a hands-and-feet scramble up to the first ridge and a glum trudge to the second as the damp wriggled into my boots and clamped cold hands around my trouser bottoms. As I climbed the second ridge I noticed the air above was brightening, the gray thinning to a pearly smoke. Now there were cobwebs of light in it, a fretwork of gleams. With every foot climbed the translucence changed, now paling, and the cloud all around me was blue. Blue mist! Near the crest of this second ridge there was clear sky directly above me, but every other way was azure and opaque. Up two more feet and the top of the mountain appeared, a bright momentary vision, reclining in the sun. I turned around and started: I was staring across a great sheet of mist, like a deep-sea diver breaking through the surface of a glass-flat bay. And there, miles away but intimate, in their revelation, were the peaks of the Brecon Beacons, red volcanoes rising out of a vast white sea. For the next half an hour I sat on the shore of the air as waves of light washed the ridge, sometimes ivory, sometimes blue, with the Beacons vanishing and reappearing like spells, and I marveled at a cloud of bright luminous sparks, specks of light that swam before me, like stars dancing in the air.

Though I feel I have crossed every foot of it, it is never the same mountain twice. In another mist, a dark, predawn blanket, I climbed it after a day and a night of rain. Everything slipped and wept and trickled; under feet and fingers the slopes gurgled and squeezed, like the flanks of a dormant slug. Blind, I felt my way across it, a mite traversing a mammoth, and could hardly believe it when the sullen dawn came up and I found myself at the entrance to one of the old sheepfolds, exactly where I had aimed to be. I felt vindicated, as if I truly understood one thing, this mountain.

Monday August 14th. Fair. Jack and I drenched 83 or so *beautiful* yearlings. The days are shorter and going TOO QUICKLY.

Wednesday 16th. Day of the clouds. Noel and Lesley and I, all of us talked about them to Pim and Twinky individually. This has been the summer of the redstarts and the summer of the clouds. "Don't forget it's the summer of the earwigs too," said Pim. I thought I had lice when I woke up this morning. Had a bath and the shampoo top rushed away down the plug hole thus upsetting the works again. A wonderful dramatic day. Noel on the roof— now some rafters off also—kept stopping to watch the light changing over the Beacons—and the showers rushing towards us through shafts of sun. Cold at night. Enormous moon.

Thurs. Aug. 17th. A sparkling morning. Not one single cloud. Hard china blue sky, sharp light sun vaulting over the hill. Some dew. "Hay making," I thought. "This minute." Phoned Peter

Evans at 8:30. He came and, as the clouds appeared in the west, cut our meadows. Rowan and the first red berries of autumn—Lords and Ladies. Twinky and I stood in the yard under a duck egg sky and the evening star, listening to owls and watching our bat. We whispered to each other. A glorious day. Every time it looked like rain we sang our anti-rain song.

Friday 18th. Peter arrived early to finish cutting and began "woofling" the Far Meadow. Watched the clouds all day but bright sun and fair wind from the south. In the evening went with the boys to the old castle. Harebells are growing in its walls, violet blue against the pinkish stone. Pim and Twinky ran up and down the gallery and then we piled off to the Tower, stopping to play Pooh Sticks on Robin Hood's bridge—much kissing at the kissing gate, and then round the tower we ran in a bright cool wind, and watched young Friesian bullocks trotting over the grass as the farmer sent his dog to call them in. Pimmy said "I'm doing something daring and dangerous and mischievous" as he climbed over the wall and into the meadow. He stood by the weir and then came running back before the bullocks and we watched the swallows dipping their wings as they skimmed the water. Came home and I trimmed the boys' hair and tidied the house just in case Robert should come for his birthday.

On August 19 we hauled the hay in. The great highlight of the summer, the climax of the year, hay-making could take days, ideally in a week of sunshine. In the period running up to it Jenny's forecast worship escalated to a peak of devotion, and the London weather center's tweed-toned, gnomic pronouncements, delivered by the radio, threatened to drive us all mad.

"Unsettled! *That's* no good. . . ." or "Did you hear that? 'Another fine day'—and look at it—look outside! Are we supposed to believe him when he says the outlook's good? The poor little man's mad or he's just making it all up. . . ."

She ran in and out, staring at the sky, listening to the forecast, calling the premium-rate weather line, and the harvester, and tried to make it all match.

After the crucial decision to cut, the grass is first turned and then woofled: the tractor tows a machine like two spiked spinning lobster pots that whirls the hay, drying it and shaking out seeds for next year's crop. Woofling leaves the herbage in thick shaggy lines, which at last the baler scoops up, its elbowed steel arm pumping up and down, *chung-bung, chung-bung, chung-bung,* up and down, while bales drop out of the back. The rhythm of the machine and the chug of the tractor are accompanied by the buzz of insects and the thump of new bales on the sward, and a heavenly smell hangs over the meadows. Freshly baled hay reeks of clover, old suns and cut grasses, rain and earth and dew.

In the afternoon we drag the bales into clusters, ready for collection later, and laze about in the shade of the hedge, dizzy with sunlight. Alexander and I chew grasses like proper farmers and watch the hay maker steering his tractor like a horse, looping around at the end of each pass, sometimes raising his eyebrows or grinning at us in greeting. The day draws on to teatime and the last evening, when we all follow the tractor and trailer around the field, and everyone who can throws bales up onto it. This is called hauling the hay, and I like it best when it goes on into nightfall, with the last load bumping and swaying slowly up the track to the Big Barn, where the stack now reaches up toward the swallows' nests, the lightbulb, and the spiders, dangling on their dusty threads.

The rising scents and dimming shapes of a blue summer night all around us, we came up to the Middle Meadow gate that Saturday night, the beams from the tractor's headlights groping toward the house. The trailer gave a lurch and the load slipped, collapsing in a cascade of hay and cries of alarm. Jack, who had been sitting on the very top, came tumbling down, landing on and in the fallen bales.

"Jack!" someone shouted.

"Jack!" Jenny cried as she scrambled to him in the silence and stillness of the jumble of lumps below the trailer. There was a pause, then, slowly, Jack stood up. His cap had come off. He put it back on, looking as shaken by the fuss as by the fall.

Then Alexander stepped backward off the track and fell into a thick clump of nettles by the gate. He screamed. Falling into a lot of nettles is horrific, especially as a small child: the vicious, stinging, burning pain is like standing in a wasp's nest, as Alexander knew: he had done that, too, in the garden in London. He was rescued and comforted and hustled home for a bath: nothing really helps, not even dock leaves, as much as the fact of being treated.

Meanwhile the bales were reloaded, lashed, and the work carried on until the last was hauled off the trailer, lugged across the floor, and heaved to the top of the stack. There were tired cheers and then a nervy consultation about leaving the barn doors open: hot, damp haystacks have set themselves ablaze, and we all imagined waking to smears of smoke, then gouts of flame, bursting out through the roof and slit windows.

"Do you think it will be all right, Pete?" Jenny asked anxiously as we surveyed the sweet heap. To me it was as though the hay was a God, so much worried over, so much debated, installed now in its shrine but perhaps not yet appeased.

The adults stuck their hands in between the bales, felt around, sniffed samples, looked at one another. I copied them.

"Aye, should be," was the verdict, and the hay-making was done. We went inside and began trying to clean up, sluicing hayseeds out of our ears and noses.

The next day I went down the track with a good whippy stick and the promise of righteous destruction speeding my steps. Slashing down nettles with sticks, scythes, boots, anything, was one of the few acts of destruction our mother approved. I reduced the clump that had hurt my brother to a tangle of bleeding black stalks and wormy yellow roots. Nettles follow human and animal doings; around gates and pens, at the doors to barns and sheds, at the edges of streams, around feed racks, wherever sheep or men have been, nettles are, poised to strike at the merest contact. A really good sting can burn all night and still be there when you wake. Alexander and I became familiar with all the various levels of venom different plants contained (the little dark autumnal clumps were the worst), and connoisseurs of the lumpy rashes they inflicted. Amazing to us, Jenny seemed able to ignore them; sometimes she pulled them out with her bare hands. "Ouch! Doesn't it hurt?" we cried. "Ow, Mummy! Stop it!"

"Oh, I'm used to it," she said wearily. We were deeply, unreservedly impressed.

We did a great deal of nettling over the years, and it was very satisfying, particularly with a sharp scythe. Nettles were bracketed with crows, maggots, flies, magpies, thorns, thistles, barbed wire, rain, the Tory party, and the east wind: to be loathed and feared.

Friday. Another wonderful day. To the river in the evening. The tops of the beech trees are turning yellow in the woods above the estate. The corn harvest is nearly done and the squirrel in the wood is making premature raids on the hazelnuts and leaving the shells all over the lane.

Walked round the flock to check the poor castrated lambs. A disgusting and shameful business. Annie rushed up followed by her daughter (now called Ella) and I amazed to note how jealous she is if I stroke other ewes. Twice she elbowed them out of the way. The rowan trees are burning bushes, flaming berries bright as jewels. The badgers have been excavating too, and at the entrance to one bury, heaped with a frantic pile of new-turned earth, there were bones, two sheep shoulder blades (one of them lamb size) and some chicken bones. This industrious badger has probably dug his tunnel into the back of a fox's den which lies adjacent. I watched the ravens croaking spirals to each other as one climbed and climbed in circles to join its mate soaring miles above us. And almost invisible because so high was a flock of birds flying south. Could they have been the swallows? I have missed them in the yard these last two nights.

Saturday. Dull again, rain in the morning. No water. Made rowan jelly after much desperate boiling potted it like mad and fear having examined one for 4 hours later it may not be jelly but juice. Walked the ewes. The Quoiker yearlings are quite beautiful. Elegant, long-legged, confident, in the pride of their youth. Lovely animals—they gaze with heads high standing still as you walk by, and sometimes wicker a greeting. In them I place my monetary hopes. They have grown so fast this summer. Autumn has definitely come—golden and promising many apples—Jack has harvested his precious onions.

*

Thursday August 31st. A week of sun—mists in the mornings but bright later. Lesley and Noel worked like mad on the roof. Tiles still off. Polythene cover at night—plaster and wood dust in the bedrooms and in the beds if I am slow to make them. Still no water—dust and dirt horribly depressing. Children need a bath. As do I. Today dull and actually quite cold. Drizzle and low cloud. Jack and I gathered Hill Fields and weaned their lambs. Annie knew she was losing Ella. For the first time I watched her come and bleat for her lamb at the gate dividing them, and then she looked at me with anxious reproach. And another thing. Passing the Patch I said, "That lamb looks miserable—perhaps it needs a drench." But I'm sure now that it was grieving for its mother (the young ewe with Gid) who has been dying at the bottom of the Patch and whom at LAST Jack consented to kill. Lesley and Noel to London leaving plastic flapping. Hope we don't get a strong wind. . . . The swallows haven't left quite yet! Saw them flying into the stable this evening.

Not quite the end of the summer of earwigs and clouds.

Friday September 1st. Drenched our beautiful yearlings. Had planned to do it in the morning but Mervyn delayed and in the event the afternoon was better. Sunny and warm—jerseys off. Sheep very hot when they arrived at the dip. Waited a good half hour. They gasped as they swam, just as bathers when the first wave breaks. Pim found some small blackberries and then Twinky wanted some but there weren't any, only wizened green beginnings. So he ate groundsel instead.

The weaned lambs have become scared without their mothers but they look quite happy in the meadows though jumpy—bunching and running at the slightest excuse. Pim and I watched Jack walking home in the cool golden sun—walking steadily, surely, exactly at his own pace across the meadows, flat fields of canary yellow. We sat on a hay bale in the yard and a single swallow flew by. The green woodpecker has been laughing these last days. Lark has gone. The apples grow larger, tipped with red. September will be luscious with fruits. My instincts are to harvest and preserve everything these days. Memories, pictures, not only berries. The rowan jelly hasn't set but at least I've caught its taste and colour.

Saturday. Went early to town to look for Lark. She was seen by the bowling green, upsetting the players and chased away by an off-duty policeman who complained that she "wouldn't go away." The sun so bright rolling along the top of the mountain, the distances and edges of hills and trees so clear. Pim remarked on the darkness and length of our shadows. We all wandered around outside and sat in the sun. I could hardly bear to go inside to make breakfast.

Monday. Constable Clayton telephoned—Lark found near Forest Coal Pit. In town overheard conversation in the butcher's shop—
     Butcher: "Whose funeral is it today then?"
     Woman: "The neighbour's. Two pork chops, please."

Wednesday Sept. 6th. Vet came to do the castrating at 9:30. Went to collect Jack—the swallows are *still* here after all—and we chased lambs up and down the First Meadow. After rain, mackerel skies of great height and speedwell blue. Squirrels nutting more busily than ever. Jack picked last of the peas. The corn is in now. Valley seems quiet—we have finished with tractors for the moment it seems and wait now for ploughing and chain saws. Twinky and I walked in the First Meadow in the evening to stir up the poor stiff wethers. The bracken is just turning on the mountain, the heavy bottle green tinged with brown. More rain tonight. Tomorrow perhaps we can have baths. Noel woken at 1:00 a.m by "torch flashes" in the yard.

Thursday. Went to town in the morning with Noel, Pim and Twinks. Noel in the newspaper shop actually heard someone say, "How much is that dog in the window?" There was also a hot gospeller who misguidedly placed his soapbox near Pat's shop. An unfortunate choice of venue, giving rise to much ribaldry and scorn.
     Twinky and I chose fish in the market. He stroked the smoked

cod because he liked its brilliant orange colour. I chose white cod. Shopped and met Betty for coffee. Met Mrs. Thomas, who said, "I thought you'd already left."

Came back for fishy lunch and afterwards as the skies cleared and blue appeared Jack and I set off to shift sheep. In the end after MUCH sweat (Jack so afraid of catching cold because he'd sweated so) we achieved 127/125 ewes up on the mountain, lambs and old ewes in the Horse Fields and Lower Meadows in two groups awaiting dipping on Saturday. Walking the ewes up the mountain, pushed by Lark through forests of bracken, was hot— the lights and shades, the iron black clouds against turquoise bands of blue and plumes and mares' tails of silver overhead and the incredible golds and bottle greens of the valleys beneath us made me breathless also. The grass up there has blades thin as needles, but there are whinberry leaves and if they forage they should find enough to live on. How well and creamy they look now, but a month of hard living will reduce that no doubt. Twinky and I watched the evening and the sunset in the yard. Pim and I made wishes to the new moon. He wished for peace in the world, and for wings, to fly. In the distance the rams were fighting—we heard the *clack-clack* of their horns as they clashed, we watched the rooks fly home down to the valley from the mountain, we heard the thin "tinking" of a blackbird and the twittering of high-flying pipits—the sky cleared and grew palest blue—a wind got up and it grew colder as dusk fell. The swallows have left now. Not a bat to be seen. So very quiet and still tonight. Summer all but gone, and so am I, and how desolate the farm will be—Jack and Thistle and Bart all alone again after almost 10 months of living here. Jack is very morose these days.

And with that, and an entry for Friday, September 8, about selling twenty-six yearlings for £37.50 each, taking the ewes up the mountain a last time and packing a suitcase, and noting that a ewe called Crosslegs had been bitten—by a snake?—Jenny took us back to London.

❖　❖　❖

Now we went to school in Kensington. My father would walk me there, across the park. He and Jenny never argued aloud; any conflict between them was conducted either in silence or formality. They were polite to each other, and apparently kind and considerate, yet they were utterly separate: two individuals, sharing only us and the basement flat.

Friday afternoon meant squatting on the school steps, looking out for the car. When our mother appeared, often slightly breathless, we piled in and set off. Down Kensington High Street, across to Holland Park, and down into the jams at Shepherd's Bush. Via Hammersmith flyover and Chiswick roundabout, soon we were on the motorway and passing Heathrow. I lectured my mother on the extraordinary size of the jumbo jets flying over us—as long as the Eiffel Tower is high, I claimed—and then we all eyed the first flock of sheep outside London: black-faced things on the side of a reservoir south of the carriageways.

Once she had settled into the drive, my mother would begin to tell us stories. Shakespeare's plays told as tales and historical adventures were favorites: Drake and the Armada; great battles of the Royalists and Roundheads; Charles hiding in his oak tree; the exploits of Bonnie Prince Charlie; the story of the Scarlet Pimpernel. The heroics and tragedy of Owain Glyndwr and his great dog, Gelert, held us in breathless attention. One of the most gripping stories was *Hamlet*, told on a dark night somewhere in Wiltshire as we rolled past roadworks in a thickly coned slow lane. "It's a black and eerie night on the battlements of Elsinore, and the sentries are jumpy. They think they've seen something in the dark . . . they're scared. They think they've seen a ghost."

Sometimes it did not register with me that these were not true stories, and occasionally I lost the connection between a familiar story and its author: the source of many déjà vus in English lessons.

When the stories ended my brother and I started waving to other drivers and punching each other. A tall radio mast at one of the service stations was traditionally hailed as "halfway," though halfway between what and what I was never sure. We glanced over Mum's shoulder, not quite believing encouragements like "You're doing very well" and "Not long now," and started punching each other again. The dead arm and the dead leg were a large part of our childhood. A good solid blow, trapping the muscle against the femur or upper arm, causes sharp pain, followed by an amusing numbness. Pile in another blow on top of the first, or add a dead arm to a dead leg, and your opponent can be reduced to a sort of giggling agony. The game could be played either freestyle, taking shots at each other at random, or more coldly, like Russian roulette, each taking a shot and giving one in turn. This could make us scream as we refined it, drawing gentle circles with our fingers on each other's thigh or arm: "It's going to go right there, into the middle of this circle . . ." one would inform the other as the victim convulsed with anticipated pain and near-hysterical mirth.

The approach to the Severn Bridge filled us all with relief; we wound the windows down for a blast of dark sea air, a tradition Robert started, and gazed at the great channel, its vast and smoky waters, and the light buoys balancing their little lanterns on the coursing tides. We were "weekenders" again, until the next lambing. Jenny made only one entry for that period at the farm:

The lambing in the bitter spring of 1979 was terrible: a battle half lost. Appalling weather. Indifferent/disastrous "help"—mistakes— incompetence—exhaustion—starving ewes and lambs—pneumonia. Lambing sickness, one case of Black's disease, scrapie. Marigold dead. Lambs with eyes taken—lost/frozen twins. I dread the next lambing already.

The diary begins again in the summer holidays. The summer was good, then poor, then good again. Monday, August 27, 1979, was, my mother wrote:

The Most Glorious Day of the Whole Summer. It's come back— the summer, I mean. Pim and Twinky and I woke to see the blue sky reflected in the Big Barn roof. We leapt up and stepped out of the kitchen door into brilliant sunlit morning—the sky cloudless clear blue, translucent as the sea. Quiet and still, dew on the grass, ravens rowing across the sky to the larch wood—a kestrel hanging above the mountain, and the sheep sitting in hot sun just outside the hill gate. The boys and I had breakfast, then took them up, high this time, onto the mountain. The thin grass up there was gold in the sun; the whinberry wires shiny green cushions. The sheep bleated disconsolately.

Before they found the farm my parents were looking for a weekend place. Many of my mother's friends had such an arrangement—though, as my father pointed out, most of them were rich. My friend Adam's family had houses in Kensington and Florence, as well as mid Wales. Going to see Adam and his mother, Clarissa, at their farmhouse meant friends, wonderful food, vast supplies of Lego and Star Wars and Smurfs, a trampoline, and a taste of the good life, one that I assumed to be normal, something inaccessible but not entirely out of reach.

Wednesday 29th August—To Clarissa. Helped to haul her hay. Twinky slept in the grass. Jack and I raked hay cocks. I asked him—as we rowed up the hay with our wooden rakes, as the shadows darkened as the slanting late summer sun turned the grass golden and the hills around us glowed—whether this reminded him of his childhood. He said it did. He said too he couldn't bear to see wasted swathes left behind the baler. "It's like fire on my back, you understand." He picked up a handful of grass and clover—"On a frosty morning, for a sheep, this would be wonderful." I raked less desultorily after that—but it was hot as we loaded the bales and rumbled to and fro to the barn on the trailer. The boys loved it. Everything. The people, the food, the weather made a lovely generous day. Twinky "found" a white pony named Taffy. "Oh Mummy," he said, "I do wish I could ride it. Adam does, without a helmet." He had serious doubts when the animal stood over him, haltered and ready. In the end, I got on and held him in front of me. His first ride. He was most nonchalant about it afterwards. Jack "really enjoyed" himself also.

At the end of the school holidays we went back to London again: perhaps Jenny meant to offer the possibility of some sort of partnership based on children and proximity. It was much too late. Along the shelves in the hall were long white spaces where my father's books had been. He was there to welcome us, but he was quiet and subdued. I resolved that I would get up early the next morning so that he might walk me to school. They did not share the same bed; Mum slept next to me in mine. The next morning I leaped up and ran next door to the double bed, and found it empty. The covers were arranged as if it had not been slept in. I knew then that something definitive had happened, but I checked anyway, and he was not in his shed, nor in the kitchen, nor the bathroom.

I came back, crying, and Jenny sat up in bed, and looked at me with such sorrow and sympathy.

"Where is he?" I wailed. "He's gone! Where is he?"

"Oh, dearest," she said, shaking her head, her face despairing. "He's left us. He's left me. I'm so sorry. I'm terribly, terribly sorry."

And she told me that he still loved us, and that of course we would see him again soon, and that she and he were friends, of course they were: it was all going to be all right.

In that terrible moment, as I stared at my mother, we confronted a flat and simple truth that we had both been avoiding. My father's disappearance was wrenching and desperate but it was not an ambush: it was a confirmation. My mother must have known some sort of end was coming, and perhaps I had been waiting for it too, as I emulated her, carrying on, child and parent acting, for each other's sakes, as if things would improve. But I half believed, half hoped that, imperfect and tense as they were, things would nevertheless go on forever; that my father would always come home from work, tall and beautiful in his suit, his smart shoes and long dark mac, with a Hamley's bag under his arm, which he often had, and our mother would marvel at the presents he had brought my brother and I, complimenting him, reaching out to him through her approval and praise of the toy cars and soldiers. And sometimes, I expected, we would go on trips together, like the time we went to Brighton, when my mother chatted happily in the passenger seat, pointing out a hundred things, and my father smiled gently and said "Hmm" and "Oh yes" as she remarked on something, and I lolled in the backseat beside Alexander, watched the clouds above us, studied the flanks of the buses and cars beside us in the traffic jams, and felt safe and completely content. In the evening she would tease him about watching a western or an action film on the television. "Your father wishes it was him!' she said as Fletcher Christian flourished his sword at Captain Bligh, and he smiled, and I smiled, because as far as I was concerned that was him. Then they put us to bed, and read to us, and sometimes, if there had been a model aircraft kit in that week's Hamley's bag, my father would work away at it while I slept, so that the first thing I saw when I woke was a gleaming fighter plane standing, poised for action, beside my bed. What a lucky, happy child I had been in all those moments. But now the big bed was empty, and my mother was sitting, disheveled, in mine, and everything was lost, and wrong.

And she must have known that her sentence "He's left us" was not the whole truth, or not the only truth, and though I think I sensed the concealment and simplification of the words, I went along with her. At that moment it was entirely his fault. It was a crude solution, like giving up a hopeless struggle with some intricate knot and pulling the longest string, reducing everything to a small, mean bead.

So I wailed in shock, but not in great surprise. I can still see the dim bedroom—the light coming down awkwardly from the pavement level—and recall an apprehension of the emptiness and uselessness beyond my grief, the sensation that there was nothing below it, no hope that it would alter anything. My crying was agonized but there was something else in it too: wrapped in the vivid unreality of the disaster there was a consciousness of it; I was not swept away in unreasoning sorrow. Beneath the tears there was a feeling of conclusion. The fracture had started long before that moment and ran on long afterward, but in its revelation, in the way it split open, in an instant, the world of the basement flat, it exposed the worst of itself and left my mother, my brother, and me standing more or less where we already were. It was the worst thing imaginable, but we had already imagined it. Uncertainty was crushed, vain hopes extinguished; the days of quiet tension and loud silence were over. It was as though he had died, as if the three of us who were left had suffered a disaster: the disappearance of our father and the death of our family. Whenever he reappeared, more curious and desirable than ever to me, it was like passing an afternoon with a ghost. Life continued in a strange, breath-held way: it seems now like a time of grief and mourning, the world robbed of the possibility of joy, underlying calm whipped away, leaving a permanent need and a desolate question, "Where's your father?" which we would be asked so many times in the following years, and which nothing answered, and which could not be exorcised by shouting, crying, or accusation, because we all felt ourselves responsible for it.

We did see Robert soon, and they did seem to get on better now, putting on a cheerful front for us on the Wednesdays and Saturdays when he came. That autumn they sat together in the garden with Alexander, in the sun, as I ran around and around. We made the best of it all, in that terrible, repressing English way, but there is a photograph of Alexander and me, taken at school, that sums up the time. Our hair has been washed and brushed, our uniforms are neat, and the photographer has posed us side by side; the picture is mounted in an oval frame. The photographer was a friendly, elderly man who tried hard to make us smile. In the picture, we gaze out at him, and we look utterly miserable: solemn and stone-still. We associated cameras with our father; this unfamiliar old man seemed a bad parody of him, a confirmation of what we had lost. Everything about Robert became special, desirable and fleeting. He took us to the swimming pool with him, the parks and the museums, and I watched him intently, and inhaled his smell from the miraculously clean white handkerchief he always carried, with which he wiped our ice-creamy mouths or running noses. I had an exceptionally good memory as a child: from the moment he left, almost to this, I remembered whatever he said as if it were gospel. I began a relationship with him then that would take us over twenty years to resolve: half unconditional adulation; half concealed but furious reproach.

We had only one conversation about what had happened, sitting on a bench in one of the playgrounds in Holland Park as we watched my brother exploring a large climbing frame, which was made of hollow green plastic cubes. Alexander's expression was downcast, as was mine, and sitting on that bench under a mulberry tree, my father decided the time had come to talk about it.

"Look," he said, "I know this is very hard for you, but do you understand why I'm not living at the flat anymore?"

"Yes," I said. "Why?"

"Well, I just think it will be better for all of us if Jenny and I don't live under the same roof. I'm not going to disappear; I just think it will be better like this. You can understand that, can't you?'

"Yes," I said. And of course I did not. I understood that he was taking responsibility for the fact of what had happened, for the decision, but there was no sense of why he had made it, except in the overtones. "Better for all of us if Jenny and I don't live under the same roof." The implication was that somewhere there was an inexplicable, insurmountable fault. But where was it? What was it?

The day we finally left the city Mum took Alexander and me on the Thames on a boat. It was an uncertain London afternoon: glimpses of clear sky between chapped clouds, the river sulking somewhere between brown and gray. When we returned to the basement flat we found the front door broken in.

"Wretched man, he knew what he was doing," Jenny lamented, having established that almost nothing had been touched. "Grandpa Joe's dueling pistols have gone . . . probably the most valuable things we owned. . . . It's pretty well the final straw. . . ."

The police dusted my tin toy box for fingerprints, admitting as they did so that it was pointless, and we climbed into the car once again. Jenny wriggled, settling herself into the driving seat, then turned and looked at us.

"Well, good riddance to London, I say—Wales, here we come!"

We rallied smiles, hoisting hopes in answer to her grin. Wales! Windy skies blew through the word, wild seas chopped its edges. "Wales, here we come!" we echoed, and away we went.

6

The Mountain for Good

W E ARRIVED WELL AFTER NIGHTFALL, THE WOOD LIKE a Gothic fairy tale, its pale fingers steepled above a goblin legion of knotted trunks and boles; civilization reduced to the glints of the village lights below, then extinguished, as the road turned upward again, toward the mountain.

The rushing, empty cold of the wind made me shiver as I opened the far gate. The rough turf of the track undulated in front of the car; rocks and ruts shook the steering wheel in Jenny's grip, as if to repel our arrival. The walls of the barn and house were ghostly white, a silent answer at the very end of the questing road.

Standing in the yard for a moment, in the dark, with the smell of the wet fields in my nostrils, I stared to the south, over the mountains, at an orange-indigo glow in the sky. It came from the lights of Merthyr and the Valleys, and looked ominous.

Seen from space, on one of those maps of the lights of the Earth at night, South Wales blazes as brightly as anywhere in Europe. We were just beyond the rim of it, in the dark, but only just. The wash from streetlights and headlights has banished darkness from the sky above the Valleys and the coastal plain, but what you see now is merely the latest term of that banishment, which began during the industrial revolution. The last time the lights went out down there was during the Second World War, but the curves of the coast make the Bristol Channel simple to navigate from the air; Hitler's bombers had no trouble finding the great shipping termini of Cardiff, Newport, and Barry Dock. From his lookout on the old hill fort at the top of the valley, where he curled up with his shotgun and some cider, doing his bit, keeping watch for German paratroopers, Jack watched the conflagrations in the sky, saw the colors of the flames playing above the horizon like a fiendish aurora. It was not the first time hell had come to the world beyond our hills. During the industrial revolution, when the mineral wealth of the South Wales valleys was bled and sweated out of the ground to fuel the changing of the world, chroniclers record that the density of the workings and their ferocious industry made dark the day and lit the night sky with fires.

The front door scraped over stones swollen by rain and damp, opening to the dank smell of mold that lingered around the door. In the kitchen the cooker needed lighting; Jenny began half an hour of cursing and prodding the oily old machine as the wicks refused to hold the flame. Upstairs, the bedrooms were divided by thin wooden partitions that were papered, inexpertly, with jolly flowers. The ceilings were wooden planks lagged with old newspaper: above Alexander's bed you could see between the boards a little picture of a bull and lists of stock prices at some market of long ago. The cracks always made me think of snakes, ever since Jenny told us a story about a night in Thailand when she had been advised that there were snakes in the rafters: "They said sleep with your mouth closed and you'll be fine! Sleep with your mouths closed, children," she teased.

She tucked us in and answered the question I always asked her: "What are you going to do before you come to bed?"

"Well, I'm going to have a cup of coffee, and listen to the radio downstairs. Then I might sit by the cooker for a bit, and then I'll come up, I should think."

I asked her to turn off my light when she came up, so that if I woke I would know that she was in bed. If I woke with the light on I leaped out of bed, zipped through my brother's room, down the stairs, through the sitting room, running over the sofa rather than round it, and arrested my flight only at the kitchen door; opening it very carefully, I sidled in, dreading that she would not be there.

"Hello, darling, everything OK?" My mother smiled, reassuringly.

"Yes," I puffed, while the world settled back into its right course. "Are you coming up soon?"

"Yes, I am. I'll see you in a while."

If she went out without telling me, or stayed in the fields with the sheep after nightfall, I suffered fits of worry. Suppose she broke her leg and couldn't get back? Suppose she met badger baiters and they attacked her? Suppose Something Happened. It was not just that I loved her and worried about her: she was all there was between my brother and me and the wild, indifferent world, and without her I knew I would have to take charge, and I feared that responsibility.

Jenny tried to calm me with loving, sometimes agonized reassurances: "Don't worry, don't worry, I'll always come back—don't I always come back? Have I ever not come back? No. Well then . . . I'll never leave you, I promise I won't. You're my boys. . . ."

When this did not work she tried dismissing my fears, airily. "Oh, stop fretting. It's quite ridiculous! Nothing will happen, and if it does just call Ursie, she'll come and sort it out." By the telephone there was a bent and yellowing postcard bearing a list of emergency numbers, an ominous precaution. I had a strong relationship with it, formed the evening Jenny came in from the fields with a clutch of different mushrooms. She loved mushrooms but was inexpert in their identification. She held up various specimens, comparing them with a wall chart of edible fungi.

"Hmm, not sure, not sure. That one's definitely all right, and this one might be a blewit . . . but what about these? I must say the drawings aren't very good. Where's that book?"

"I wouldn't touch them if I were you," I huffed. "They're probably poisonous."

"No, I don't think this one is, or these—they might be delicious."

"But you don't know!"

"I'm pretty sure. I'm going to eat these three anyway."

"But what happens if you're wrong?"

"Well, I'll be a bit sick or something."

"Don't eat them!"

"Look, if you're worried, here are the numbers—if I start foaming at the mouth just pick up the phone and say, 'My stupid mother's eaten a toadstool!'"

It was funny and terrifying. She fried the beastly things and ate them defiantly as I sat, waiting for the first sign of disaster. It did not come, and the incident seemed further confirmation of her bravery, which I knew we all needed, and her mercurial foolishness, which I both loved and feared.

Adult life was a mystery to me. What did they get up to, by themselves? What was she thinking about, sitting by the cooker? It was as though she was on watch. What was she watching for? Nothing, there was nothing to be scared of. She was careful to maintain that line, and waited years before telling us some of the things that happened when we were at school, or after we had gone to bed.

One rainy equinoctial night, the gray dimness outside having tipped into a wet black, Jenny, having put my brother and me to bed, was sitting in front of the fire, kneeling close to the hearth on the rug, absently picking wood chips out of its spark-pitted fibers and flicking them into the flames. Lark had been dozing on the sofa, but now suddenly pricked up her ears, growled, and barked. Jenny stared at the curtained window, in the direction of the yard.

"What is it, Larky?"

Even as she asked it there was a deliberate double knock on the door. Lark barked furiously and leaped up. Jenny's heart thumped in her chest. There had been no sound of a car. Whoever was outside had walked up to the house, through the rain and dark. Knock knock, it came again. More barking.

Jenny was on her feet now, approaching the front door. The walls were three feet thick and the door was bolted, but it was only a few old wooden planks. She thought, for an instant, of the shotgun, upstairs under her bed. Too far away, too terrible.

"Who is it?"

"Only me." A man's voice, low, local.

"Who are you?" Jenny heard anger in her own tone, and a sort of archness, not quite disguising her fear.

"Huw, Jen."

"Huw!" she cried. "Goodness sake, you gave me a fright."

Huw was a surly but not unfriendly farmer who lived two valleys away. Even as she reached out to unbolt the door she thought, almost said aloud, What on earth does he want?

Huw was wearing his cap, tweed trousers, Wellingtons, and an old jacket. He was soaked, smelled of damp and mothballs and tobacco. He grunted about his boots, and slipped them off.

"What is it, Huw?" she asked as he brushed away Lark's inquiring nose.

He straightened, looked at her, sharp dark eyes in a thin, weathered face, and said, sorrowfully, "I miss her something awful, Jen."

His wife, Mary, was two years dead.

"Oh, dear. Dear Huw. It must be awful for you."

"Aye," he said. "Terrible lonely."

He went and stood with his back to the fire. "Have you anything to drink, Jen?"

"Erm, no," she said, thinking of the whiskey. "I'm afraid I haven't. Tea?"

"Proper wet out there," he said, turning slightly to one side, as if to warm his thighs. "You must get lonely, Jen, don't you?"

She ignored the question.

"Well, you must go home and get dry, luvvie. You shouldn't be out in it."

"Don't seem to care what happens," he said quietly, shooting her a look, "since she went."

"Poor Huw. You get warm for a minute and I'll make us some tea, then you must go home and look after yourself."

She ducked into the kitchen, shutting the door behind her. She put the kettle on, shaking her head. How to make him go without making him an enemy? She lit a cigarette. The kettle boiled; she made a perfunctory cup of tea and went back to the living room, determined to be brisk.

Huw was standing in front of the fire in his socks. His trousers were stretched along the hearth; there was no sign of any underpants. His penis was long, and pointing at her feet. He looked her in the eye.

"Don't mind if I dry my trousers, do you, Jen?"

She stood absolutely still. "Actually, I do rather, yes."

He continued to look at her. She didn't know where to put her gaze, so she looked at Lark, who was looking at Huw, with her head on one side. I absolutely must not laugh, Jenny thought.

"Do you want it, Jen?"

She shook her head. "No. I don't."

"Don't you miss it, Jen?"

She shook her head again, looking at her feet. "Please put your trousers back on, Huw."

"They're all wet."

"Put them back on, please. You must go now, dearie, please."

For a long moment they both stood still, then he turned toward the fire.

She looked away while he picked the trousers up and put them back on, with a wince. She was still holding the cup of tea she had made for him, she realized, and put it down. She moved his Wellingtons a couple of inches toward him and stood back while he put them on, then she opened the front door, and stood back again.

"Go carefully," she said.

He gave her a brief, still look.

"Good night."

He said nothing. She shut the door behind him and slid the bolt across. Then she turned around, stared at Lark, and put her hands to her head. Her jaw dropped and she gave a silent squeak of horror, relief, and near-hysterical amusement. Lark barked and wagged her tail.

"Oh, my Lord, Larky! Did you ever . . . ? I mean to say . . . ! My *God*! Shh now, you'll wake the boys."

While she was downstairs, "listening to the wireless," my brother and I talked, occasionally raided each other's beds for a pillow fight, and read. Once we cracked reading, and with no television to distract us, it became a shared addiction. Mum brought hundreds of books with her from London. Everywhere there were books, and since we loved to reread, there was never a chance of us getting through them all before we grew up. We were both awake and preoccupied when Jenny came up, carrying her wireless under one arm, not missing a moment of Radio 4's evening schedule. Roald Dahl's *Charlie and the Great Glass Elevator* was the first novel I read, from first word to last, for pleasure and without being prompted.

"I've just read this book," I announced, as if I had just learned to fly but was trying not to show off about it.

Mum was gratifyingly delighted, and I remember the elation coursing through me as I lay in the dark, listening to the shipping forecast murmuring out of her room. "Scram!" the murderous space egg-worms had spelled out to Charlie, as he stood gawping at them. "Scram!" said the Vermicious Knids.

Enid Blyton and her ideal children, with their absent parents and their adventures, which always began with the discovery of a hoard of tinned peaches, and always ended with a lift home from their grateful friend in Interpol, came next. Willard Price's boys, Hal and Roger, became favorites—they were in the business of capturing and shipping dangerous animals to zoos and safari parks, on behalf of their absent father. It was reassuring to find that many books featured children in the wild, answerable to no one, and that most of our heroes were as emotionally close to animals as they were to humans. Tintin had Snowy, Obelix had Dogmatix, and the best thing about Enid Blyton's interchangeable children was their parrot, Kiki. Animals were just as good as humans, we felt, if not better: you could not read Roald Dahl's *Fantastic Mr. Fox* without siding forever with foxes against certain kinds of men. The essential elements of adventure, our books suggested, were wilderness, diminished authority, and animals; we had the lot, and soon acquired the animal companion to beat them all: Toss.

Including the cat, Thistle, a thin old tabby with terrible teeth, and Lark, and Vivian (the mouse that turned up at breakfast, and sat behind me as I guzzled cereal, and watched us eat, chewing companionably on spilled lentils), there were six of us, until Lark became pregnant. She gave birth on the sofa to four moley little creatures, two black and two gray. Jess, Toss, Floss, and Tess were all, supposedly, given local farm dog names. During one of their early moves around the sitting room, Toss fell off the low sofa and landed gently on his head. This, Alexander maintains, explained what happened subsequently. Though his siblings grew up to be bright, talented dogs, and his elder sister, Jess, became the star of a large farm in mid Wales, Toss never seemed to notice sheep. Inevitably, he was the puppy we kept. When his mother ran around to gather a flock Toss went too, bouncing along at twice her speed, snapping happily at her ears, trying to knock her over. He had small topaz eyes which shone with mischief and mystification; he was as quick as a greyhound (timed at forty miles per hour for a few flashing moments in the wood, going downhill); he was friendly but he never threw a fight. His missions in life were to beat the car and attack any intruder. He confirmed his complete rejection of his ancestors' genes one afternoon, scorching ahead of us up the lane, when we ran into a group of Derwyn's strappers. Toss did not check his speed but tore straight into the middle of the terrified sheep and jumped clean over the biggest ewe, who had no time to get out of his way. He had a broad curious nose, twitching ears that never stood up for long, and huge paddy paws. His sex drive never definitively surfaced: either he was gay, and all those fights were the fallout of failed advances, or he never progressed beyond puberty. Toss was like a third brother to us, and with his arrival the crew was complete. It came as a comic shock to discover that his name was crude slang. I muttered my discovery to Alexander. He did not believe me at first, then his eyes widened as he saw I was serious, and he began to laugh and laugh in amazement and glee. "Oh, Toss! Typical!" The innocence, foolishness, and offense of it all seemed characteristic of the animal. "Toss! What have you done now!" Toss took a break from licking himself and grinned. No wonder people looked startled when we shouted at him in town.

By the time we came down to breakfast Jenny was already up, pushing back the curtains, and boiling water. On warm days, with the kitchen

door open—it led out to the rough ungrazed area we called the garden or the back patch—all the light and buzz of the day would slant
in, calling to us. We ate fast, with our eyes glued to books or the backs
of cereal packets. These were important spaces of cultural encounter—
I discovered pop music, in the shape of the Police and Abba, on the
backs of cereal packets. It all looked very good, but as it was silent, or
merely rustled, I missed its point. Having no television or commer-
cial radio and there being no billboards in town, the toys and tie-ins on
cereal packets were the only advertisements we saw. Their hyperbolic
claims and colors were intriguing but, without tunes, toyshops, or
other children to expand on them, utterly mysterious.

When we had done, and with our trousers tucked into our wellies,
Toss and Lark busy on reconnaissance ahead of us, plunging along
dozens of scent trails, and our favorite sticks swinging in our hands,
we set out to see what we could see.

Fallen trees and old machines were bases for endless games. We
were pirates, or German soldiers on the point of changing sides. We
were snow leopards, Romans, wolves, highwaymen, Highland clans-
men. We climbed trees, wormed our way into hollow trunks, used an
old sheep dip as a moated fort. Sometimes we based ourselves on or
near one of the old machines.

Tangled thickets of rusting iron sinking slowly into the earth, the
old machines were probably seed drills, hoppers, and ancient mowers,
but it was hard to tell; they spoke obscurely, in a lost language, of past
time on the mountain.

Ranging over the acres we found empty shotgun cartridges in the
wood, windscreen wipers stuffed into a hedge, and the shell of an old
boiler in the stream. There were several implements of unknown function, and on the mountain, if you knew where to look, there were
unexploded mortar bombs.

Our father once brought a couple of these projectiles home, presumably to entertain my mother, who was horrified and called the
bomb squad. Robert was amused. The squad arrived, after a while, in
combat jackets and a camouflaged Land Rover, which got stuck
halfway across the meadow. (It always infuriated Jenny very much
when someone, balking at the track, attempted to cut across our best
grazing and got into trouble. So on top of their disrupted evening and

the humiliation of their mishap, the soldiers received a brittle welcome.) Jack rescued them with a couple of planks and a bit of sacking under their wheels, and the soldiers took the oxidized but still intact bombs away with them.

Alexander and I loved the idea of explosions: we often heard the hillsides echo with the crump of artillery and the hammering chatter of automatic fire, but we made the racket in our heads as much as our hollering mouths.

We ran around, shooting up cohorts of invisible enemies, the whole mountain transported, in our imaginations, to central Europe, until someone real appeared, whereupon our first instinct was to level our sticks and shoot him too.

"Someone's coming up the track!" we shouted.

"I see him!" Jenny called back, from the yard. "Get hold of Toss!"

Visitors to our outpost were often themselves people of the margins, or those who wished they were. A motorcycle gang appeared in the wood and set up camp around the abandoned cottage. "Who are you then?" Jenny demanded, cheerfully, of their leader, as we peered over her shoulder, eyes on stalks at the wings and skulls, the leathers and spikes, the chrome, ponytails, and exhaust. "We're the Surrey Hogs," came the reply.

"Well, hello, Surrey Hogs!" she said, gaily, before muttering to us, "Derwyn's terrified of them, everyone is, but they're sweet really, see?"

Then there was the man who came to sell us ironware. "It's the gypsy!" Jenny said as his van approached. "A dear man. I wish I could afford all his hurdles." He had a nose like a Roman and eyes like an eagle and a soft-burred voice. After they had done the deal the gypsy lingered by the gate for a moment, staring into the view. He had a look, at once peaceful and longing, that we recognized; Derwyn had that look when we ran into him, standing on the track, tamping tobacco into his pipe. There was something about that wide, deep prospect, the way it fell and climbed, like a symphony, to the peaks of the farthest mountains, that made you both happy and wistful.

"Isn't it beautiful, Derwyn?" Jenny said. "Aren't we incredibly lucky to be living here? Aren't we blessed?"

He put a match to the pipe and drew on it. "Oh, aye," he conceded. "But you can't eat the view, can you?"

A reluctant, thoughtful look spread across our mother's face. "No," she said slowly, "I suppose not." It was as though she did not believe him, as though she was thinking "Of course you can!" but trying not to be rude. "We can be jolly grateful for it, anyway!" she concluded.

Jenny began phoning all the local schools. Now we were here for good, she was determined that we should attend the best school available. She found one she liked, and started trying to talk the headmaster into taking us, though it was a good nine miles from door to door, down the valley and over the river, a drive that would take us past the village school and the large primary in town—both perfectly acceptable, in the headmaster's eyes.

"You'll never keep it up," he said over the telephone, having established that she was a single parent with a sheep farm to run.

"I will, I will," she vowed. "Please, Mr. Williams, I really want you to have them."

"Well, all right then," he said, doubtfully. "If the children are prepared for it too."

We were mucking about in the sitting room behind her as she spoke to him, and she turned around, her hand over the mouthpiece, and said, "Mr. Williams says he'll take you. Are we going to do it? Everyone sure?"

I had the sense of a world balanced on the end of my tongue, the future suspended between yes and no. "Yes," I said, and that was all it took. She turned back to the telephone. "Yes, Mr. Williams, yes, we're sure!" she cried, and I marveled at how easy it was to choose a new life, and how strange it was to do so when you had no idea of what it might hold. I shrugged and went back to the game.

"Come on, come on, get up!" Jenny exhorted us on the first morning of school. We had already been up once, piled our clothes onto the battered brown radiator in Alexander's room, and dashed back to our covers to wait for our undershirts and shirts to heat. We dressed, then presented ourselves in the kitchen. Jenny attacked our chaotic heads with a brush, which had the effect of making our hair stand on end: the soft water, the complete absence of pollution, and Mum's money-saving home haircuts (administered with the kitchen scissors and styled, apparently, after the Beatles) combined to give us a look like startled hedgehogs. "Hopeless!" she cried. "Put water on it! Come on, we can't be late. . . ."

We piled into the car, fighting for space with the dogs, and rattled down the track. "Buzzard! Buzzard on the post!" we shouted, in the wood, as the great bird watched us approach his telegraph pole, his gold-ringed eyes disdainful, launching himself into space only when we were right beneath him. I wished I could change places with him, and spend the day cruising the air currents, and he looked as though he knew it.

"This is better than the London traffic, isn't it?" Jenny exclaimed, waving a hand at the dappled valley, the cloud-shadowed hills, and the pitching fields. "So much better than the Tube!"

"Shut up, Toss!" we yelled, in town, as the hound went wild at the sight of another dog. There was a terrier he hated who lived on a certain corner. He associated its appearance with the use of the turn signal, and then, with beguiling but infuriating logic, associated the signal with the idea of the terrier. Every time we turned left or right he would leap at the windows, whining and barking, wondering where that terrier had got to.

"Now, children, here we are. Be good. Have a lovely day, and I hope you meet lots of nice friends. And remember, we're getting free school meals, so eat as much as you possibly can. Gobble it all up! OK? Good. Off you go."

Mr. Williams, a round, bald Welshman who kept a cane on hooks above the girls' entrance, met us. He never had to use it; its only reported sortie was supposed to have involved a boy who threw a book. We did not throw books. We were introduced to the deputy head, Mrs. Morris, a woman as loud and warm as summer thunder, and as terrifying as two storms when she was angry. After assembly my brother and I were separated and introduced to our new classes.

"Stand up and tell everyone your name," the young teacher said, and she smiled at me encouragingly. The class craned for a better look at the new kid with his ludicrous pudding-bowl haircut.

"Hello," I said in my plummy BBC Received Pronunciation, inherited from my parents. "My name is Horatio."

My classmates' faces ranged the spectrum from puzzlement to delighted disbelief.

We sorted out our relationships according to a set of principles, the authority of which was both mysterious and somehow self-evident. I had a silly name and both my brother and I had English accents. We were therefore posh. Everyone else had normal names and normal (South Welsh) accents.

"Mum!" I complained, miserably. "They call me posh!"

"Well . . ." She didn't seem worried. Indeed, she smiled gaily. "Well, you are!"

"I am not!" I howled. It seemed the greatest possible betrayal.

"What does 'posh' mean?" I demanded.

"It's about the passenger ships, the liners. The best cabins on the voyage to Africa or India were on the port side on the way out, and the starboard side coming home—on the side facing away from the sun. Port Out, Starboard Home—POSH!"

I stared out of the car window, imagining us in our cabin, in the sun, with everyone else on the other side, calling us posh. I considered this difference and it never quite made sense. For one thing, my friends and classmates had better cars than we did, and televisions and, soon, video recorders. We could not afford any of that, even if the mountain had not been in the way and we had been able to get a TV signal. How, then, were we better off? They had carpets, suites of furniture, kitchens full of gadgets, stereos; even the kids had modern record players. What was so posh about our cabin?

When finally I heard the mysterious term *class* I asked my mother about it—what class were we. Middle?

"Upper middle, Granny would say. Upper middle," she said, with complete certainty. That gave me some confidence, anyway. There was obviously something ludicrous going on: it sounded as though Granny, famed in the family for a certain battiness, was making the whole thing up (the entire class system, not just our place in it), but at least the solution seemed straightforward. Presumably most people were "middle." If we kept Granny's "upper" bit quiet we should fit in fine.

As well as free school meals we had child benefit, a state payment for single parents on a low income, which Jenny collected weekly from the post office. "We're on the breadline," she said. "But we'll do just fine."

"Marrowbones!" she flourished. "It's a brilliant wheeze. If you're ever poor and hungry, go to the butcher and ask for some marrowbones for the dog. They'll give them to you for nothing, then you take them home, boil them up, and you can make a delicious soup!"

We economized in every way she could think of. "Shut all doors and turn off all lights," she chanted. Curtains were drawn at the first hint of nightfall: "Just as good as double glazing," she explained. Moldy food was salvaged whenever possible: "It's only penicillin!" she exclaimed, with withering humor, if you objected.

Any unfinished food at the end of a meal made her miserable. It was a contrast we always noticed when we stayed with our father.

"If you don't want it, you don't have to eat it," he would say, after a first attempt to encourage us to finish up. But he was less familiar to us, and we were anxious not to disappoint him. Jenny had to work much harder.

"Please finish your supper. Come on! Clean plates!"

"Don't want any more—full up."

"Oh, do! It's a long time until breakfast. Have a little bit more, just to please me."

"No, I don't want to—"

"Finish your supper!" she shouted, banging the table.

When she was not looking we slipped leftovers to the dogs. Consequently, we ate our meals with Toss and Lark by our chairs, sentinels at attention, watching every forkful traveling between our plates and mouths.

"Oh, these dogs! These endless mouths to feed. . . ." Jenny lamented.

There was no question of the sweets and crisps everyone else munched at break times, so Alexander and I pretended we were buzzards, and scavenged off our friends. Sometimes we appeared to be worse off than we were: I broke a shoelace, one morning, found it frayed beyond repair, and replaced it with white string. It looked ludicrous by itself so I replaced the other with some of the same string and hurried to the car, where my mother waited, rolling her eyes. The dinner lady who supervised us at break time was scornful. "Look at you! Look at the state of you! Got your shoes done up with string!"

I snarled, but one of my friends came to my defense.

"It's not your fault, it's because your mum's poor, isn't it?"

There were few secrets in the small town, where the contents of Jenny's shopping basket revealed us as clearly as a daily interview: cat food, dog food, milk powder for the lambs, frozen battered fish thumbs for supper, bread and cereal for our breakfast, whiskey and cigarettes for Jenny's nights alone in the kitchen. We all became thin. On one beach holiday my aunt watched us, as we emerged blue and shivering from the sea, and took her sister aside. "They're not getting enough to eat, Jenny," Ursie said, solemnly. "You simply cannot economize on food!"

"Oh, Lord, Ursie! Do you think they're starving? How terrible . . . !"

We may not have been overfed, but we were extremely healthy, and barely ever ill. If I wanted to miss school, I had to feign, and I was adept at it, particularly on school sports day.

"I don't feel very well, I think I've got a temperature. . . ." I ventured, and sucked with all my might on the thermometer.

"Well, this is saying normal but [her cool hand on my forehead] . . . if you don't feel up to it, stay where you are—I'll tell Mrs. Morris."

My brother wished me a dubious "Get well."

"Thanks," I returned humbly, and while he was driven away to win races I jumped out of bed, dressed, and set off up the mountain. Reflected in the puddles around the hill gate were vivid fragments of the sky. The bracken was taller than me, a sunny forest of green stalks and fronds, all its fingers uncurled; wherever I trod on it sticky white sap leaked from the broken stalks. Beyond the skyline, where the ferns thinned out, the hummocks of pin-thin grass smelled of dew and peat, as though they steamed invisibly in the sunlight. Protruding here and there were pale rocks already warm to the touch, and higher still were the whinberry bushes, exquisite collages of tiny red and green leaves, the berries like purple pinheads, brushed with a fine silver bloom. So small and so deliciously sweet, they stained my lips and fingers purple-red. When we climbed the hill together Alexander and I rolled around in these soft-spiked bushes, eating constantly, guzzling like legless sheep. We were particularly pleased with the vertiginous effect of lying on our backs with our feet higher than our heads, so that the distant mountains formed an upside-down horizon. Then we would double back to the edge of the ridge. From there the farm was a kingdom to admire. Every sheep we owned seemed to be visible, spread evenly over their fields, grazing or sitting in the sun. The hill grasses sighed, a wishing sound, under the long, soft wind. The muttered boom of the Concorde setting out for America rolled in from behind the Beacons. And then, coming up the pitch, I saw Mum in her little white car. I felt like a young eagle, with the world at my feet, and I had a feeling of utter completeness, strangely conscious that this scene, this moment, was fixing itself in my brain. I was caught out, of course—you could not climb the mountain with a temperature—but I would say, wanly, that I felt a bit better, and my mother would let me off.

Mrs. Morris knew I hated school sports, and she was not fooled for a moment. She probably thought Jenny was too soft on us, and in many ways she was. Jenny was aware of it too, and used to explain it to us.

"My mother never hugged me," she would say, "and she never told me she loved me, and I'm just not like that. I love you both with all my heart, you know that, don't you?"

"Yes, Mummy," we chorused. "And we love you."

"Granny was a hopeless mother," Jenny continued. "She had no idea. And I think she missed out terribly. The wonderful thing about having children is that you can at last forget yourself, forget your own wretched problems, and love and be loved back. And you never have to worry that they're going to turn round one day, and say, 'I'm off, I don't love you anymore,' not like boyfriends when I was young. It's just wonderful!"

We nodded, and thought about those boyfriends, and about our father. She said she and he were still friends, and she wanted him to see us as much as possible, and said he was a good man in many ways. But when she was cross or desperate, or when the money was tight, and he had turned down a request for higher maintenance payments, she would rage against him: how cruel he had been, his dark side, how weird he could be. "I mean, if it was me, making all that money, I'd want to give it to my children!" she'd burst out. She never believed that he was not making a fortune in journalism.

"The problem with him is, he always, always puts himself first," she said darkly, and Alexander and I became very grave. We did not know what to do with the criticism; he was in London, following his life, and Jenny was here, struggling for the benefit of ours, and yet . . . and yet.

"She's living her fantasy with her sheep, while I go to work every day. I can't afford to give her more money, and why should I, even if I could?" he said when I asked him about it. He looked hostile, his face cold. I quailed. "I'm not getting at you," he said, more softly. "But seriously, if Jenny wants more money, she should think about earning some." I could understand his argument, as I understood hers, but in my mind I automatically defended whichever parent was absent, excused them from any attack, whether I could articulate a defense or not. It caused a kind of speechlessness, a flat, internal denial. An attack from any other quarter was a comparatively easy thing to repel.

"Your mum can't drive!" someone said at school. It was not the first time I had heard this. There was a small traffic circle on the way to school that she considered ludicrous and irrelevant, and she liked to go the wrong way around it, if no one was about, then nip up to the school gates, especially when we were late.

"Yes, she can!"

"She can't. She's mad—goes the wrong way round the traffic circle!"

"Shut up!" put in one of my friends. "She's just a bit—eccentric, isn't she, Ratio?"

It made me almost tearful. It was sweet that he thought that, and felt protective and sympathetic about it, but was it true? Was it sad, if true?

On the very rare occasions someone came with us after school, all the way home, by special arrangement with their parents, they loved it. Darren, the class bad boy, came home with us and had his head spun. This was a slightly mad child my brother and I liked and feared—he had dark eyes, which glinted like an adder's when he had it in for someone, and he was big, and pretty fearless.

"Come and help me with Penis," my mother said briskly. Darren looked at me, eyes widening slightly.

"Penis is a ram, Darren. There's something wrong and he can't get his penis back in, so it hangs down and gets covered in mud. See, he's in here. Hello, poor Penis."

Darren helped her catch the stricken animal, and watched, fascinated, as she washed the mud off with soap and water, leaving the offended organ shining pinkly. Mum said he had done very well, catching and holding the sheep, and Darren inquired solicitously after the animal's health the next day, having told everyone the full story. There was generally some drama to show people, and if our mother was guaranteed to reconfirm the posh thing, then at least she was popular; our friends always liked her.

I do not think Alexander had my class complexes, but he had his own problems. He went through an unhappy and bad-tempered patch when he threw a chair at another boy—they were both in kindergarten at the time, and no damage was done. He had problems with his work; in the face of endless English and math exercises his dyslexia made him confused and frustrated and his handwriting was a complete mess, as was mine. His teachers, our mother, and even I took him aside and gave him talkings-to; extra lessons and a special-needs teacher were arranged, and Alexander rapidly came around. He was an unusual child. He outraged Mrs. Morris, when still very young, by calling another boy a parasite, an insult so effective it made the target cry.

"Alexander called me a parasite, miss!"

"Did he? Well, Alexander doesn't even know what that means. He's just saying something he's heard. He doesn't know what a parasite is."

"Yes, I do," my brother put in. "It's something that lives on something else, like a flea."

The teachings of Tintin, of course—Captain Haddock, to be precise. Parasite, poltroon, guttersnipe, pickaninny, jackanapes, bashibazouk—we had them all off by heart, and we knew what most of them meant. We learned to swear, too, of course, but idiosyncratically. Someone, Darren or Shane, called someone else a wanker. What a word! I had no idea what it meant. That night, during a tussle over a boat in the bath, with my mother lightly scolding us and both giggling, I tried it on Alexander, who was amused and impressed by its sound. The effect on my mother was dramatic and terrifying, but it now seems she was not sure of the meaning either.

"Oh, you wanker!"

She whirled around. "What did you say?" she hissed, furious. I froze, terrified of the change. "How dare you!" she shouted. "Don't you ever say that again!

"Wankers go to prison!" she added witheringly.

Alexander adopted slang from Asterix. He particularly liked the confused and stammering Roman legionaries, receiving a beating from Obelix.

"*Quid? Quid?*" he put in.

Soon we swore like brigands. Though adults regularly complimented Jenny on how polite and well-brought-up we seemed, she knew how fluently crude we could be in private. She often chided Jack for swearing in front us, because "bugger" and "bloody" were two of his standbys, but our vocabulary plumbed deeper than that.

"I think you picked it up from Mr. Brown," she sighed.

Mr. Brown farmed beyond the larch trees. He kept sheep on the mountain most of the year; from the back of the house we watched him riding up the ridges on his pony, with his dogs hurtling through the bracken, and his sheep bundling away. As Mr. Brown worked his animals the mountain rang with fantastic bellows and wails, growled cautions, and sudden roars of fury. The sound came to us in long ropes of vowels looped around occasional consonants, but though it seemed wonderfully strong you could not actually make out any words.

Jenny told a family friend that we were swearing too much. In what must have seemed a clever piece of reverse psychology, he informed us that the worst word in the world, much worse than the f-word, much worse than anything, was *quark*. "That's the one you mustn't say," he told us, soberly. "That's the real baddy."

Alexander and I stared at each other, awed. We hardly dared ask its meaning, and readily accepted his refusal to say any more about it. Of course he could not tell us, it was the worst word in the world!

When he had gone we discussed it. We tried to think of what it might mean, but our minds would not supply images to match the appalling syllables. "Imagine saying it at school!" Alexander marveled. "That would get them!"

"Yeah, you bloody quark!"

We giggled, scandalized. "You quarking quark!" we whispered fiendishly. It was like being entrusted with a nuclear weapon for the playground, or being shown an entirely new color. At last, the ultimate word. "Quark!"

"Don't say it!"

"No, you're right, we mustn't."

"Terrible," Alexander said. "Imagine if Mrs. Morris heard you say it. She would tell Mum, wouldn't she?"

"Definitely."

"What do you think would happen?"

"You'd be expelled."

We shook our heads. "Right," I said. "Whatever happens, we must make a vow that we will never, ever say it. We will never say 'quark.' Never. OK?"

"Yes," he said. "I promise I will never say 'quark.'"

"Me, too," I said.

And we never did.

❖   ❖   ❖

At school we guarded our tongues, watched the classroom clock, and waited for home time, half term, and best of all, the holidays, which began with the battered car at the school gates, our mother's smile behind the dirty windscreen, and the dogs grinning out at us.

"Up the airy mountain," Jenny sang as the car heaved us back up the hill. "And no school tomorrow, hurrah! Look, mackerel sky—a change of weather."

The barred armada of silver clouds really did look like a shoal, combining to form a huge speckled fish belly, hove-to over the hills. Below it the martins and swallows were a weaving, twittering swarm that copied the tumblings of their prey: the flecked, tottering towers of flies and midges above the fields.

"You see, nature is all patterns." Our mother pointed, waving her finger as if tracing echoes in the air.

Looking for patterns, Alexander and I lay facedown in the meadow, staring into the microscopic universe of the grass, where, if you kept it up, ants became as big as cats, and beetles were rhinos, and a grasshopper was Pegasus. We were careful with grasshoppers, because my grandfather said he thought he might come back as one in his next life. Wasps, though, were the enemy, because when he was very small my brother trod in a nest of them in the back garden in London, and they nearly killed him. The discovery of a nest in a tumbledown wall behind the house made us itchy with fear and affront; we were relentlessly drawn to the insects' stone gateway, where they alighted for two seconds before crawling inside. We dashed in and struck, fled and circled, dashed in and struck again.

"Will you *please* grow up and stop being so stupid—live and let live, or they'll sting you," Jenny shouted up from the yard. "You're asking for it, and you'll get no sympathy from me."

But the little warriors with their gas-mask faces seemed to be asking for it too; there was a brutal excitement in squashing them on the stone, and a horror that you could assuage only with the thrill of another attempted murder, in the same way the ghastly, broken struggles of an injured wasp demanded another blow. When they came out in a swarm we ran for our lives.

"Boys! Come here, please, we need you to help!"

Shamefully relieved, we went. Jack was in the kitchen, sipping tea.

He seemed in a rightful place there, at the pale kitchen table which his grandfather had made from planks of beech, relaxed in the high-backed chair, puffing his pipe, his fat rubber boots resting on the flag-stones.

"We're putting them up the mountain today, children, so it's all hands on deck."

The old man smiled slightly with his eyes as he watched us listening to instructions. On the wrong day, he knew, we could take as much marshaling as the dogs. But "putting them up" was a certain thrill, and we had a responsibility to behave. "It will be tremendous fun!" Jenny said. "As long as we all keep our tempers."

The flock was gathered into the yard, all the best ewes assembled in a belling white crowd, their ears twitching, their urine puddling, as they nibbled tops off the nettles and gaped hungrily into Jack's garden. We shooed them around behind the Big Barn, up through the long grass under the larches and on toward the hill gate. They streamed like a routed army, following one or two leaders, treasured animals, clever and calmer than the rest, that always seemed to understand our intentions. After the leaders came the younger ewes, overexcited, pushing to the front but too timid to break away. Then came the body of the flock, their heads nodding with their strides, cropping grass as they went, occasionally adding their tongues to the racket. At the back were the tamest sheep, one or two pets that waited for my mother, charged the dogs, and never stopped bleating.

"Go on, Hoppy! Get on with it, Snowdrop!" Jenny shouted, flapping at them with her sweater. Jack yipped, the dogs yapped, and Alexander and I ran about, cutting off the escape routes of bolting troublemakers. At the hill fence we held them as Jenny went ahead, wrestled the old gate open, and counted the flock through. Counting sheep is a trick, because though some file through at a steady pace, most dash in twos and threes, and others stop dead in the gap and bleat, as if trying to make you count them twice or not at all. As the last two passed her Jenny lifted her head and nodded.

"Eighty-four it is, Jack. Remember, everybody, eighty-four. Right, let's go! Boys, someone, stop that lot. . . . Go on, Lark, get away out!"

The dog bounded up through the bracken, turning a party of escapees that came haring back on pounding feet, uttering strangulated bleats. Following their leaders, most now seemed to remember where they were going, taking the uphill path in a flowing, flyblown stream. Whenever one threatened to break away Jack hissed and swished his stick; Alexander and I uprooted and stripped long stems of bracken to wave in emulation. We felt part of the huge view. The framing mountains had different personalities. To the left were "the tops," the flat green hills lying along the head of the Valleys. You went "over the tops" if you went that way, up a switching road, to a flat moor Jenny called "the roof of the world." There was a quarry there, and the sound of it came to us over the dome of the sky, rumbling up and rolling down. The tops were industrious but old-fashioned. Life went on there, but not quickly.

In the middle was a mountain of the kind we drew with our coloring pens, a huge, lazily conical hump like an ancient, long-retired volcano. I believed a Lancaster bomber had flown into it during the Second World War, and I imagined a flare of yellow light, and a twist of smoke like an extinguished match, and the mountain, massively, mournfully impassive.

To the right of it were the ridges, peaks, and plunges of the steepest Beacons. The Beacons were dramatic, powerful, and godlike. Wodin or Thor might live among them, making weather. They were mountains that could make your spirit sing in May and kill you in December. To stare at them was to face fate, beauty, and terror. Beside the Beacons was the Pisspot of Wales. A valley thus christened by Jack, because, he said, if it was raining anywhere in the country, you could be sure it was raining there.

At a certain point, where the bracken was short and the sky appeared low down between the hills at the head of the valley, Jack and Lark pressed forward. They overtook the leaders and turned the flock toward the successive ridges that receded, up and farther up, to the top. For a while the path was lost, the sheep scattered and we shouted and ran back and forth as Lark did her best, barking and rushing, pursued by Toss, the white tips of the dogs' black tails marking their charges through the fern.

"Stop it, Toss! Good dog, Lark, get away out! *No!* She's missed three there, get away *far* out, far out, dammit! Boys, go and help her, quick or we'll lose them. *Quick!* Well done. . . ."

By the time we regained control the flock was split in two, with Jack in the middle, but now the paths were wide and clear and they led straight up the ridges. We panted and smiled; the tricky bit was over. Now the ewes walked steadily, and we followed, matching the rhythm of their climb. Attuned to the flock, which was calm now, we relaxed our watchfulness a little, and took in more of the mountain's day. On the highest saddle three specks crossed a cloud: walkers on the skyline. On the wide gray scree below them were two horses and a foal. To the right a kestrel dipped, rose, slid, and stilled, as if she wrote music over the hillside. High to the left a glider scudded, riding the long ridge winds.

We drove the sheep in a long rising zigzag, following the sheep tracks up the side of the first ridge, back across its top, through long blond grasses, then up the next. Now we were higher than the hill that formed the western wall of the valley, and the lands beyond were revealed: a gently pitching sea of fields, old Radnorshire, cross-hatched with hedge lines, fading into the haze of mid Wales. Here, above the bracken line, the sheep began to fan out, their bleating silenced, replaced by the soft, ripping sounds of their grazing.

We caught up with Jack above the prow of the second ridge, and all took a breather, Alexander and I sprawling on the hummock-sprung turf, the world on each side dropping down and away; we lay on a lip between giant bowls of air and stared at the mosaics of the valley. Toss sat down, tilted his head back, and fixed his gaze on the clouds. He watched their slow turning, twisting, and tearing, as if he, too, wished for wings.

"What do you think, Jack, a bit to pick?" Jenny pinched out some bright blades and tried one between her teeth. Alexander and I plucked bents, and bit without severing them, halfway down, so that the ends stuck out of the corners of our mouths. By smiling repeatedly we forced the ends together, so that they opened and closed like the mandibles of giant insects. We sat face to face and battled with our mandibles, giggling as we tried to get the ends into each other's nose and eyes. Jack prodded the ground with his stick.

"Aye, there's a bit about if they'll look for it. Should do for a while, anyway."

"Yes, it should. What a relief!" said my mother. "We should go now, and very quietly, because if they see us they'll follow. That's enough, boys, please. Come on, dogs, down we go, nice and quiet."

We set off at a trot, Jenny and Jack following. At the bottom of the steep ridges, where the ground sloped less fiercely, Alexander and I broke into a jog, then a run, going faster and faster until we hit a breakneck charge, the bracken flying by on both sides, our feet slapping the paths in a wild drumbeat. Toss passed us like a missile, his long pink tongue waving crazily around his open jaws, grinning up at us he overshot, skidded around, and came pouncing back, ready for combat.

"Oh no, Toss, no!" Alexander cried, and we laughed in wild despair as the hound went for us, and we all crashed into the bracken, panting, rolling, and scuffling.

Jenny made furious "Be quiet!' gestures, so we stopped fighting and started down again. But by the time we reached the hill fence the first plaintive bleats could be heard from beyond the ridges, and soon after that the first white beetles appeared on the skyline. After a moment's pause two of them started trundling down the path.

"Oh, blast. *Blast!*" Jenny moaned. "They're after us, the bloody things. Rusty and that other one. Typical! Come on, run! I just hope the whole lot don't come after them or we'll have to do it all again tonight."

It was a warm afternoon. Our shoes were full of the little spines of dead bracken and under our hair we itched with midge bites; Alexander and I headed for the stream.

"Let's dip our heads!"

In the bole of shadow beneath the alders I gripped the caldron's overflowing iron rim and received a vivid warning through my palms that made me wish I had not suggested it. The scalping plunge through the surface seemed to peel my head from crown to neck; it drove icy claws through my ears into my brain, and my chest heaved with the shock of it. In the few seconds I could bear, I could hear the *rumble-burble* of the stream flowing into the caldron a few inches from my neck, the pressure drumming through my head, as though I pressed my ear to the mountain's stomach. I came out in a rush of gasps, rivulets of pure cold eeling down my back and front, to see my brother laughing with delight and dread.

"Aah! Aaah! Cold! it's *so* cold—your turn!"

"Are you numb?"

"Yes! Completely numb!"

"Your face has gone red!"

"Yours will too in a minute. Go on!"

Alexander knelt on the wet stones. He gathered his courage and plunged, held his head under, and emerged, spluttering and shuddering. We ran around, trying to warm up, then went higher up the stream to work on our dams. We spent slow hours peering into the water, at tiny jackknifing shrimp and the chrysalises of the caddis fly: minute stones cemented into a jeweled tube, like perfect sarcophagi. Then we hurled rocks, broke bottles, and killed horseflies. When we reappeared in the kitchen we were streaked with red mud, there were ragged tide marks around our necks, and our feet squelched in our shoes.

"Oh no! Look at you! What a mess you've made, and those were clean clothes too! And now I'll have to wash them all again. Poor Jenny! Poor bloody Jenny! Washing washing washing! I hate washing, it's such an endless bore!"

"Sorry, Mummy."

"Are you really? Or are you just saying it?"

"We are, really!"

Toss hid under the table, the cat squeezed her eyes almost shut, Lark was tactfully, typically absent, and we blushed and dripped, waiting for her anger to abate.

"Huh! Well, I suppose you'd better go and have baths. And I'll slave away cooking your supper!"

We were truly remorseful now.

"Go on. Don't worry," she cried with airy sarcasm. "Don't worry about me."

We made our way upstairs and held one of our conferences. We must do better, we agreed, we must think of Jenny and try to help. When she asked us to help with the sheep we would concentrate. We would try to keep our clothes clean. We would tidy up the shoes in the hall. We would feed the dogs without being asked. We would draw curtains without being asked. We would fill the woodshed, lay fires. We could take her tea in bed.

✤ ✤ ✤

I was sometimes the instigator of mischief, sometimes the evangelist of improvement. I was aware of unnatural undercurrents in my relationships with Jenny and Alexander: there were aspects of the husband in the way I listened to her troubles, and a hint of the father in the way I tried to impress better behavior on my brother and me, through him. Alexander felt the peculiarity and the injustice of this: "You're not Dad!" he protested.

"No," I said solemnly. "But Dad's not here, and someone's got to say it."

"You're just as bad as me!"

"I know, but I'm trying to be better. We must both try to be better."

"All right, I know," he growled. "Just don't blame it all on me."

"OK," I said, and reached for our verbal olive branch: "*Pax! Pax* means peace."

"*Pax,*" Alexander conceded. "*Pax* means peace."

Robert occupied a particular place in our minds, like a ghost, sometimes present and sometimes unimaginably far away. He was separated from us by so many removes—the mountain, the Bristol Channel, the motorway, and the mad warren of London—and yet he was just there, in nine digits on the telephone, in our thoughts and conversations, and in the smooth white envelopes that contained his letters, and appeared in the box at the bottom of the hill. His strong handwriting addressed us so intimately, and spoke so clearly in his voice, that you could hear him and feel his presence. "Dear Pim," ran the briefest note in one package, "I thought this might be up your street." And there was *The Machine Gunners* by Robert Westall, the prequel to my all-time favorite, *Fathom Five*. He could not have chosen better. It was as though he was there with us, as though he knew what I thought and did. "Our father," we said every morning at school, "who art in London," I sometimes said to myself.

Once or twice, at night, before Jenny came to bed, Alexander and I dialed Robert's number from the upstairs extension. The first time his voice was so tired and withdrawn that we put the phone down, having said nothing. The second time, I said "Hello" in a funny voice that he did not recognize.

"Who's there?" he said irritably, and I cut the connection.

We loved to talk about him, and best of all, to hear Jenny speak fondly of him; when she did it brought him closer. "Your father's so clever" (or "handsome" or "funny"), she would sometimes say, and we loved to hear it. The better he was the better we felt, and the better we felt ourselves to be.

"Oh, he used to make me laugh," she said, the past tense moving him further away. "When we were going to work on the Tube he went through a phase of sitting opposite me and sticking out his tongue. Just a little bit, just the tip. It sounds silly but it used to make me laugh so much I cried! And people never knew what I was laughing at—when they looked at him his tongue would have disappeared, and he would be smiling, you know, looking sort of mystified. I used to beg him not to . . ."

It sounded idyllic, like a golden age, a fairy tale that should have ended happily, but which, in failing, comprised and revealed his one tragic and mysterious flaw.

"Why did he leave?" I asked the question in dozens of different ways. Jenny's answers varied. He did not love her. He met someone else. He didn't want to live at the farm. They were not complete or comfortable answers, she knew, and we could tell. She shifted around unhappily. "He still loves you, though, you can be sure of that," she would add, with conviction and relief.

But he was with "someone else"; a woman he had known for years, his girlfriend at university in South Africa. She was kind to us when we met, but though we found no fault with her we could not like her much.

"I expect she's very nice," Jenny said, encouragingly. "I suppose she's very pretty, is she?" We shrugged. We liked the woman's sons, who were older than us, and cool North Londoners, but there was something unreal about seeing our father filling in the gap in their family. It made him seem more isolated than ever, more individual and alone, and it further colored my perception of his departure. We were not surprised when, eventually, it did not work.

Since it was he who was not there, who had not been there that morning, and he who had moved on to someone else, it seemed to follow that Robert was responsible for the separation. But the simplicity of this troubled us all. Jenny was anxious never to set us against him, but sometimes she fell into dramatic despair, lashing herself for our predicament: "I'm so sorry I couldn't keep him, I'm just so sorry, for your sakes."

"No, Mummy," one or other of us would say. "It wasn't your fault."

She shook her head: "I'm sure I talked too much. I used to think, You're talking too much, you'll drive him mad. And I think I loved you two too much, that's one thing. I think he felt left out. I don't know! I suppose I bored him."

"No . . ." Alexander shook his head.

"I don't think so," I said, faintly annoyed.

"Yes," she said, "I did. But I didn't leave him. I said 'until death us do part,' and I meant it."

Seeing us pondering this, she hurriedly intervened: "But sometimes things just don't work. People can't help that. Dear Robert can't help who he is."

And, she said, soothingly, he was good really, and good at whatever he did. He was very good with sheep, she remarked, which surprised me. "Yes, yes, very gentle. He's a dear person, really, Robert," she would say. "Smashing! If only he wasn't so selfish. . . ."

I tried to picture him farming: I could remember Jenny going to the *Evening Standard* on the Tube, but I had only the vaguest images of Dad working on the farm. When he asked after Emrys or Derwyn or Jack it always seemed strange that he knew them. One weekend, when he was visiting, he ran into Emrys, and I was struck by the affection between them, the fluency and intimacy of their conversation. In his absence I had constructed for Robert a life concerned with London, and the news, and important, faint things like the world, politics, and money. I felt like the child of a distant king, so it was amazing to me that he had such an understanding of the lowly business of farming.

He was a rebel, too. When he took us to explore the riverbank we passed a sign that said "Private Property, Keep Out."

"Come on, chaps," he hissed. "Let's see how far we get before they shoot us!"

Down by the river we bombed bottles with stones, teetered along ledges and wreckage at the edge of the current, and marveled at tiny, frantic mallard ducklings whizzing across the water after their mother. We chased pheasants through the woods, trying hopelessly to catch them with our bare hands, and later whirled back through the lanes in his clean, comfortable car, listening to Mozart or Schubert or Bach.

"Your father's quite wild," Jenny said affectionately, shaking her head, when we told her about it. "He had to be saved by the mountain rescue people once, in the Lake District."

Any outing with him might turn into an adventure at any moment, and I recognized him instantly in the last lines of Roald Dahl's *Danny, the Champion of the World,* in which the great man wrote that what children really want is "a parent who is sparky!"

Partly in emulation, Alexander and I were quick to scramble over fences, venture across other people's land, and take liberties with the out-of-bounds. We spent a great deal of time jumping out of windows and climbing things; it was the right training, I felt, for our father's sons.

There were other adults in our life too. As well as the lambers, in 1980 Jenny's prayers were answered, and David Hughes came to be our lodger.

David's typewriter sat on the table in the Beast House bedroom, his pictorial map of Manhattan hung on the wall. David slept on top of the three mattresses between the curling iron frames of the huge bed—frames that Robert and Jenny had rescued from a hedge, years ago, and proudly painted white. David's routine included a few hundred words first thing, then a lope down the track to meet the morning, an exercise he occasionally underscored with joyous whooping.

"There's David, greeting the day!" we said, at a snatch of weird hollering. Then came breakfast, then feeding sheep or helping out, and a retreat to the typewriter. Around six o'clock, and the weather forecast, he would appear in the kitchen, smiling, and at some mysterious point, when the "sun" was deemed to have dipped "below the yardarm," he and Jenny would award themselves a whiskey. They lis-

tened to the radio news, conferred, and often laughed. David seemed
to understand and entirely sanction the way we lived: he was not
fussed or bothered; he loved the views and the space; he would stand
and gaze—really looking—at the many places that made up the land,
and he understood the depth of Jenny's sympathy with the animals.
There was still not much money around but it went further. David
struck up relationships with various food and wine suppliers, and soon
boxes of "provisions" appeared, to be lovingly unpacked. It's not just
all right, his smile seemed to say, it's . . . *fun!*

David had not been with us long before another friend of my
mother's turned up, chauffeuring a drooling setter called Humphrey
in a lime green Renault 4; a beautiful, gay young woman called Elizabeth. Very quickly and completely, Elizabeth and David fell in love.
She moved into his room, and though David's routine did not change
outwardly, the afternoon sessions in the Beast House were now sometimes accompanied by the popping of corks.

Jenny felt terribly left out, in the moments when she allowed
herself to be, and bemused to have a love affair ignite in her spare
room. "My nose was a bit put out, but it was a wonderful thing, of
course. . . ."

The Beast House bedroom had a certain power over couples. Noel
and Lesley, the lambers, married after their term under its chill,
steepled ceiling, as did Jon and Gay, also lambers. Indeed, my mother
and father were the only people not to have married happily after that
bedroom. It was a very romantic place, especially in the summer, with
the windows under the eaves open and the light and drowsy sounds
coming through them, at shin level, and spreading across the floor of
the room.

We explored the bedroom when no one was in residence; it had an
enduring mystery. There was the enormous wardrobe, stuffed with a
beautiful fleece belonging to Frosty (the black ewe with a white-
dusted back), and our parents' old clothes from their previous lives:
lacy dresses, furs, and flares. In a box of books I found *The Joy of Sex,*
which was intriguing, though I did not linger over it, as it all seemed
rather bizarre.

The Facts of Life were straightforward as far as they applied to
sheep and adults; their implications for small boys, though, my

mother was obliged to explain. The only lesson I remember clearly involved wet dreams. We were years away from them, but Jenny was anxious that the absence of a man should not condemn us to ignorance, so the instructions were given well in advance of their time.

"As you get older and your body changes, you might find, one night, that you have a sexy dream, and wake up with the bed all wet. Don't worry, don't panic. Just go to the bathroom, get a cloth, and mop it up. It's perfectly normal, no big deal at all, nothing to worry about, OK?"

Unfortunately, in the mists of my mind, these instructions became confused with what you should do if the roof started leaking, and you woke with water pouring onto the bed—a much more likely event, given our ages and that of the house. Conflating the two, I formed the impression that as your body changed you might have a sexy dream one night, and wake up to find fluid dripping from the ceiling. In which case, the trick was not to panic, but to put a bowl under it and fetch a flannel. It seemed a little odd, but not impossible. After all, I woke up one night to find a black-faced lamb at the foot of the bed, bleating and sporting a pink bath towel, which it wore like an enormous shawl.

"Mu-um! There's a lamb here with a towel over its head."

She retrieved the beast. "Oh good, he's woken up! He was freezing to death so I put him in this box by the radiator. There you go, lamb, stay in there, sweetheart. . . . Very good! Back to sleep, everyone, good night, good night, children."

David's novel grew rapidly, and he gave us discarded drafts, piles of pages blank on one side, which we welcomed with our felt-tips and crayons. I went to work on one chapter, obsessively drawing the same enormous bird, body like a boat, huge scimitar wings, eagle-billed and taloned, on the back of each page. Jenny was reading to me when David knocked on the door and presented my mother and me with a sheaf of papers. There were my discarded bird drawings, but now there was a stanza typed below each picture; a poem reflecting the changing aspects and wonky expressions of the bird, which David christened the Brecon Beak.

THE BRECON BEAK
by David Hughes

The Wild and Woolly Wowl of Wales
Has a beak like a razor and wings like sails.
It gets very cross during westerly gales.
It has wool like a sheep and claws like nails,
It puffs up the hills and hoots down the dales,
When they hear it coming the family pales.
"To-whit-to-wool," cry the furious males
And the boys all hide behind buckets and pails
As across the sky in threatening trails
The Wild and Woolly Wowl of Wales
Dives down to attack small boys—and fails.

Its beak gets caught in hawthorn trees,
The smell from the clover makes it sneeze,
Its wings get tangled in the breeze,
It trips over roots and falls on its knees,
It bumps into flowers and is stung by bees,
It blinks its eyes and all it sees
Are tiny things like boys and fleas.

So Wales's Wild and Woolly Wowl
Is a very pathetic species of fowl.
So worry not, the Wowl you spy
Is only dangerous in the sky
When the winds are blowing cold on high.
The moment it comes down to try
And eat up boys it starts to fry.
Its fleece is hot, its beak all dry,
It squeaks and sweats and with a sigh
Decides it only wants to die.
But if you give it apple pie
And orange juice the bird will cry,
"To-whit-to-wool—and now, goodbye,"
For fruit's the best thing to untie

Its muddled wings and let it fly. A drink is all
   it needs—that's why.

The Wild and Woolly Wowl of Wales
Has a mind like a razor and thoughts like sails,
It has dreams like a sheep and nerves like nails,
It thinks on the hills and broods down the
   dales
While telling itself all kinds of tales
As across the heavens in narrative trails
The Wild and Woolly Wowl of Wales
Tells stories about itself—and fails.

It was a happy time. The cooking improved dramatically—now there were roasts and hotpots: vats of cheese, bacon, and onions, padded out with golden spuds. My brother and I became "those boy-y-s," a rolling, mischievous appellation, the way David said it, in his baritone, and we mucked about inattentively as the grown-ups discussed politics and books and their various friends. They smoked and drank and laughed at the weather and the drudgeries of farming. It was a hard winter, but there was excitement more than fear in their faces when they heard the forecasts. "It's just so wonderful to have *help*," was my mother's mantra, meaning it was wonderful to have company.

Then they decided to stop smoking—David went to bed a lot, and though his relaxed, amused expression barely frayed, Mum went gently mad, bursting into tears for no reason. They assayed nicotine gum and spent a lot of time comparing dosages. Mum said the little yellow cubes made her feel sick, as she chewed them ferociously, and that she hated the bloody stuff, though she was pleased to discover it set hard and waterproof, excellent lagging for ill-fitting pipes. Soon she was addicted to the gum and back on the cigarettes, alternating one with the other.

Alexander and I stared up at men like David with great attention, and I was conscious, early on, of my instinct to look to them for surrogacy.

And all the time, Robert revolved in our imaginations: sometimes he was a perfect hero, exciting, loving, and bountiful; at other times, when we were unhappy, he was a remote, flawed figure, uncaring and distant. Whenever he came to see us he turned the landscape into a playground, in a way Jenny could not, but when he came to the farm, and he and Jenny were together, I watched him with nervous attention: Was he happy? Was he having fun? I tiptoed around him, desperate to please, as though in fear of an angry instant when he would open his mouth to tell us why he had not stayed with us, and everything that was wrong with us would come out: we were lazy, self-indulgent, unrealistic, eccentric, on some sort of permanent holiday, he might say in his calm, rational way. He never did. He would laugh and talk and play; he was perfect, when he was expected, and on his way, and climbing out of his car, with his beautiful smile and gentle kiss, his cheek cool and stubbled against mine and his smell delicious. And at the same time he was miserably inadequate, in his somber leave-takings, and the smile and the long look he gave you just before he left, which seemed to say something kind and clear and detailed; at once an explanation, a confirmation, and a farewell, but all in a soft silence that forbade speech. Then he was away down the track.

I distinguished between Dad and the space he left, urging my mother to marry again, for all our sakes, to fill his empty place. I understood that we were her confidants. And I knew we were inadequate substitutes for a man her own age, just as she could never quite compensate for our missing father. Because the adults we had most contact with, our teachers and Jenny, were women, I came to feel that I understood them better than men, and for a long time I was more at ease in their company. Men were more unpredictable and more distant, but they were also more interesting. They understood me easily, instinctively responding to my needful gaze; I adopted many as role models. Our Welsh teacher, who was fun, with a fearsome temper; our new headmaster, who made amiable jokes and puns; "Indiana" Jones, whose dry humor and love of action reminded me of my father—men were strong, often solitary, willful, and very funny, I established. I remember leaning on the cooker one evening and encouraging Mum to marry again:

"Anyone! It doesn't matter as long as they're nice. . . ." I badly wanted someone to look after her, and us.

"I understand, sweetheart," she said. "I wish there was a man in the house too, but there just isn't anybody. There's no one around who's my type, that's the thing. . . ."

Someone her type? That was that, then, I decided. She obviously did not have a type, or we would not be here, like this. So there would never be such a person. I was absolutely sure.

David and Elizabeth helped Jenny with Alexander and me, taking us for walks, reading to us, playing games. One afternoon when Jenny was away we played cards at the kitchen table while outside the daylight turned cloudy green: the sky, the air, and the rain took on a darkly glowing undersea hue, through which lightning flashed pink-white and there came rolling blasts like mountains exploding. Alexander and I jumped, Lark tried to sit on David's feet, and David looked thrilled, and tried to keep still, but finally could not stop himself and dashed outside to revel in it. The thunder seemed to be stooping over the house, stamping its giant feet somewhere among the larch trees, beating its furious cudgel against the low green clouds.

"Come back, David!" I squeaked. "Tell him to come inside!" I implored Elizabeth.

She was reassuringly untroubled: "Oh, don't worry, he loves it, he'll be fine. . . ."

You can't stop men, she seemed to be saying. They just do these things.

It went on and on. Then the rain came down with a great ripping, hissing sound, as if a dragon had doused his fiery snout in the clouds. I knew where the local beast lived—among the great compressed sandstone blocks, as mighty as any granite, that made the mountain's forehead. Looking across the valley to the Beacons on a stormy evening it was easy to see the dragons: their smoke rising from the pine forests; their wings in the torn black clouds; the horizon bloody with their fires. Such grim nightfalls made us shiver. I locked the front door and bolted into the kitchen, determined to get my back to the cooker.

❖ ❖ ❖

It was not unusual to "get spooked" at the farm. Although the whole place felt charged full of ancient, benevolent energy, there were sinister patches. A corner of our Quoiker never felt quite right to Jenny. And she dreaded passing that dark shadow behind the barn. Some nights, when nothing moved or called, everything seemed to be waiting for something. On certain days, when no birds sang, the slightest noise in the wood would set your heart racing. Sometimes under a cold moon we heard weird cries and terrible shrieks—a fox, my mother would say, with an odd note in a voice, or "Don't worry, it's just a rabbit, caught in a snare."

Coming down from the hill one night, Alexander and I took a shortcut across the fields, following a path that led into a small wood. We went slowly in the dark. Suddenly there was a crash in the branches above us, and an alien, grating squawk. The hair on my neck stood up, and Alexander froze.

"What was that?" he demanded.

"A bloody crow or something probably, I dunno," I said, and heard in my voice that same note of lightness, tinged with dread, that I feared in my mother's speech.

"Didn't sound like a bloody crow to me," he retorted, and we ran.

David and Elizabeth stayed with us through the winter, the lambing, and on into early summer. They dissolved all our money worries, our fears of ghosts and strangers, and seemed to applaud our isolated, unworldly life.

They gave off gaiety like light. One day they took Alexander and me to the reservoir, and while we swam, they laid out a feast of foods and wine, and kissed each other and laughed. When we emerged from the water there were rosy prawns heaped on a plate, with tiny black eyes like berries, crackling pink armor, and extraordinary insect legs. We had never seen prawns like this before. We watched, amazed, as David cracked one open and peeled it, raising an eyebrow at us in conspiracy, before devouring the white flesh with a lip-smack of pleasure.

"Haven't you had prawns before, boys?" Elizabeth asked.

"No. . . . Not like that!"

"Here, this is how you do it."

We stood up to our knees in the reservoir, and littered the bank with shells and legs and heads. We told Jenny about it later, with great excitement, and she rejoiced with us. How lucky we were to have lodgers!

When they left we felt more alone than ever; Jenny's isolation was underlined, and I understood that our friends had not extinguished our worries, merely sheltered us from them. Now all that remained of them were rituals, like the sun-downing whiskey. Jenny began to lean on it more heavily.

I woke one night to find my light still on, and crept down to bring her upstairs. She was in her nightie and a threadbare orange dressing gown, pacing the kitchen, with a cigarette and a whiskey, and she was crying.

"What's wrong?"

"Oh, dearest, I just don't know what will happen to us. Sometimes I feel so worried, sometimes I just despair." She wept. "Oh, dearie me. . . ."

"But it's going to be all right, I'm sure it is," I pleaded. "You mustn't worry, it will get better!"

"Yes, I expect it will, of course it will. . . . Oh . . ." She wiped her eyes and nose, but now the tears came again, and she spoke through heaving sobs, her expression terribly broken, like a child wailing in a playground. "It's just sometimes . . . I think it was a terrible mistake . . . bringing us all up here, up this mountain. . . . I don't know how we're going to manage. . . ."

"It wasn't, Mum, you know it wasn't. It's wonderful, really, isn't it?" It sounded hopelessly thin.

"Yes, yes, it is, but . . . ohh! Dear me!" She smiled damply. "It's just the drink making me cry. We'll be fine, we'll survive somehow. Don't worry."

She stopped pacing and returned to her station by the cooker, sniffing, wiping her eyes. Now I began to pace, moving over the flag-stones in the way I always did, one, two, and one to the side, the way a knight moves in chess. I curled my feet so that I walked on my heels and the tips of my big toes, keeping the soles away from the cold floor. My gaze roved over the kitchen, the thick walls, the ranks of jars on the shelves, the empty wine rack, the cobwebs slung like dusty hammocks in the corners, the calendar on the back of the door. It all seemed so secure when Jenny was happy, and so terribly vulnerable now.

"Is it money?" I asked tentatively.

"Well, yes. It is partly money . . ."

"But, so, how much do we have?"

"Well . . . not much. A bit. Enough to be going on with. We'll be OK if we get a good price for the yearlings."

"Do you think we will?"

"Yes, yes, we should do. They're jolly good little sheep, anyway," she said with defiance in her voice. "I should think they'll do just fine. Come on, it's no use worrying. Go back to bed before you freeze. I'm coming up now too."

It was one of the bleakest nights of my childhood. Not long afterward all three of us addressed the question of happiness.

"Life is all ups and downs; think of it as hills and valleys," she instructed us.

"Why do there have to be valleys?" Alexander asked.

"Yes, why can't it all be hills?" I demanded.

"Because you can't have hills without valleys, my darlings. Because life goes down as well as up." She drew a series of humps in the air. "The important thing when you're down is to remember that it goes up, too. However bleak things seem, remember, you must face with courage whatever the future brings, and trust that things will get better. All will be well."

"But will it, though?"

"Oh, yes." She nodded over the top of her coffee mug. "Always!"

The day of the yearling sale came. Jenny and Jack gathered thirty-two of the best into the pens. The buyer was a friend from mid Wales who ran an extensive farm. He would not buy as a favor, but if he liked the animals he would give a good price for them, and by coming to us he

saved Jenny the auctioneer's fee and the cost of paying Gwyn to take
them to market.

Jenny and Jack hovered anxiously by the gate as the shepherd
made his inspection.

"Do you want my honest opinion?" he asked after a while.

"Yes," said Jenny.

"They are very good," he said.

"Oh, Jack!" Jenny cried. "What a compliment to you!" Jack tried
not to look too pleased.

"How much do you think they're worth?" Jenny asked the shepherd.

"How much do you want for them?" he returned.

Jenny took a deep breath. "Well, last year they sold for thirty-eight
pounds each, but I thought, well, I wouldn't *mind* forty pounds this
year."

"Right," said the shepherd. It was done. When he had gone Jenny
did a little wiggling jump for joy and hugged Jack.

"I know what! Let's go to the pub. I'm going to buy you a beer to
celebrate."

"Oh, no, can't really," Jack demurred. "I haven't shaved, see."

"No, I insist, I'm kidnapping you. Come on, boys, everyone into
the car! It's a celebration!"

We sat in the near-empty pub. Alexander and I had juice and
crisps, and Jenny worked out 32 x 40 on the back of an envelope.
When the check arrived a few days later she propped it on the kitchen
windowsill behind the sink.

"Look at that boys! One thousand, two hundred and eighty
pounds! It looks good enough to frame!"

It was a double celebration, because the yearlings had been sold to
breed; they would have happy lives on their new farm, Jenny said.
When sheep went to the abattoir it was a miserably different story.
Then their panic at being chased into the back of Gwyn's trailer was
terrible to witness. When the door was slammed shut behind them
they peered out through the slats in the sides and cried, and Jenny's
face was haggard as she turned away, drawn and haunted. 'They know
I'm betraying them," she whispered. "They can tell."

"Don't think about it," we urged her. "It will be over very quickly, Mummy."

But she shook her head, and as the trailer lurched away down the track she wept.

"I'm a hopeless farmer!" she wailed. "Robert always said I was much too sentimental, and he was right!"

The worst were the old biddies, old friends going for a few pounds. She held back as many as she could, more than she could afford, to spare them the horrors of slaughter. "I want that one to die at home," she would say, "where I can look after her."

She had a large collection of these old animals, and whenever Jack or Gwyn raised an eyebrow at them she was loud in their defense. "They make lovely mothers! They have perfectly good lambs, and they're much easier to work with than mad young ones—I don't know why everyone doesn't keep a few. . . . You're laughing at me, Gwyn!"

The last days of the old were spent in the Patch, the steep field below the pens, where they could be watched from the yard. Under the hazels at the bottom of the field the ground was checkered with their graves. When one died as she hoped it would, quietly, without pain, Jenny was as happy as if she had witnessed a new birth: "She went in her sleep! No fuss—just perfect. Wonderful! I so wish they all went like that."

Found dead in the morning, the corpse would be left all day, to make absolutely sure, as Jenny said, that the old biddy was definitely, definitely dead. At some point in the late afternoon the body would be transported, wobbling, bouncing, and beginning to smell, to the bottom of the Patch.

The burial party consisted of the corpse, swelling gently, its weight swaying the wheelbarrow, which was pushed by Jack and followed by Jenny and Alexander and me, dragging tools.

Mum reconnoitered the ground. "We don't want to put her in on top of any of the others, and we don't want too many stones. How about here, Jack? That's not too close to Calpurnia, is it?" Jack cast an eye at the gentle depression of Calpurnia's grave, shook his head, and set to work, cutting foot-square turfs with the spade. He removed each with great care, setting them in a stack like a pile of parcels, leaving a red rectangle of naked earth. This he attacked with the pickax. "Stand back, children!" Jenny ordered as we pressed forward to watch the spike stab and rip. Jack paused to rescue earthworms, which writhed frantically between his gentle fingers.

"Good for the ground, worms," he explained, and I nodded, as if knowledgeably.

In my eyes Jack was the ultimate authority on this mysterious, almighty thing, the ground, and Jenny was his apprentice. He was the source of our most common mantra: "Good for the grass," someone was sure to say, quoting him whenever it rained.

"Jack says there's liver fluke in the L-Shape," Jenny said. Even after she explained that this meant there was bacteria in the marshy grass of that field, it still sounded like a kind of spell, a rune in the turf that only Jack could read.

He began heaving out hills of red soil with the shovel. When he rested we joined in; he watched our efforts tolerantly before reclaiming the grave. The thumps and scrapes of the pick and shovel drew the attention of the hedgerow birds. A party of great tits passed squeaking comment, and a blackbird chinked, indignant at our presence there, in the quiet at the end of the day.

When he was up to his hip in the pit, Jenny said, "I think that's enough, dear Jack, don't you? Such hard work, you've done wonderfully well."

"Bit more, I should say," Jack grunted. "Don't want any resurrections."

Jenny laughed at the question marks on the faces of my brother and me.

"The foxes will dig them up if you don't put them deep enough," she explained.

"On the third day she'll rise again," Jack intoned.

The climax of the enterprise was the moment when the body was lowered into the pit. Nearby sheep stopped grazing and watched, incuriously, as the stiff white form, with its clouded eyes and mucus-trailing mouth, was swallowed by the field, leaving a whiff of rotten egg.

Alexander and I recoiled, protesting.

"It's only methane!" Jenny sighed. "Perfectly natural!"

"It stinks!"

"Yes, and if you hung around for three days and nights you might see a green cloud of it coming out of the grave," she said. "Sometimes you see it burning in marshes—people used to see the light and think they'd seen a ghost."

Wrinkling our noses, we took up spades and joined in with the conclusion, heaving the cones of soil back into the hole. It was somber work at first, as the earth fell on fleece, shoveled lumps bouncing hollowly on the inflated rib cage and settling around the head. When the body disappeared it was better, and when the hole was nearly filled Jack did a grave dance, stamping, bouncing, packing down the earth with his boots. At last the turfs were replaced and trodden in, and we loaded the tools into the barrow.

"Thank you so much, Jack, and well done, boys. Well done, everybody!"

In the gloaming we made our way back up the Patch, my mind swimming with green gases, ghost lights, and sheep's souls, ascending on the third night.

We drove Jack back to his cottage, and returned to the now dark farm. "Do you think we've got ghosts here?" I asked as Jenny bolted the front door.

"Oh yes, I should think so, very friendly ones." She smiled. "You can feel the spirit of a place when you go into it, and I felt wonderful when I first came here."

"Who do you think they are?"

"Some lovely old farmer and his wife, I expect, keeping an eye on us, keeping us company. You're not scared, are you, boys?"

"No!" we said. "Never!"

It was nearly true: we were more often enchanted than scared. Doing a round of the meadows one night, Jenny was amazed to see a fiery orange light, like a big blazing fruit, which appeared over the wood and cruised across the meadows, rising up to follow the contours of the Quoiker before disappearing over the northern skyline. It made a rushing sound, she said, and it was climbing parallel to the rising ground: it was no meteorite, nor ball lightning. Perhaps it was the Tanwedd, a legendary Welsh apparition like a flying saucer.

We saw the great shimmering pillars of the aurora borealis, one winter, like pink and green searchlights probing the northern sky; another night, to the west, we watched Halley's comet on its weird, stationary plunge through space. Derwyn showed us the entrance to a hidden tunnel, leading straight into the mountain, and high up above us on a distant ridge was the split gravestone of the notorious villain Macnamara, whose shade, it was said, haunted the lonely heights.

"Don't worry about ghosts!" Jenny used to say. "We've more to fear from the living than the dead!"

It made sense, and though the lengthening of the shadows and the coming of night made me prickly with the sensation of awakening spirits, in daylight the sown ghosts of the landscape made it rich and fascinating. The heap of rocks in our lowest field, all that remained of Ty Newydd, seemed to await the return of its builders. The abandoned cottage in the wood was so perfectly sited, under the arm of a tree-topped bank, that it was almost an effort not to see smoke curling out of its cracked chimney. The crumbling stone exclamation of the ruined castle still commanded three valleys, and demanded all travelers acknowledge it.

On the other side of the mountain lies Llyn Safaddan, a lake that abounds in fish, particularly large pike and eels, and myths. As well as a record of changing color, to a livid red, "as if blood flowed partially through certain veins and small channels," as Gerald of Wales reports, and to an eerie green before times of war and desolation, the lake has been seen covered in buildings, pastures, gardens, and orchards, and, when frozen, heard to emit terrifying sounds; as Gerald says, "resembling the moans of many animals collected together."

There are stories about drowned villages. Archaeologists have discovered evidence of extensive ancient settlements around the reedy shore, including the canoes and tools of Bronze Age lake dwellers, who built their homes on stilts above the water.

Gerald also tells of a prophesy that says if the natural Prince of Wales were to come to the lake and order its birds to sing, they would immediately obey him. In the reign of Henry I, Gerald writes, three men, Gruffydd, son of Rhys ap Tewdwr; Milo, Lord of Hereford; and

Payn FitzJohn, Lord of Ewyas, were passing the lake, and jocularly discussing the prophesy. Milo and Payn went down to the water's edge and took turns commanding the birds to sing, and were ignored.

> And Gruffydd, perceiving that it was necessary to do so in his turn, dismounted from his horse, and falling on his knees towards the east, as if he had been about to engage in battle, prostrate on the ground, with his eyes and hands uplifted to heaven, poured forth devout prayers to the Lord: at length, rising up and signing his face and forehead with the figure of the cross, he thus openly spake: "Almighty God, and Lord Jesus Christ, who knowest all things, declare here this day thy power. If thou has caused me to descend lineally from the natural Princes of Wales, I command these birds in thy name to declare it"; and immediately the birds, beating the water with their wings, began to cry aloud, and proclaim him. The spectators were astonished and confounded; and the earl Milo, hastily returning with Payn FitzJohn to court, related this singular occurrence to the king, who is said to have replied, "By the death of Christ [an oath he was accustomed to using], it is not a matter of so much wonder, for although by our great authority we commit acts of violence and wrong against these people, yet they are known to be the rightful inheritors of this land."

Gruffydd's people have always looked at incomers with mixed feelings. At the bottom of the scale, in our time, were the second-homers, who bought beautiful farms, sold off the land, and visited but rarely, in the summer and at Christmas. They inflated land prices and denied homes to the next generation of locals. Theirs were the houses that were targeted by Meibion Glyndwr, the self-proclaimed Sons of Glendower, nationalist arsonists who burned out a few second homes during the 1970s.

Next came the weekenders, who would keep a few acres around the house and rent out the ground; befriend the farmers; buy a few pet horses or sheep; and boost the pub's takings. They were tolerated or welcomed, as were the straggling lines of walkers, pony trekkers, and holidaymakers.

We were of the third kind, immigrants who had exchanged their distant lives for Wales. My mother reckons it took her twenty years to be accepted as a fixture, if still an incomer. Among our peers my brother and I were identified as incomers by our accents, which seemed to bar us from ever being Welsh. But as we became accustomed to a permanent life on our mountain, which we had known on and off all our lives, we felt ever more at home, and as rightful inheritors of the territory as any true Prince of Wales.

One bright morning I stood in the back patch and stared at the spiny, tousled crowns of the larch trees above the house. I could not see him, but there was a cuckoo in there somewhere, making an almighty racket. In between shouting his name he was rattling out a series of clucking squawks; he plainly wanted everything with ears, near and far, to hear and admire his hullabaloo.

I felt an amused aggravation with this bird, shouting as if it was all somehow his doing, this paradise of warmth and promise, the fresh sunlight and the dreamy view.

"Cuckoo," he shouted.

"CUCKOO!" I answered.

"Cuck-coo?" he replied before he could stop himself.

"Cuckoo," I affirmed.

There was a doubtful pause.

"Cuckoo," I prompted. "Cuckoo!"

And then he let fly. "Cuckoo! Cuckoo!" he cried, and I answered him, and he answered me and chatted off a squawk for good measure.

My mother came out of the kitchen, laughing. "He was talking to you!"

"Yes," I said, coolly. "He was, wasn't he?"

Talking to the birds did not seem in the least strange to me, in a world where everyone talked to their dogs and their sheep, but not necessarily their neighbors. Every little mountain farm is a kingdom, as particular and unalike in character as each farmer is from his neighbor: all were in some sense eccentric, but some were definitely more eccentric than others.

7

The Realm

JENNY HAD PINNED THE SPEECH GIVEN BY ELIZABETH I TO her troops at Tilbury on the bathroom wall. I used to read it when I sat on the lavatory:

> . . . though I have the body of a weak and feeble woman I have the heart and stomach of a king, and a king of England too, And think foul scorn that Parma or Spain or any prince of Europe should dare invade the borders of my realm. . . .

Our Parma or Spain was Idris Baines, who farmed the mountain miles beyond us, but whose ragged animals were forever appearing on our precious grazing.

"I bet he's putting them in on me again," Jenny hissed. "The little bugger."

And there he was, in his cap, a still shape on the skyline, waiting for her to do something about it.

"Come with me, children. He's better when you're around."

Idris's face was a red tide of broken veins; his voice spiraled up from squeaky hails when he was calm to enraged shrieks when he was angry, and he was nearly always angry. His memory of the insults his family had suffered stretched back to his grandfather's time; his grudging eyes seemed to be calculating your good luck against his misfortune. Animals belonging to Idris went in terror of all humans: his sheep ran for their scraggy lives when you stepped into the field and his dogs were savage and scared. At his most relaxed he puffed on the tiny butts of roll-ups, which he carried in his pocket in a tin; Alexander and I stared, amazed, at the little glowing buds that stuck to his lip, leaking smoke into his mustache; he was like the pirate Blackbeard, who wore tapers in his hair. When our cars passed in the valley his lips moved, but you could see he was not mouthing greetings.

"They've jumped in again, Idris," she called as we approached him, allowing herself the thinnest note of bleakness, which sounded like provocative sarcasm to me, as her voice chimed loudly across the top of the Quoiker, over the tops of the thistles. Was she trying to set him off?

"Aye," Idris shouted in his wavering way. "Bloody things won't come from there!"

"I'm fed up with it—they're eating all my grass!"

"Ah. Can't do nothing with them. Seem to like it though, don't they?"

He watched with a half smile as we chased his sheep, which bolted over the fence like fleeing thieves and dashed into the bracken. Idris's dogs stiffened, pointed their muzzles at the strays, but did not move.

"See? He runs them at the fence," Jenny muttered to us under her breath.

"Do you think they'll stay out this time?" she demanded, plaintively, as she tugged the rusty wire erect once more and began to knit its top strands together with a length of baler twine ("farmer's friend," Jack called it: bright plastic string that holds hay bales and the poorer part of the countryside together). She looked at him and raised her eyebrows, emboldened by his silence.

Idris smiled. "Might do."

When the rain and sleet set in, you would see his animals standing on mud for days, bleating to be fed, but no Idris.

"He lies in bed watching the television," Jenny sneered. "And his animals starve!"

"I'm scared of him," she said after another encounter on the hill fence, just the two of them under a beaten gray sky, by the dripping blackthorn, Idris hysterical, screaming something about being cheated by the Davises and the bloody Joneses too, as his dogs flattened themselves to the rain-fattened hill and Jenny looked at her feet, her voice quiet, soothing. "Yes, Idris, no, Idris, I don't know about that. . . . Poor Idris. Look, I've got to go now, the boys will be worried. . . ."

"I'm sorry for him, really, but I'm scared he'll hit me, one of these days," she said when she returned.

"No, he won't!" I said.

"He'd better not!" Alexander said, hotly, as if our glowering tempers were enough to hold him back. We were only ten and eight but if he ever touched our mother, by God, we'd go at him together with our fighting sticks. We went out the back to hack and swing and roar.

On your own ground you could almost believe you might win a fight like that, but in someone else's farmyard you went very quiet. Going to see Idris was like volunteering for a nightmare. The road went up over a ridge, past polyethylene feed bags strewn about like oil-slicked birds, past rusting rolls of barbed wire, past a dead car, drunkenly titled on blocks, and on, into his yard, into the blast of barking dogs and the gaze of broken windows, patched here and there with more feed bags, some of them ripped. Then, as you waited for him to come out, you tried not to stare at the torn corrugated iron roofing and the streams of oiled water running straight into the buildings, and when Idris appeared you smiled in your most friendly way. He never asked us in, and we never guessed aloud at what might go on in there. I imagined squalor and weirdness, which was exactly what some visitors must have thought when they came to us.

"Oh, Lord! Look at the dirt!" Jenny cried when the year's first proper sun came out and illumined the blotched downstairs windows, where Toss had pressed his nose against the panes, and where Alexander or I had squashed flies, leaving their innards in little yellow smears on the glass. She was happier drenching fifty sheep than cleaning a room: "I know it's grotty, but the fact is I haven't got time, most of the year," she announced, one sleeve rolled up, flushed and flustered by the annual spring clean in a way that she never was in the pens. "Life's much too short for housework—it's just so boring!"

Of course we agreed; we made a great deal of mess and hated hoovering. "I suppose I ought to do something about those cobwebs," she sighed, "but why should I?" She brightened, defiantly. "I love spiders!"

She shrugged at the mud that trailed her into the kitchen. "The point is, this is a working farm!"

"Yes, Mum," we affirmed, and knew that we colluded with a wildly idiosyncratic set of values. Mud, sheep shit, and broken furniture were dismissed with a wave of the hand. No one ever made a fuss about dirt or germs. "Oh, microbes," Jenny said. "What can you do?" But a brash dress, an ugly vehicle, or a nasty piece of new building in town caused shrieks and retching noises. At the other end of the scale from the farm was the mysterious and ludicrously disinfected and overclean land of the "bijoux" and the "chi-chi," the capital of which, for some reason, was a particular London suburb.

"Golly, it's like something out of *Virginia Water*," she exclaimed in the face of certain objects and attitudes. Fussy clothes were bijoux; smart cars were chi-chi. Expensive flats in London were bijoux; microwave ovens and duvets were Virginia Water: ugly things, conspicuous bad taste, suspiciously—dangerously—convenient, and devoid of class.

I had no idea what Virginia Water might actually be like, but I had a clear picture of what it was not: Vivian on the kitchen shelf, nibbling red lentils and depositing piles of his little black droppings; Toss, stretched out across the entire sofa, on his back, fangs grinning, paws kicking gently in the air as he dreamed of catching squirrels; fleas pinging off him; ranks of penicillin and antibiotics fighting the milk for space in the fridge door; giant syringes of colostrum in the freezer, snuggling up to the fish; my mother squatting in the grass out the back, keeping an eye on the skyline in case Mr. Brown should catch a half-mile glimpse of her urinating; my brother lying flat on the ground in a tantrum, pounding the mountain with his feet and fists;

me, with a hammer, smashing one of the old henhouses to pieces in an act of entirely gratuitous vandalism, for the sheer pleasure of it; my brother and me play fighting so fiercely in his room that our combined weight drove the leg of the double bed to pop through the carpet, slip between the floorboards, and smash through the ceiling below, into the living room.

"Oh no, oh no, oh no!" I gasped, trying in vain to heave the bed back up through the floor. "It was an accident . . ." Alexander began, shakily, before trailing off. An agonized, amazed noise came up from below. We exchanged a look like a farewell, then slunk downstairs, trembling like curs.

Our mother stared at the small but darkly ragged hole in the middle of the ceiling, then us, in silence. We braced for the tempest, but when she spoke she was terrifyingly calm.

"Well, you've finally done it, haven't you?" she said. We flinched. Enunciating every word with a terrible clarity, she said, "Pushed the bed through the ceiling!"

Our stammered apologies were utterly inadequate. She gave a defeated shrug.

"It's pretty well the final straw, I reckon."

The coming of the final straw had been threatened before, but this was surely its moment: the dark wooden limb poking obscenely into the room even looked like it. Shocked and remorseful, Alexander and I pulled the bed back into the bedroom and turned in all our savings, which came to about eleven pounds.

"Well. That's not going to help much, is it?" she said tiredly. We were already so distressed that further chastisement must have seemed pointless.

The next day she climbed onto a chair, holding a rectangle of white cardboard, which she carefully taped over the hole. She seemed to find it quite funny.

"There you are. That'll have to do, I'm afraid! Looks sort of all right, doesn't it?"

We nodded, dubiously.

"Good!" she said brightly. "Perhaps you'll be a bit more careful in future. It would be nice if we could keep the rest of our ceilings. . . . You pair of prunes! Luckily it's quite a small hole. It will be fine, as

long as no one looks up. Trust your mother to sort it out!" she said
with a laugh, and tapped the side of her nose with a finger.

We laughed, but as I looked up at the cardboard and the sticky
tape, part of me longed, silently and treacherously, for something like
Virginia Water. Alexander and I shared occasional moments of weakness when we fantasized about warm houses in which all the doors
were left open, the stairs were carpeted, white bread was toasted for
breakfast, and the days ended with television and warm duvets. Jenny
dreamed of a life free from Wellington boots.

"I hate wellies!" she groaned. "I hate tramping around in them all
day. So boring and ugly and your feet get so hot. . . . Oh, I used to
wear lovely shoes!"

Sometimes her previous life jangled into ours through the telephone.

"Hello? Hello!" she cried. "Golly, how are you?" And there would
follow a laughing conversation, conducted in warm and excited tones.
"Well!" she said when she had put the phone down. "That was my
dear friend Angus, the Canadian oil millionaire. Ringing from Cal-
gary, Alberta, to make sure we're all right—isn't that just amazing?"

Her past did seem amazing: there were Christmases in Welsh castles; spine-chilling episodes in a Boston terrorized by a figure called
the Strangler; precarious travels around Europe in a tiny plane. . . .
There were E-type Jaguars, famous boyfriends, proposals of marriage,
last-minute changes of heart on airliners. When she washed our hair
she would lather it and then tease it into vertical spikes, so we looked
like the Thai children she had seen in Bangkok. She knew how to live,
and she knew how to tell stories. They came with morals, and not boring ones, either.

"When chances come, my darlings, you must seize them with both
hands. Grab everything!"

There were one or two simple formulae for the most enjoyable kind
of life: Cambridge or Oxford, followed by London in your twenties,
and lots and lots of parties. She did not seem to have many regrets,
except when she knew there was a party somewhere. "It's awful thinking of all that fun, and not being there," she would say wistfully.

These longings fell with sudden intensity, like cravings for honey
or chocolate; they surfaced on our returns to the mountain after we

had visited our cousins or friends, to be rapidly submerged under the farm's next requirement, whatever it was.

"Boys, I need to put a post in—would you mind giving me a hand?"

We groaned.

"Come on! It won't take long!"

All our friends were probably watching television or riding around on their bicycles to see each other. Nothing would ever take long, according to her, but we knew that everything did.

Patching up a stretch of our boundary took a couple of trips back and forth across the fields, between the toolshed and the collapsing fence, carrying—when Mum was not looking, dragging—posts, the sledgehammer, and the iron bar. When everything was ready, and she had chosen the spot where the wire was feeblest, we took turns wiggling the crowbar into the earth, then positioned the post above the hole. One of us knelt down, praying, and steadied it while Jenny hauled the sledgehammer up to her shoulder level, and half dropped, half lowered it onto the target, the small flat head of the post. We could all imagine what would happen if she missed: the lumpen hammerhead arcing down toward your skull, shoulder, and restraining arm, the thud, the shrieks.

"That will keep you out for another week, won't it?" she shouted at one of the Norsters' ragged ewes, which stared insolently at her, the wool trailing off its unshorn back.

"Blooming strappers. Jack says they leave a bit of wool as a marker for their friends," Jenny remarked, tugging the tell-tale strands off the sagging wire. We eyed the strapper, which snorted and stamped its foot at the dogs. Lark twitched one ear; Toss ignored it completely. "Go home!" we shouted at the sheep.

It was impossible not to identify shepherds with their sheep: a glance at Jenny's coddled, vociferous white bundles spoke tellingly of her, just as the whistling, fleeing figures belonging to Idris or the Norsters betrayed them. When farmers fell out they prosecuted their disputes through one another's animals. In one incident a man enraged by his neighbor's continuing failure to keep his strappers under control seized an intruding stray and broke one of its forelegs, snapping it with his hands. One of Gwyn's enemies imprisoned a pregnant ewe belonging to Gwyn in a barn and starved it almost to death before slipping it back, little more than an animated corpse, to die in front of its horrified shepherd. Another trick was to round up offending animals, put them in a trailer, and drive them miles away, then let it be known on the grapevine where they could be found.

"It's bloody medieval around here," Jenny said, shaking her head.

Warring neighbors tore down each other's fences, stole hay and hurdles from remote barns. Or they marched, toting a shotgun, into a hostile farmyard, to murder dogs suspected of attacking their sheep. At the climax of one confrontation over a collapsing fence, two sets of brothers fought a battle on the hill. In a perverse, self-spiting insult, the losers chained one of their own dogs to a stake on the mountain near the disputed boundary and left it there, eating its own feces to survive.

The police and the animal protection authorities were never involved—to inform on a rival, however hated, was simply not done. Jenny's love of animals was well known, and she grew used to being suspected of telling tales.

"You'd better feed them soon, or someone will see and report you," was her ultimate sanction. When someone did see, and did make the call to the RSPCA, she would naturally be blamed, though the reporters were almost certainly walkers, appalled by the starving or mistreated victims they had stumbled upon.

When Jenny had finished knitting the wire to the new post with baler twine she declared the job done.

"Aren't we brilliant? We did it! What a team—we're the three musketeers!" she exclaimed, and we laughed and felt bigger.

"See? We can do anything if we put our minds to it, and all help each other," she continued as we made our way home, lugging the tools through our own private evening. The valley filled with shadow half an hour before the sun left our uplands; up here every thistle cast a long shadow, midges still danced in the lanes for us, and our bats came out to hunt them, skiing wildly through the warm air, little black flickers against the still sky.

From the meadows came the thrum of pounding feet: the lambs were running races, forty or more hurtling along beside the hedge toward an invisible finishing line, some leaping, kicking, and twisting, others pouncing in a joyful, stiff-legged dressage, before they all turned and bolted back the other way.

Alexander pointed. "Look at the moon!" It was waxing, a silver crescent supporting a blue shadow.

"Oh, yes," Jenny sighed. "Isn't that wonderful—the new moon with the old moon in his arms. . . . Goodness me, aren't we lucky?" she breathed. We paused and gazed about us: she encouraged us to stop and drink in beauty, to set sights in our minds like postcards. Two herons, standing on the church tower one morning, seemed to be doing the same thing. Wild sentinels in gray morning dress, their drooping crests like warriors' plumes, they looked like pagan conquerors who had dressed for a wedding then seized the church, now surveying their demesne.

When the three of us stood like that, attempting to grasp the glow of each moment, the true, full being of the place, it was as though we were all the same age, child-adults, knowing nothing but wonder.

We all sensed it, but Jenny made it explicit: "Age doesn't mean a thing, you know," she said. "In the great scheme of things we're only here for a millisecond—if you look at it that way I'm pretty well the same age as you!"

I turned this thought over. It had serious implications, which I broached one night in the kitchen as she struggled through the sheaves of paper in the cardboard box that somehow directed our lives: her "admin."

"I don't understand how you become an adult," I said. "How do you know how to do admin and pay bills?"

"I don't know, darling! But don't worry about it—as you grow up you will understand. It just happens."

"Can you teach me now?"

"No, I'm afraid I can't! I'm hopeless at it—that's why I have an accountant!"

It was as though the gap between our ages changed constantly.

When she attempted admin, pulling her hair, muttering to herself, she did not seem much older, or more competent, than a sixth former. But once she had passed the front door, the moment she confronted the farm, she became, in a trice, commanding. Then she was in charge again, at the head of her troops: like any good officer, she was keen to develop their capacities.

Alexander and I began as little more than self-propelled barriers, slightly cleverer than dogs but not as fast. We progressed, via fencing, nettling, gathering wood, grave digging, and lamb feeding to catching and holding. This was properly useful, and could mean hours in the pens, sliding around in the muck, buzzed by the flies, infuriated by the sheep, and subjected to the long, soothing monologue Jenny kept up, talking to and about each animal as you grabbed it, subdued it, and presented it for drenching, maggotting, or vaccination.

"Hello, lamb, aren't you beautiful? Who's your mother, then? Oh, I know, you're one of Hippo's twins. You've done very well considering your mother is so hopeless. Dear Hippo, I've never known a sheep with less of a clue about parenting. First she tried to adopt someone else's, then she abandoned it, and then she damn near abandoned you, didn't she, sweetheart? Hold still!"

The monologue was broken occasionally with terse commands to me: "Watch out!" "Don't hurt her!" "We've already done that one." Her mind was entirely absorbed in the task, and each animal's well-being. Your tiring limbs, shortening temper, and circling mind did not exist. Many, many times I raised my eyes toward the sticky canopy of the sycamore tree that shaded the pens and thought darkly of my father's departure and decided that there was no mystery to it at all. He probably resented being used as a sort of sheepdog with arms.

"Good! That's the last of this lot—only one more lot to go and we'll have done it! And you can stop looking so sorry for yourself."

"I hate sheep!" I shouted. "I hate farming and I hate sheep. They're so stupid!"

"They are not," she shouted back. "Some of them are very clever, as a matter of fact. Now, stop fussing and come and help, please."

"No! Why should I? I don't ask you to help with my homework, do I?"

"If you won't help me," she said, bending toward me slightly, with narrowed eyes, "I won't help you. Then you can cook your own supper, and wash your own clothes, and get yourself to school. Or you can go and live with Robert. It's absolutely up to you."

She turned back to the sheep. I sent a beam of pure fury at the quilted back of the green body-warmer she always wore, a tatty sleeveless thing with pockets full of nuts that the sheep adored, and were forever nuzzling, and did as I was told, impotently, pointedly sulking.

It was not quite true: I did not hate sheep. I loathed one or two, when we could not catch them, and detested small bands that insisted on running the wrong way. I devised an imaginary instrument for herding them, a machine gun that would fire clay pigeons. As the operator and inventor I would enjoy setting it up in a corner of the field, and demonstrating it, firing streams of bursting, leaping projectiles in a flailing ribbon across the field, a line no sheep would ever dare cross. A burst on the left, a burst on the right to turn them, a little squirt behind them to get them going.

"Will you please concentrate! Think what you're doing, sweetheart, or we'll be here all day!"

I gave up that fantasy, guiltily and forever, the day one of our rams was faced with a real gun. He was dying in the First Meadow. I did not know what was wrong with him, but Jenny was quite unequivocal, and very busy.

"He's a goner, I'm afraid, the poor old boy. He's in pain too, so I've asked the vet to come and kill him," she explained. She was being deliberately brisk. "Jack doesn't want to, and I don't blame him."

Jack shook his head. I felt a shameful disappointment, having hoped for a glimpse of his famous Humane Killer, the bolt gun that he used for stunning pigs, a darkly precious instrument that he tried never to let me see, lest I should try to touch it. The Humane Killer remained wrapped in its oily sack. "We've got to deal with a minor crisis in the barn," Jenny went on, "and the vet is on his way. The thing is, I'm worried about that ram, lying out there by himself. I'm scared the crows will come and get his eyes. Would you mind going down and keeping them off him?"

It was a gritty gray day, spits of rain in the wind. The ram was the only animal in the First Meadow. He lay on his side, bloated and wretched. As I approached he shifted a little but he could barely kick his short legs. His flanks heaved as he watched me come; we stared helplessly at each other. I was sure he knew what was going to happen and feared he thought I might be his death.

"It's all right, boy," I said. "It's all right." I sat down next to him. He looked at me. I stroked his head. Sitting beside all his size and smell and plight, I felt the warmth of him through his wool, his snorting nostrils, his licking tongue. I looked at the mud between his clees, and thought it would still be there when we dropped him into his grave, and marveled that death should be so certain, and so near.

Three crows glided down from the hill fence to the Lower Meadow, thirty yards below, shouting angrily as they came overhead. In the lower meadow they shouted again—*Kaaa! Kaaa! Kaaa!*—then they came back up, turning their heads toward us as they flapped past, lascivious and impatient.

For a while I talked to the ram. I told him it would be over soon, and that I was sorry, and I burst into tears. He stared at the dank field. I felt ridiculous, stopped crying, and picked a handful of dull winter grass, which I held under his nose. He did not want it. I was horribly relieved when the vet arrived.

The vet brought a pistol. Jenny was appalled: why not an injection? The vet had some reason. Mum hustled my brother and me into the car, contriving a mission to town, but as we came down the track above the First Meadow she slowed, unable to pass the sight of Jack and the vet standing over the animal. I understood: there was something unconvincing about the tableau, about the way the vet held his gun. Jack retreated.

"Oh hell, he's going to make a mess of it," Mum blurted, and the vet fired. Jack started to approach the body but the vet held up a hand to stop him, and bent over the animal again. He fired another shot, and, after a word with Jack, a third.

"The stupid . . . incompetent . . . wretched . . ." Jenny ground out, "hopeless . . . bloody . . . fool!" she shouted to us.

"Goodness me, I'd like to give him a piece of my mind! But if I do he'll never come back. And one day we'll need him again, heaven forbid. Don't do it, Jenny. Bite your tongue."

We all adopted this sort of running commentary, which was part conversation, part performance, and part self-instruction, so although there were only three of us we lived in a babble of conversations. There was barely any distinction between talking to a dog, a cat, a sheep, or yourself. Alexander could often be seen talking to Toss, I murmured to myself whenever I was alone, and Jenny, when she was not chatting to the sheep, thought aloud as a matter of course, especially when problem-solving. I discovered the many merits of this as soon as I was old enough to be sent alone into the lambing fields at night, to do a late round.

"There's one thinking about it in the Far Meadow, just the other side of the hedge," Jenny said. "If she's having trouble give me a shout. She's a very good little ewe, though, so it should just slip out. Wake me if there's anything. Wrap up warm!"

Outside, under the protective yellow penumbra of the yard light, I tried out the heavy lambing torch. The sliding switch was temperamental.

"Not too far forward and not too far back," I muttered at it, and flashed the long white wand into the cavern of shadow behind the Big Barn before heading down the track. One of the old biddies at the top of the Patch belled a question. "Good biddy, only me," I answered. She repeated herself. Her noise seemed to expose me, and I was already jumpy. As I passed her I tried to sound quietly confident.

"It's only me. I'm just going out to look around the meadows, and then I'll be back, all right? Be quiet." She called again.

I kept the torch off but my thumb was tense against the switch. There was some scattered bleating from the Hill Fields. "It's just a fox . . . passing through," I announced to the night breeze, making it so. The Middle Meadow gate made its familiar double rattle. I advanced into the dark field. The hedges whispered, tapping their twigs and creaking.

"Now, where are these sheep?" My voice sounded warm and orderly, pushing back the not-quite-formless dark.

I switched on the torch and turned a slow circle. Molehills looked black-red, like fat scabs; sheep's eyes glinted blue-green. Beyond the range of the torch the darkness thickened and seemed to contract. I stared down the blade of light. The flock was settled and peaceful. I spoke to the sheep, reassuringly.

"I see, you're all down there . . . chewing your cud . . . so you're not doing it . . . nor are you . . . everyone's OK . . ." As the eye of light fell on them they stopped chewing for a moment, turned their heads slightly, and waited for it to move on. "Good . . . very good. . . . What was that?"

A choked whickering sound from the middle hedge. "She's doing it," I thought, with a surge of adrenaline. "Don't run," I told myself. "Don't frighten her."

She was down on her side, a bulge of flesh pinkly distending under her tail, which was bloody and wet. As I approached she tried to stand. "It's all right, sweetheart, all right, girl, stay there, don't get up, don't get up," I garbled, but at least the tone was right, low down, part reassurance, part supplication. I was with her quickly, on my knees, hand on her side, and she was not trying to get away now; there, bulging out of her, yellowish and covered in slimy fluid, were the nostrils and the tiny hooves of her lamb. The night seemed to funnel down through concentric circles: in the vastness of the dark was the tiny splash of torchlight; in the light was the little puddle of flesh and fluid. "Nose and feet together, that's good," I said, my heart thudding, knowing I was not going to go all the way back to the house and fetch my mother to what looked like a perfect birth. "Good girl! I can almost get my fingers . . . Push! There, there, there you are, good girl, push!"

I worked at the tight ring of muscle, easing it back a fraction, just enough to get finger-and-thumb purchase on the soft, tiny feet. The ewe groaned; I heaved. "It's coming! It's coming. Good girl, very good . . ." Now there was an inch of leg behind each foot and a centimeter of nose above the nostrils. A gentle pull had no effect at all. The ewe was panting like a runner and I was shivering with nerves.

"Right, I don't want to hurt it, but it can't stay there. . . . This lamb needs to come out and breathe. . . . I'm going to give it a proper pull. . . . Are you going to help me, biddy? Come on, come on, girl!" Wincing—to ward off the possibility I might pull the baby's front legs out of their sockets—I pulled, building up the draw until it took all my strength. "It's coming!" I cried, and there it was, long and yellow and sliding out now, an entire lamb, perfect from end to end, finished with fleece, ears, tail, toes, eyes, and even lashes, flopping out onto the dark wet grass, a small, impossibly complete sheep, half in and half out of the glistening cape of its amniotic sack.

"Clear the nose and mouth," I told myself, and pinched the slime away from its head. "Now it has to breathe," I added, "or I have to rub it to get it going." But there it was, a miraculous, spluttering cough, and the lamb threshed, and its legs seemed to engage suddenly, like gears, and then it was wriggling up onto its knees and trying to stand. The ewe was on her feet in a moment, all over it, whickering and muttering, nuzzling and licking madly, nudging and kissing and guzzling the slime, and as she talked to her baby it answered: a high, bewildered cry, which carried far across the dark fields.

I poked my head around my mother's door before I turned in, and proudly told her what had happened. "Wonderful!" she said. "And did it stand and . . ."

"Yes," I said, because I knew the last line. "It suckled. It had its first drink!"

Alexander and I were taught an eclectic range of subjects, Jenny's interests. We both became quite good at stars. On a cloudless night the three of us stood outside, a little way down the path toward the hill, so that we were clear of the towering ash tree that guarded the house, and tilted our heads back, like the dogs when they had treed a squirrel. Jenny pointed up as if the heavens were a great blackboard.

"The big W?" she prompted.

"Cassiopeia."

"Good. Easy one—that group of little stars, how many are there?"

"Seven! Seven sisters."

"Good. What's their other name?"

"Pleiades."

"Good. Alexander, what are those three?"

"Orion's belt!" he said, and went on to quote her precisely: "And there's his bow, and there's his dagger hanging down."

"Very good. And what's that saucepan?"

"The plow."

"Yes. Now, where's the north star?"

"There!"

"Good. So why can't either of you learn flowers?"

We laughed. We were intimate with foxgloves (and the trick of gently pinching shut one of their pink trumpets behind a visiting bee, for the outraged buzz the insect made before you released it) and with honeysuckle, which we suckled. We all delighted at the lemon-cream eruption of the primroses in the exhausted, after-winter Lower Meadow, and the harebells that appeared behind the house, pale lavender and exquisite, tiptoeing, tremulous as fairies. But we were hopeless at hedge flowers. In May or June, as we bowled along the lanes in the car, the questions would start.

"Now, what's that white plant, children?"

"Uuummm . . ."

"Oh, do wake up! It's Queen Anne's lace! My favorite!" She brought the car to a stop.

"Twinks, what are those white stars in the hedge?"

"Celandines?"

"*No!* You know they aren't! White stars in the hedge—come on!"

"Stitchwort?"

"That's right, poor man's buttonhole. Pim, what's that?"

"Vetch?"

"No, it's herb Robert."

"Herb Robert!"

"Yes. So what's that lovely thing?"

"Campion?"

"No, that's vetch!"

"Ahh! That's vetch!"

"I don't know, it's hopeless," she sighed. "You can do fauna, why not flora?"

Fauna was more exciting. Animals and birds did things, ate

things, moved, died, left traces. I became obsessed with tracks and signs, picking up eggshells in spring and feathers in summer, poking at droppings and prizing owl pellets: "Shit Exploring," my brother called it, as I made haphazard guesses at the kind of bird that had left this particular turd.

"Why can't we play a game?"

I was merciless in imposing my crazes upon him, and he was usually forgiving. He did get very fed up with my insistence on walking everywhere quietly, though.

"Shhh!" I hissed. "Step around the sticks, and don't let these branches brush you."

"Why? Why do we always have to sneak about?" he roared. "We're not hiding from anything, are we?"

We knew the land so well that we often wished we were hiding: if only an enemy would come and chase us, we could use our territory to defeat him.

The only unannounced intruders we had now were those who did not know what they were getting into, and the police, who came once or twice, cautioning us to keep our dog under control. Toss turned into a first-rate guard. He established a fearsome reputation for biting people, and we were not sorry. When friends and neighbors came, they telephoned ahead or waited in their cars until assured "that dog" was inside. It was our fault. At first we thought it very funny, when the dots appeared on the skyline, to see Toss take off like a rocket, hurdle two fences, streak straight up the mountain, and, moments after his little black arrowhead intersected with the silhouettes, inspire distant shrieks and screams.

"Bloody walkers! Good dog!" Toss went for the color red. Anyone wearing red hiking socks and blundering across our fences was in trouble. Jenny developed a redemption strategy, which involved running victims to the hospital for jabs and then pressing cash on them, to pay for ripped trousers and bloodied socks. They might also get the standard lecture, if they had been caught on our ground, about trespassing.

"Where do you come from?" she would ask.

"Luton [or somewhere]," came the reply.

"Well, how would you like it if you found me climbing over your garden fence in Luton?"

It was not a robust strategy, and Toss lived, obliviously and near permanently, on his final warning, and we all dreaded the day he would go too far, and "they" would come and get him.

"They" were a puzzling enemy, comprised of all the faceless human forces who were not on our side. They dug up the roads in inexplicable places, making us late for school. They wanted our sheep to be earmarked, an identical mutilation of every animal, which was supposed to make them harder to steal. They cut the hedges with vicious flails, destroying birds' nests and leaving thorns in the lanes which punctured our tires. They cut down trees, ripped up the old field boundaries, set snares, hunted foxes, trapped and baited badgers. They flew fighter jets low over the mountain, terrifying our animals and us. They were wedded to fertilizers and chemicals, forcing us to dip the sheep in poison twice a year. They believed in the Bomb and nuclear power stations; they beat and broke the miners. And then they had the gall to traipse across our fences, practically inviting Toss to bite them.

No one we respected ever spoke up for them, except our father, whose clear-eyed comments could cut through all our peculiar philosophy. During one of his visits we were walking down the mountain on an inclement day when we encountered some walkers. Before we could stop him, Toss nipped one of them. Dad made a mortified apology, then turned to us, angrily, and said, "Your dog's a bloody menace."

There was suddenly no denying it. Toss was a savage, and we were savages too.

Another time, driving with him farther up the valley, I looked at a particularly wild stretch of mountain and announced that I wanted to live there.

"But how would you make your living?" he countered, curiously.

I had no answer. The idea of making a living had barely occurred to me. As I understood it, you did what you wanted to do and your living somehow made you. He was the only person we knew who had an office job, and we questioned him curiously on it: What do you do when you get to work? What's it like, where do you have lunch, what happens after that? He answered us patiently, but the world he described seemed unreal. On one visit to London he led us at a jog up a long, dirty spiral staircase out of the Underground, remarking, "I don't take the lift—this is the only exercise I get every day!" He laughed sadly as he said it, which allowed me to take it as a joke. I could not seriously believe that anyone, least of all my father, could live such a deprived life.

He bridged the gap between us and them, and however perverse "they" seemed, anything associated with him was, to me, sacrosanct.

The farm was scattered with his doings: Robert's roof, Robert's bit of fence; the swings he set up in one of the larch trees behind the house, which were amazing, allowing the rider to hurl himself off a collapsing old wall and fly out, with the shed roofs, the yard, and the whole valley whirling away between his feet. Even the bulb in the yard light was his, since only he was tall enough to approach it, via the extendable ladder; it was an annual ritual that on one of his visits he would climb up to replace it. I loved to be compared to him. If one of my jokes made my mother laugh she would sometimes say, "That's so like your father. Gosh, he could be funny, so dry . . ." In the Lower Meadow one evening, I was standing among tall thistles, lost in some thought, waiting for Mum to tie up the gate, when I noticed she had finished and was looking at me. "You looked just like Robert, just then," she said. "Exactly the same." I tried to work out how I had done it. My brother, who is very handsome, and sometimes melancholy, was often compared to him.

We both wished he would stay longer than he ever did, and Jenny did too, for our sake. "Can you stay?" we always asked, though we knew. Even now, the word London, the summons and finality in its heavy syllables, reminds me of his answer.

With time, I came to accept that the three of us were sufficient to ourselves, and that it was unlikely Jenny would meet someone else. Robert's feeling was that occasional meetings for significant periods would be better for everyone than "little and often"—weekend encounters and truncated visits. We accepted this, too, and Alexander and I would count the weeks, days, and, at last, hours until he came again, and the sight of his car cresting the pitch and advancing toward us was one of the most thrilling of our childhood.

He always came on Boxing Day, with presents wrapped in beautiful paper. When we had unwrapped them, and eaten a second Christmas lunch, our fabulous new toys were carried back to his car, we climbed in, and the three of us set out for London, and a week of him, and theaters and cinemas and television, in a city glittering with lights and Christmas trees. On New Year's Eve we drank champagne. "Cheers, chaps," Dad said, and winked as we downed the bright bubbles. Jenny spent it alone.

Almost the New Year—Robert took the children away on Boxing Day, at 3 in the afternoon, for a week in London. I am pleased they are surrounded by radiators and central heating and television and museums, and, hopefully, films and pantomimes. I am here, quite alone except for the animals (350 sheep), surrounded by tinsel and holly and ivy inside, and snow and strips of ice out. It is odd to be without the children. Awful really. But I have a battle to fight with the weather keeping all the animals alive, and that is tremendously extending and takes my mind off my loneliness. And I think of John Eskell now that Betty is dead, and he so lonely now, and also, there are the desperately brave and valiant Poles holed up in their mines hanging on to their Solidarity. Being alone on a Welsh mountain is rich really. I'd rather be here than alone in a flat in Chelsea. And I remembered to buy a bolt before Christmas, and when the children went away I spent some time trying to nail it to the bedroom door. I feel much safer now when I go to bed even though I couldn't get the screws to go right in. A freezing fog. The yard unfrozen and awash in deep brown sheep droppings (because I've allowed 70-odd to live in the buildings during these three weeks of blizzard and cold) and outside the back door and blowing in billows a thick white fog. In the morning I heard a sheep bleating high on the hill, so, in thick mist and dusk walked the hill fence. Followed the four-leaf clover tracks of a small fox. In the Quoiker, Lark discovered a perfect, fresh sheep's front leg. It was white, loose, no smell. A murder. A world of pathos in this beautiful, softly fleeced limb. I looked, slipping on ice, the dusk changing to darkness, for the rest of the animal. Like tracking a murderer, trying to read clues in the snow. But in the white fields and deep snow I couldn't distinguish it. I'll look again tomorrow. I need to know the mark on the fleece. Derwyn, and Mr. Brown, I know, both have killer dogs. I felt so hungry when I came back. I sliced off a piece of cold lamb shoulder and ate it with a cold roast potato.

When we came back from London we pulled the decorations down and threw the holly in the fire. It burned with a rush so fierce that the flames were almost white, as if all the cheer of Christmas was released and spent at once. Now we faced January together. Garnet, one of the farmers at the bottom of the hill, waved as we passed him in the lane: "See you in March then, Jen," he said. "Different world up there. . . ."

One night we saw a sunset like an icy apocalypse; over mountains as still as rigor mortis a flash of gold bled out of a murderous sky, as if the last hope for the world was retreating. It was to be a hard, hard winter.

8

Great Snow

I N THE COLD THE MOUNTAINS LOOK LIKE CLENCHED FISTS, bare, lined here and there with white where the paths have frosted and the streams frozen. At night planets like tiny fires blaze, red-blinking Mars; Venus, the evening's fiery pearl. In the morning Sirius, the Dog Star, shines brighter than the fading moon. Snow is heralded by a slight alleviation of the cold, and a certain yellow light on the far horizon, which we learned to take as a warning. I was out when snow clouds came suddenly, roiling in from the northwest, tumbling over themselves like angry waves, submerging the sky. I hurried inside as the moonlight faltered and faded, and the hills disappeared, and the flakes came spiraling down.

Jenny listened to bad winter forecasts with dread for our fortunes as much as those of the animals; we could stand any rain or wind, but ice and snow meant leaving the car in the valley and walking down to it, then lugging ourselves and our supplies back up. We did it for weeks when necessary: Jenny walked us down and drove us to school, then did the shopping, climbed back up with carrier bags, fed the sheep, walked down again, and drove to fetch us, before finally shepherding us home.

The trek to school was wonderful, all downhill, with rabbit tracks and fox prints to identify and untangle. Jenny showed us the tiny footmarks of mice and the four-twig tracks of crows. We pictured all the night's goings-on as the sheep greeted us hungrily, yellow against the snow. Down the lane we slithered, and on into the wood, where we found rooks turning over the snowy leaf litter beside the road: they exploded up from the cover as we approached, ragged and wet-looking purple shapes, like djinns incarnated from the dark mulch under the snow, cawing protests about the interruption of breakfast.

The walk back up was not so good; tired at the end of the day, we wanted nothing more than to settle down with our toys, as we clambered out of the car at the foot of the hill and started up the opening section, the thigh-searingly steep first pitch.

The glimmering wood seemed to listen as we trudged through it, following our own tracks. The tangled trees darkened against the stippled white; somewhere among them snow slipped off a branch with a noise like a poacher stumbling.

"Come on, darlings," Jenny said. "It won't be long now and you'll be bigger than me, and I'll be saying please, please wait for me!" Alexander grumbled at the pace until Jenny clipped Toss to a leash and handed it to him: the dog pulled him on like a husky.

When we were not at school Alexander and I hurled ourselves into the drifts, snow in our sleeves and hard-packed down our boots, snow down our necks, the cold crystal taste of it in our mouths, our cheeks burning, our bodies hot under layers of clothes and coats.

Days after most of the area's roads had been cleared, a plow would arrive, spurting gouts of white, or a council digger appear, patiently scooping the drifts out of the lane and dumping them into the fields. Ice might keep us walking for days after we were dug out.

Jenny developed a winter routine: she stocked up supplies, lagged the water tank and the pipes above the bathroom, turned up the radiators, moved the sheep to fields best sheltered from the expected direction of the wind, and waited. She called on Jack and warned him not to try and reach us if it snowed. The village cottages seemed to huddle together for warmth, smoke rising from their chimneys like breath. "Wish us luck, dear Jack!" Jenny instructed him. "And make sure you keep warm for goodness sake!" We knew she dreaded the snow, but Alexander and I looked forward to it.

"Gritter!" Jenny shouted as we drove to town for supplies. The sight of one of the council's bright-striped lorries was an omen as powerful as the yellowish light in the sky. "It must be bad if they're out!" we agreed as the vehicle rattled past, flashing its orange strobe and pelting the road with reddish lumps of salt. On the way back from town the first flakes came; we eyed the ground and studied the sky. "Will it stick?" we pondered. "Too wet, I think," Jenny decided. "We'll chance it tonight."

We cheered. It was a miserable sleety night to have to walk all that way, with the shopping too. The next morning the fields were mottled, snow covering the roots, the grass like green fur on the back of a white beast, as if winter were pushing itself up through the ground. Still the flakes fell, sometimes fast, sometimes slowly, sidelong slipping through colder air, careless, unhurried, as if the weather were shifting from foot to foot, waiting.

"I'm taking the car down to the bottom," Jenny announced after she had heard the lunchtime forecast. "It's coming, my dears."

As she walked back up the hill it began to fall heavily; now there was nothing warm anywhere in the world, except her sheep in their coats. They called to her as she passed.

"Good girls, sensible sheep, you stay there. You'll be warm under that hedge."

As Big Ben struck six, Jenny turned away from the radio and toward the supper she was making, frowning. The forecast was not good—we might well be walking for a week, she thought. Had it given any true impression of what was coming, she might have been tempted to evacuate us and drive the flock off our land, down to our neighbors' lower fields. Instead we ate, played, and built one of our great fires. We filled the grate with a wigwam of branches over crumpled newspaper and twigs, lit it, and basked in the heat of a roaring conflagration, which sent skirls of sparks swirling up the chimney and flung ruddy light into the cold sitting room. We perched as close to it as we could, until our clothes were almost too hot to touch and our clammy backs felt feverish, as though they, too, were glowing red. The crackling branches spat sparks onto the rug, and we stamped them out, tutting mildly at the little black pits that remained. With the drafts on one side and the fire on the other you could feel two temperatures at once. When the blaze had burned down to its embers we went to bed, and the next day the storm arrived.

"Blizzard," said Jenny tersely, peering out through the bedroom windows.

Term had not yet started, so after breakfast we dressed up and went out to see what was happening. It was a near-whiteout. I got as far as the bottom of the yard before turning back. The wind came from the north and east, driving the snow off the mountain, straight down the gully and onto us. It was like being under a pressure hose of snow— snow blowing horizontally, vertically, and diagonally, snow coming up at your face from the ground as you bowed your head under the blasting, strengthening wind. And the cold was like a punch in the ear. As Alexander and I retreated to the living room, arming ourselves with toy guns and preparing to exchange fire between defensive positions behind the sofas, Jenny set out to feed the sheep.

It was already drifting in the lanes, forming waves against every wall, hedge, and bank. The world was changing shape. The cold soon drained the strength out of Jenny's arms and legs, but she did what she could, dragging out bales and cutting their restraining strings. The wind spun armfuls of hay away into the white, swirling it off like so much dust. She made it as far as the Lower Meadows, ducking lower and lower under the blizzard. Peering about her, she realized she was nearly lost, in a field she knew intimately. She turned back. She followed the gradients back up toward the First Meadow with nothing but the feel of the ground underfoot to guide her. There was a cold tapping against her cheek: icicles were forming in her hair where it escaped from under her hat.

Halfway across the First Meadow, she stopped briefly to rest and get her bearings. But there was nothing to tell her where she was: the whiteout was complete. The field, the gentle little meadow nearest the house, was gone. There was nothing now but wind and the infinite, clinging snow. She staggered on, going slower as the freezing air plucked her strength out of her and little drifts tugged at her legs. She sat down for a moment to recover her breath—"I'll just get my strength back," she thought, peaceably, and the moment stretched, and she was less cold now, almost warm, everything was better. Sitting there in the snow was strange and beautiful, and the wind was a little gentler nearer the ground. Perhaps she might close her eyes for a minute.

She jerked suddenly, lifting her gaze to the mazy whirlpool of flakes.

My God, she thought all at once. I have to get back to the house right now. I have to get back.

She stood once more, bent her head, and began to trudge slowly up across the field, toward the place where the house must be.

We looked up from our game as she came in, pursued by a gust of snowflakes. Her hair was clotted with icicles.

"Look!" she cried. "Look, children, I've got icicles in my hair!"

"Wow!"

"I think I nearly died in the First Meadow!"

We did not know what to make of this, so we stared at her, and her icicles, and made sympathetic noises. "Truly!" she said. "It was touch and go, I promise you! It's really dangerous out there. Batten down the hatches. We'll just have to wait until it passes."

The storm came on all that day, licking under the doors with its white wet tongues; pouring down the chimney; coming up through the drains. The plug holes and overflow holes in the sinks and the bath spat icy drafts. Finally the windows froze over inside and out, and the world beyond them disappeared.

As the light began to go, in midafternoon, Jenny scratched a hole in the coating of one of the panes and peered out. For a moment she could not comprehend what she was seeing: huge white shapes moving across the back patch. Then she realized what they were: whirling off drifts, which stirred like waves, were twisting pillars of snow, stalking silhouettes, circling the house.

"Golly!" she muttered, and closed the curtains. "I think we might be here for the duration, my dears," she announced, tugging the curtain tight. "Just listen to that wind. . . . Have you ever heard anything like it?"

As we looked at one another the pause between us was immediately swallowed by a roaring noise like a train, a noise that rose to fall and rise again, on and on, raging and tormented. How puny and temporary we felt as we listened to it, and how thrilled, too, in our little fortress of stone and wood, as it defied the terrible elements.

"I hope it won't pull the roof off," Jenny said, rolling her eyes, partly in mischief, partly from nerves.

"No, Mummy," Alexander said, smiling uncertainly. "It won't, will it?"

"No, it won't. It's stood for centuries. Nothing to worry about. Except the poor sheep!"

The fire hissed and twisted in the grate, battling the drafts and flakes in the chimney, and my brother and I went back to playing with our toys and messing around with the dog. There was a fizz in us that did not just come from being inside all day. It was a rare feeling, gleeful and nervy, as the wind howled—really howled, like an animal—to be safe but not secure from the danger outside. Jenny listened to the radio and the wind and quietly prayed that the electricity would not fail.

The lights stayed on, the phone still worked; we had supper and went to bed. While we slept, Jenny lay in bed, listening to the wind; as it flailed the corners of the house the stone moaned, raising a wuthering, fluting song. Then she slept too.

She awoke puzzled. Something had changed. As she shook off her sleep, she realized what it was. The roaring had stopped. In fact, all noise had stopped. All was perfect silence.

In the bathroom she noticed there were no more drafts coming up through the pipes. She hurried back to the bedroom and woke us.

"Time to get up, boys. It's not quite as cold as it was yesterday but it's still pretty chilly."

In winter it was always cold, even with the radiators on, the fire going, and the cooker turned right up. When Robert came to stay one Christmas, he went to bed in the Beast House bedroom fully clothed, with a woolly hat on. Jenny was in the habit of keeping her coat on when she came in from the fields, which always made me uncomfortable. We ought at least to act, I felt, as if there was a distinction between the sheds and the house. Jenny was impatient with such niceties. "But I'm cold!" she said when I objected. "Put a sweater on then!" I retorted smugly: it was one of her catchphrases.

Getting out of bed that morning we were sensitive to every degree, selecting from multiple vests, shirts, and sweaters.

"Layers!" Jenny said, throwing us each another vest. "Layers are the key!"

Downstairs reeked of dog. Lark and Toss grinned at our appearance. Jenny tried to let them out, but the back door was frozen shut. The windows had thick white curtains drawn across them from the outside, so when I went to open the front door I had no inkling of what might be there.

The door often stuck, as it did now, so I put my back into it and heaved on the handle. It opened, but I did not move. Before me was a vertical white wall, containing a perfect imprint of the doorknob and the knocker.

"Mummy! Twinks! Look!"

We stared at the snow wall. It was as though a great polar beast had died in the yard and was now lying with its flank slumped against the house. Or it was a variation of *The Lion, the Witch and the Wardrobe*: our front door now led to the back of someone's fridge. It was ludicrous, somehow. We laughed as if it were a practical joke.

"Crumbs," Jenny said. "Buried alive!"

Alexander and I exchanged thrilled glances.

"Upstairs," Jenny said. "We'll get a view from the landing window. Unless we're completely covered!" She led the way. On the landing we scraped and scratched at the window and peered out. The entire front of the house was drowned in drifts. They came up as far as the upstairs windows, huge lapping white waves with snow still falling onto them. The blizzard had swallowed us.

We went back downstairs and ate breakfast. The phone was dead; there was no more dry wood and no way of getting to the woodshed. Under the overhead lights, which we needed because the snow smothered the daylight, Jenny's face looked drawn. Her gaze shifted uneasily from us to the opaque windows.

"I don't know if I should try to go out or what. I ought to go and see how they are, but I don't know if I'll be able to do anything for them. It might not be very sensible. . . . I don't even know how I'll get out of the house!"

"Don't go," Alexander said. "It's too dangerous."

"Yeah," I agreed. "We're snowed in."

"Stay here and wait for it to melt?" Jenny exclaimed. "It could take weeks! We'd starve, and what about my sheep? We'll have to think of something." She put the kettle on.

Reassured that she was not going to try anything straight away, Alexander and I made our way up to the attic. Leading the way up the small stone stairs, I got as far as poking my head up above floor level.

"Snow! Drifts!"

Low, perfectly smooth white dunes had formed all the way up one wall, where the drafts had penetrated the eaves. We retreated to the sitting room and began a game there.

"Snowdrifts in the attic," we explained.

Jenny nodded thoughtfully and made herself a series of cups of coffee while she recalculated the food supplies. Soup for lunch, cauliflower cheese for supper, soup again for lunch tomorrow, and pasta tomorrow night; then what? Cereal, if there was any milk left.

The wireless said the army was rescuing people with helicopters, and urged anyone who needed help to write SOS in the snow.

"Fat lot of good . . ." Jenny murmured. "They'll never look for us up here."

There was a shout and a thump from the front of the house.

"Hey, what was that?"

"Rescuers!" Jenny exclaimed, rushing to the door and opening it. As we stood staring at the white wall it chipped at the very top; a small semicircle fell away, revealing a red face, hatted, whiskery, and smiling.

"Happy new year, neighbors!" Mervyn greeted us. "Stand back."

He had come up the hill with his daughter's boyfriend, wading across and around a white-changed world, found the house, found a single fencing stake protruding from a drift near the Big Barn, and with this he was now digging a hole in the blockade by our front door.

"Dear Mervyn, happy new year! You've come to save us."

"You can't stay here, Jen. Best come down to ours for a bit. Better get these boys out, eh?"

"Yes. This minute! Right, children, we're being rescued. Gear up. I want you to put on the warmest clothes you have."

We did, and Mervyn pulled us out through the hole, one at a time. Then we set off.

We walked down the yard, stumbling along, six feet above ground level. The world was unrecognizable. The five-bar gate to the track was reduced to two inches of iron sticking out of a drift. The fences had disappeared. There was no sign of the sheep. Here and there were the tops of hedges, the trees transformed into little bushes, poking out of the white. All the planes and angles of the fields had changed, whimsically rearranged by the storm. We could not walk along the usual routes, but slalomed slowly around great dunes of snow, tripping, sinking, and sliding, every step a struggle. In the Horse Fields I strayed slightly and sank immediately into deep snow, floundering helplessly, panicking, until I was dragged clear.

When we reached Mervyn's house, halfway down the mountain, we were all exhausted. Avril, Mervyn's wife, fed us baked potatoes and showed us our room; then the adults held a conference. Jenny was appalled by what might be happening to her sheep, but they agreed that it was too risky to attempt to go back to them today. Alexander and I had already found the television.

The next morning Mum and Mervyn set out after breakfast to rescue the flock. The mountain had swollen, a great pregnant shape, white and huge, its woods like stiff black hair. Jenny struggled up the hill as fast as she could, terrified of what she might find.

Meryvn had to hurry to keep up with her. They crossed the Horse Fields and the Lower Meadows and arrived at the buried fence line that marked the boundary of the Rough Field. There had been more than thirty animals there, Jenny knew, but as they stared across the field they could see nothing but waves of unbroken snow. It was as if the mountain had swallowed the flock, or the storm swept them away, sucked like spindrift into the blizzard's maw.

"Christ, they've disappeared! They've been buried alive."

They began investigating likely areas of the field, around the banks and hedge lines, in places where Jenny knew the ground dipped, scraping and digging here and there. The drifts were a dozen feet deep and more. Mervyn cut sticks from the hedges, and they poked and prodded the snow. Where the probe met resistance they dug, and found the first victims; stiff, stuck, but alive. Jenny used her scarf as a sling, working it under the bellies of trapped, cramped ewes, then Mervyn and she tugged and heaved them free. Lark began making discoveries, barking, wagging her tail and digging furiously. As they uncovered more ewes they began noticing bare patches on their flanks and rumps: denied food or movement, the animals had nibbled their own and each other's fleeces, presumably for comfort and whatever nourishment there might be in the wool. They moved the weakest cases up to the farm; the outhouses and sheds began to fill with the reek and press of sheep, just as they would have been in the old days, when the inhabitants lived directly above their animals, profiting from their warmth.

The searching and digging and feeding went on for two weeks. Jack came up to help. I remember all three of them coming down the mountain, returning from their expeditions full of stories about sheep nose-to-tail deep under the drifts, and full of amazement at the animals' endurance, and I remember too my mother's utter exhaustion, in the evenings, when she came back. Mervyn was a tough man, a builder and a farmer, but my mother matched him, stride for stride, shovel for shovel, driven on by will and worry and care. Not one sheep was lost.

The snow still fell at intervals but the ferocity of the first storm was not repeated. When the road to town was opened and term started again, Alexander and I went to stay with friends near school while Jenny returned to the farm. The attic and the roof spaces had filled with snow; when it began to melt the house rained inside. First in the bathroom, then on the landing, then in the bedrooms, water began to drip and run out of the ceilings. Jenny hurried around putting a pot, pan, or bucket under each new leak until the whole house rattled like an orchestra pit, trickling, tip-tapping, drips, drabs, and drops plinking and plunking in different tones.

When the steep pitches up the hill thawed she came to reclaim us. She blew into our friends' warm house, where we were glued to the television. We hugged and kissed and returned immediately to the screen, where the Nazis were about to do something terrible to two members of the Resistance. "Oh no, children, switch it off please," she exclaimed.

"It's OK, Mum, they won't show it!"

"No, no, it's terrible. It'll give us all nightmares. Turn it over, please."

We switched over to *Ski Sunday* for a minute or two, then flicked back. Postinterrogation, the Resisters—I think it was Violet Szabo and her lover—were now talking gingerly to each other.

"They pulled their fingernails out," our mother explained. "With pliers. Can you believe it, with *pliers*! And their toenails. I mean, just imagine the absolute torture . . ."

Alexander and I stared at each other, sharing this hideous thought. Our friends, Rhiannon and Gareth, looked horrified.

"Just terrible. And they used to drown that poor man, the White Rabbit, in a bath, and resuscitate him, so that they could drown him again! Unbelievable what people will do to one another. Sorry, I'd better not go on. . . . We'd better be off, boys. Gather up your things. I shouldn't think you'd want to leave this beautiful warm house much. . . ."

On the way home she told us about her adventures. "The water! You've never seen anything like it! It was just pouring, pouring through the ceilings. Everywhere. It was amazing going to sleep—my bed was all right, by some miracle—but listening to it dripping into all the pots and pans . . . ! There were so many drips I ran out of buckets and bowls. Hopeless, really, everything got soaked."

"Did our beds get wet?"

"Not too bad, actually, and I've had everything on full blast to dry them. I think you'll be OK. I've put the electric blankets on."

The weather abated but the snow did not leave the mountain; it hung around on the ridges in white flashes, "waiting for its butty," as Jack said ominously. (Sheep have butties, a particular friend in the flock, whom they butt and nudge playfully.)

"Oil!" Jenny exclaimed. "Quick, while the lanes are clear, we must get some more, we're low."

But neither Mr. Ferguson nor Mr. White could be persuaded to pit his nerves against the mountain. She telephoned every vendor who served the area, but none would come. Tankers were now too big, they said; very sorry, but it was out of the question.

"Oh, Lord, if I can't get oil, what on earth will we do? No cooker, no hot water! I'll try Mr. Ferguson again." She called him back.

"Please, Mr. Ferguson, please! You're our only hope."

"No, I'm sorry, but the insurance won't cover it," said Mr. Ferguson. "I can't help you."

"But what am I going to do?" Jenny cried.

"Well, I could let you have some barrels and a pump."

The barrels were hauled up on a neighbor's tractor and trailer. The red-and-black drums were positioned on the bank above the house, and their contents hand-pumped into the tank. We all took turns working that pump, and quickly came to hate it. It was a cruel labor, and we worked at it until our arms and shoulders were exhausted, sweating and swearing, the view swimming in our vision, the oil soaking our wrists and impregnating our clothes. After days of pumping, the level in the tank had risen by a dispiriting fraction.

"It's murder! But we've done frightfully well," Jenny encouraged us. "It's just to keep us going. I'm sure we'll get a tanker to come when it thaws properly."

The frost returned, and now we worried about the water. Was there enough in the tank? Would it freeze? Jenny went up the Quoiker to check. She bent over the cover of the catchment tank and heaved at it: her fingers burned against the cold iron, but the cover did not budge. "Come on!" she exhorted it, and tried again; no movement. She stamped on it, kicked at it, pulled from different angles: nothing, not the tiniest shift. She glared at the hatch cover, furious with it and her weakness. Frost sparkled at her from the rusty surface. She fumed. Defeat by physical weakness made her furious: "It's just weights!" she would exclaim to us. "If only I had stronger arms! I could do anything then."

Her hand went to her pocket for a cigarette, and paused. Slowly, carefully, she extracted a bundle of dry hay, left over from a parcel for an old biddy. She arranged it on top of the hatch cover, together with a tissue-paper hankie and handfuls of dead bracken and gorse. She squatted over the little heap, tenting it under her coat. The lighter snicked, the tissue paper smoked, and the hay caught.

She fed it and sheltered it, blowing gently and tending. "Come on, fire!" she whispered as the little red worms investigated the edges of the bracken. "Yes!" she said, and there was a single, iron ticking sound, and she thrust her hand around the rung, and heaved, and it shifted! "Ha-ha!" she said to the gathering night. "I'm the greatest!" She peered in. The tank was less than a third full, and there was nothing coming in. "No worries, children," she said when she returned, "but we'd better go easy on baths."

The freak weather brought splendor, too. After another spell of fearsome cold we found that one of our woods, the tangled spinney, had frozen into a chaotic fairy rink. A foot of ice lay locked around and linking every tree and bush, forming an undulating crystal floor, a perfect playground, so long as you did not try to stand up. The whole spinney now sprouted from a bed of curved and corniced ice, bubbled and pooled, perfectly petrified, every form of the water captured, as though stilled, instantly, by a spell. We slid around on our backs like big hockey pucks, spinning and sprawling, giggling at our own and our dogs' helplessness, then set off to explore the glaciers on the mountain.

We were moving carefully along the skyline, marveling at the sculpted drops, when a young dog fox appeared ahead, his ears twitching as he watched us. Toss and Lark immediately went for him, but the little fox was unconcerned. He trotted off, unhurried, leading the dogs straight up one of the steepest sheets of ice. Lark, ever intelligent, suddenly stopped, turned, and regretfully retraced her steps. Toss paused, but the fox paused too, looked over his shoulder, and seemed to taunt the dog. Ignoring our shouts, Toss went on, but he was too heavy, too clumsy, and as his dainty prey circled around above him, coping easily with the ice, Toss began to lose his grip; barking and whining, he started to slip. The fox sat down, tucking his tail neatly around his feet, and watched as his hapless pursuer struggled, floundered, and slid. Enjoying himself now, the hunted circled the hunter, so steady and sure. Unable to go higher, unable to turn and intercept him, Toss roared and howled, as if his barks could bring the mountain down. The fox seemed to raise his eyebrows, and with a couple of scornful glances, he skimmed away over the crest of the glacier.

✢   ✢   ✢

All living things came closer together under the rule of the cold. In the afternoons the fox trotted past the house, quite careless of being seen, sniffing the air, scenting our fire and food. Jenny's birds assembled; finches, tits, and the robin waited outside for handouts of seed or cereal. Every morning, there was Vivian, on the shelf directly above the fan heater, looking at us over his lentils with a shrugging frankness.

Upstairs his cousins were even less discreet than usual: a family of mice lived behind the bulges in the wallpaper of my bedroom. They were forever rattling off on a forage, or returning from one, squeaking and scrabbling.

It could make reading in bed quite difficult. "Will you please be quiet," I demanded, staring, vexed, at the wallpaper.

"Sorry, what's that?" my brother answered from his room.

"It's these mice! Running about and shouting—I can't concentrate!"

"You should trap them, then."

"I will, if they don't shut up." I went back to my book, *Sagittarius Rising* by Cecil Lewis: biplanes fighting in the skies over France . . .

The mice counted to six, then went back to their bustling.

It was easy, in the cold, to nab them with an upturned cereal bowl propped on a pencil over a piece of cheese. In the course of their feasting they would dislodge the prop and spend the night under the bowl. We always freed them in the morning, though: "Live and let live" was our mother's creed, and the rule of the farm, except in the case of the crows, of course.

"A murder of crows" is the old collective noun, and it has them right. In the snowy fields there were only the sheep: nothing else warm, bloody, or exposed anywhere; no grubs, no worms, and, before lambing, nothing young. Now only death would feed the crows, and they called and called to it, waiting. The ravens came over more often, flying lower-level patrols; magpies cackled and the buzzards sat around in bare trees, puffed up like turkeys, watching.

"You have to be so quick," Jenny said. "If something goes down for a second . . ."

If something weak went down it would be lucky to get back up. The knife of a beak in an eyeball would kill it through shock, and then it was a free-for-all. The yellowish corpse a berry-burst on the snow;

buzzards in their shaggy pantaloons tearing off strips; magpies raid-
ing tidbits; ravens squatting and hammering on the rib cage; and the
crows cursing them all, triumphantly.

Jenny sighed. "Oh well, she was an old one; I didn't think she'd see
the cuckoo. What a job they've done on her already! It will feed the
foxes, though, which I'm pleased about."

By the next day the corpse would have traveled down the field,
fragmenting; by the thaw there would be nothing left but scraps of
wool and scattered bones.

"Food for the foxes" was always said jauntily: it was a final compensation, a bit of good news on the other side of death. A hill farmer's relationship with death is matter-of-fact; as we grew up we learned that
the horror lurked on our side of mortality, in the bloody business of
preserving life.

"Horatio, could you help me for a minute, something rather
awful . . ."

She was looking very serious.

"What it is, I've got a little ewe with a dead lamb inside her. I've
got her in the shed. . . . The problem is, it was a head, and it's come out
and it's awfully swollen, I don't know if I'll be able to get it back in."

I held the ewe as Jenny set about trying to draw the corpse. The
protruding head was so swollen it could not be pushed back beyond
the cervix; after a struggle, Jenny decided that the ewe could take no
more—if we were not to lose her, too, the lamb would have to be
decapitated. She fetched the wicked little kitchen knife she normally
used for preparing vegetables.

"Oh, God, please let it be dead!" she said as she knelt down and
prepared herself.

"It is, isn't it?" I demanded, cloaking my queasiness in impatience:
Why did she always find something worse to imagine? Wasn't this
bad enough?

"Yes," Jenny said, slowly, feeling the mouth, prising open the eyes
and peering into them. "I'm sure it is. Oh dear, this is going to be
absolutely ghastly!"

"Don't think about it, just do it!"

"I have to think about it a bit," came the reply, and there was a harder note in it now. "I don't want to cut the ewe. How's she doing?"

"She's fine—well, she's OK . . ."

"Right. Here goes." As she worked I stared at the wet, stinking floor and vowed I would never be a farmer. I listened to the knife sliding back and forth, and Mum's single grunt as she went through the spinal cord. At last there was a fleshy, tugging sound. "Done it," Jenny said. She tied off the neck with a loop of twine and dropped the head into an empty feed bag.

"Hold this," she said, presenting me with the string and the pinched end of the neck, "and on no account let it go!" Wincing, I did as I was told as she worked her hands inside, pushed the body back, adjusted the position of the forelegs, and finally drew out the headless lamb. The ewe would live. We retreated into the house. Jenny washed her hands and reached for her cigarettes. I described what had happened to my brother. He was gratifyingly revolted, and I milked it.

"I had to hold the neck while she drew it!" I repeated, but now Alexander was philosophical.

"Oh well," he said. "Food for foxes!"

As the foxes know, most farms have their evil secrets, gloomy places, far from boundaries and footpaths, where the farmer disposes of his dead. On one walk, which had taken me far from home, into a great dark fir forest (I was looking for goshawks), I stumbled down a bank, into a sunken lane, and suddenly found myself surrounded by corpses—white spines, skulls, torn and rotting rib cages; it looked like an entire flock of the dead, and in my swollen imagination I had stumbled into the ovine equivalent of the Somme after the battle. I fled in terror.

We had two such secret places: down below the badger setts, and below the road through the wood. Compared to assisting with grotesque surgery, disposing of bodies was easy. I was unperturbed to find myself, on the way to school, dragging one by a stiff cold back leg, the head bumping over molehills behind me, toward the dizzy edge where the badgers lived.

"Bye-bye, sheep!" With a last heave the corpse went crashing and tumbling down the near-vertical drop into the dell, foul fluids spurting from its mouth and nose, filling the air with the dreadful eggy stink of putrefaction.

Jenny heaved an old one after it. As the second carcass began to tumble Jenny suddenly screeched, retched, spat, swore, and finally vomited.

"What's happened?" we yelled.

"The most disgusting thing! The most—uugh, yuk! I can hardly bear to tell you—as Elvira went over the edge a gobbet of something flew out of her mouth . . . and landed in mine!"

She raced the car into town, moaning and girning.

"It's just typical! It's the end! A parting kiss from a dead sheep. . . ."

She presented herself at the pharmacy and told her latest tale.

"Only you, Jenny, only you . . ." The pharmacist laughed through her grimaces.

"Just because it's all blood and guts out there," Jenny said, firmly, "doesn't mean we're going to be savages in here!" When we had taken our coats and boots off, and after Jenny had cooked our supper, we sat down to our daily lesson in civilization. Meals were punctuated with instructions: hold your knife and fork properly, close your mouth when you chew, never speak with your mouth full, sit up straight, look people in the eye when they talk to you, and answer clearly. Do not overload your fork; if you're doing it properly your knife should be stained toward the tip, not all the way to the hilt. Leave a clean plate, say please and thank you, wait for everyone to finish before you get down, don't say "can I," say "may I" . . .

"But why?" I demanded petulantly. "What's the point? There's no one watching, is there?"

"Because good manners are very important."

"But why? Why are they important?"

"Because otherwise people will judge you and they will think you're ignorant louts!"

"I don't care what they think."

"You will. Manners are keys, that's the thing. I am trying to give you keys which will help you in your lives. It's for your own good. Now hold your knife properly or go to bed without the rest of your supper. I'm warning you!"

Beyond the warning lay a furious shouting, which would leave Jenny on the verge of tears and the offender in red-faced silence, and beyond that, when the offense was grievous or compounded by the great but sometimes irresistible mistake of Answering Back, there was the ultimate sanction: an open-handed slap to the cheek.

Then the dogs fled, Toss glancing backward, guiltily, as if apologizing for his cowardice, and the cat stared at the floor with a magistrate's air of distaste. I sat with my head ringing, more in shock than pain, as Jenny administered a final admonishment, "Behave yourself in future!" before turning away to conceal her distress and face her guilt: now she tormented herself with a picture of a woman drinking too much, smoking too much, losing her temper, and hitting her children.

Alexander looked at me with assessment: when it was his turn, one morning, in the instant Jenny's temper snapped and we all knew a slap was coming, he dived under the kitchen table, scooted out the other side, and hared into the back patch. She went after him but Alexander was lightning quick, and kept the woodpile between him and her, circling it rapidly and defiantly.

"Come here, you wretched child!" she cried, but he would not. She darted left, he darted left, and seeing that she could not catch him, Jenny paused, her anger deflated, and she was overcome by the giggles. Alexander stumped off, more upset by her laughter than her rage.

The other constant voice of civilization came from the radio. The complexities, triumphs, and disasters of the world beyond the mountain were related to us in the even tones of BBC Radio 4. Mornings began with the *Today* program, presented by two of Jenny's heroes, Brian Redhead and John Timpson. "Good on you, Redhead!" she would cry when he was getting stuck into Some Bloody Tory. "Go on, Timpers, get him!" she would urge. When the "Thought for the Day" slot was conducted by the rabbi Lionel Blue she would hold up her hand for respectful silence and we would all listen carefully.

"I think he's a wonderful man," she would conclude when he was done. "My pinup!"

(I think the good rabbi would be surprised but not in the least alarmed to find himself in the company of the rest of her pinups, who included Gregory Peck ["Oh, Pecky!"], Harry Andrews, Jonathan Porritt, Chris Patten (the only decent Conservative, in our book), Misha Glenny, Mikhail Gorbachev, Nelson Mandela, Robert Redford, and Michael Foot.)

Sometimes our father's voice issued from the box, a tersely musical, familiar voice, which, unlike everything else we heard, did not seem to be speaking to us. He reported on social affairs; during the Brixton riots he covered race relations. His dispatches were clear and calm, but underneath the professional dispassion we could hear a tight-held anger, at the Brixton councillors who watched the riots from the town hall, like spectators at a football match; at a society that crammed its poor minorities into concrete high-rises, then goaded them, through the police, to breaking point. We knew how apartheid had banned him from South Africa; I recognized, in his description of the riot, the unequivocal tones in which he had explained to me what racism was and how it worked. We looked to Jenny when his report finished. "Phew," she said. "Fantastic! Isn't he good?" We swelled with pride and vicarious achievement.

With other reporters we splashed ashore with the British forces as they landed on East Falkland; we heard of burning ships. We listened, spooning Weetabix paste into our mouths, as wisps of the horrors of Sabra and Shatila leaked out of the box near the sink. Later we followed the course of the miners' strike, and took our anti-Thatcher convictions to school, where a game called Police and Pickets sprung up and was swiftly banned, involving as it did pitched battles between groups of struggling boys. We were transported to the desperate scenes of the Zeebrugge ferry disaster, the Brighton and Harrods bomb attacks, the Iran-Iraq war, and many other of the decade's convulsions.

Then it was half past eight, and time for *Yesterday in Parliament*, and if we were not heading for the car when the sonorous voice of the

Speaker of the House, George Thomas, intoned, "Order, order," then we knew we were late for school. Scrambling into our coats and shoes, we grinned at the thunderous hubbub of Parliament, and grimaced at the high, sword-waving bray of Margaret Thatcher, which seemed to rear up and taunt the mob of voices.

This narrow access to a single medium made me simultaneously precocious and ignorant: I could name most of the European leaders, and their political leanings, and I knew who Reagan's secretary of state was, but I would have to wait years to discover *Monty Python*.

At the other end of the day, we had our supper with *The Archers,* and when my mother came up to bed and put out the lights, the last sounds we heard before sleep were the chanted psalms of the shipping forecast.

Then Jenny would turn the volume right down as the national anthem played, and it was as though queen, country, and world were reduced to a tiny buzz, somewhere at the bottom of the mountain, and we slept.

At the weekends all three of us bounced in our beds to the jumping jingles of *Sport on Four* and the holiday program *Breakaway. The Lord of the Rings* sent Alexander and me rushing outside for our swords, to slay cohorts of invisible orcs, and one afternoon we sat around the kitchen table, transfixed, living the nightmare of nuclear war through the radio adaptation of *When the Wind Blows* by Raymond Briggs. When it was finished I went outside and stared at the silvered leaves of the ash tree, whispering and turning in the breeze, and the sagging woodpiles, apple logs dusted with lichen, and the mighty cerulean sky and the distant, anvil-red hills, and felt terribly frightened for it all, picturing everything blackened, poisoned, and destroyed.

"What would you do," I asked, soon afterward, on the way home from school, "if you saw a mushroom cloud behind that hill?"

"Well," Jenny said, "if it was coming I would get some injections from the vet, and we would go into the Beast House, if it wasn't too bad, and I'd block up the door, and if we started to get sick I'd put us all to sleep, just like we do with the sheep. It would be just fine—it's barbiturates—it's wonderfully quick and you don't feel anything."

It seems strange now that our suicide was to have taken place in the Beast House, among the woolsacks, beneath the gaze of the family of bats that hung from the rafters, swinging gently on their little hooked feet, but at the time it was very reassuring. We had a plan for Armageddon, that was the main thing.

Shriller than the rumblings of the Cold War, the noise of bitter national division came angrily through the radio. Pro- or antinuclear; for Thatcher or against—the country was polarized, opponents united only in loathing and contempt. During the general election the hedges sprouted red Labour and blue Conservative posters.

"The big farmers are always Tory," Jenny said, slowing the car.

"Why?"

"Money. . . . Get it!"

I jumped out, grabbed a Tory board, and dived back in. It was not particularly democratic conduct, but Britain did not feel like a particularly democratic country. Glimpses of friends' televisions showed battles between police and miners, ranks of strikers, chanting pickets and marching columns of the soon-to-be-unemployed. You could tell friends instantly by their "Nuclear Power—No Thanks!" or "Ban the Bomb" car stickers.

One of our friends, Jill, drove a car coated in them. Her boys were our age, ten and eight, incomers like us, and they too had English accents and an absent father. Our mothers thought we should play together. While we held fir-cone fights and small riots in hay barns, Jenny talked politics with Jill and her second husband, Guy. A tall, angular, white-haired man with a quiet voice and a great many interests, Guy ran an environmental pressure group. He researched, wrote, and distributed pamphlets with titles such as "Nuclear Power—The Facts They Don't Want You to Know."

One afternoon, as they sat in the sunny gardens of his house, Guy told Jenny the story of Hilda Murrell, a retired Shropshire rose grower who became interested in nuclear power. Hilda Murrell was preparing to deliver a paper to an antinuclear conference when she was murdered in bizarre circumstances, having apparently disturbed an intruder or intruders who were ransacking her house. An inadequate police investigation convinced many in the antinuclear lobby that Hilda Murrell was the victim of a vicious and bungling arm of the secret state.

Incredulous and appalled in equal measure, Jenny told us the story. We made disbelieving faces at each other. Could it possibly be true? A little old rose grower in Shrewsbury? Had "they" finally gone mad?

"N-o-o!" said Alexander. "Boller!" (He had trimmed down a longer word for use in company.)

I was less certain. From our mountain, overlooking the hazy valley, it did not seem impossible. The world at the bottom of the hill was clearly in terrible peril: the good and true, Guy and Hilda Murrell, were trying to save it, but they seemed frail and tiny compared to Thatcher's faceless, atomic-powered cohorts.

If it came to nuclear war I was certain the Russians would bomb Hereford, the nearest English outpost and the home of the SAS. When we needed something special, like a new consignment of pants and socks, we piled into our battered vehicle and set out for the border. Expeditions to Hereford always began in a spirit of optimism but often degenerated into fractious farce as we collided with the norms of that genteel little market town.

First there was the business of finding somewhere to leave the car: there was no question of "wasting money on parking!" as Jenny put it, so we crept and crawled around the side roads, occasionally scorning the system and reversing up one-way streets, until Jenny found somewhere cunning and close to the center. We emerged from the car, lightly dusted in seeds and strands of hay.

"Tuck your shirt in! And you do your shoelaces up! Please try and look respectable, boys, for goodness sake. . . ." She slapped seeds off our backs and winced at the state of our hair.

Clothes shopping afflicted me with truculent depression: in Marks and Spencer's I lurked, muttering crossly about not needing any more socks, while Jenny roamed the aisles. On finding something suitable she shouted brightly, "Pimmy, darling! Horatio! Come here, please. Look, they've got some really good pants!" which doused me in furious mortification.

After this came trial by women's clothes shop, which meant Alexander and I squatting, sullenly, on the edge of the window display, or listlessly drifting around the rails as Jenny hurriedly tried things on. So hurriedly, for our sakes, that she sometimes eschewed the changing rooms and stripped at the back of the shop, to our further horror. She was suspicious of being sold to, but interested in the people doing the selling: "Well, it's not my thing, dearie, really, is it yours? Honestly? With that funny frilly bit? Not me!" Prices were always outrageous, since she had no money. I remember her holding up a scarlet dress and asking, desperately, "Have you *anything* for under a hundred pounds?" The assistant was sorry, but no, she didn't. "What do you think, boys?" she demanded, twisting and turning in different outfits. "Very nice," we droned. The rare decision to buy something brought further complications, since she refused to use cash machines, and so wrote checks for everything. Cashiers' demands for a checking card were regarded as insults to her trustworthiness and means, and soon the whole of Hereford seemed to teem with petty and pathetic obstructions to our progress, designed to wind her up.

"Look, they've closed the whole street. They want us to walk all the way down there—perfectly stupid! Come on, children, follow me!"

"No, Mummy, *no*! They're working on the road; don't!"

But she did, sweeping aside the barriers and charging across the forbidden strip, to the impotent agitation of the road menders. It was as if she was sent from God to test officialdom, and it drove my brother and me beyond embarrassment, through flaring rage, into semihysterical giggles.

Finally, we arrived at the bookshop, and at last peace descended as we entered an environment we understood.

"However poor we are, I don't mind spending any amount of money on books or paints," Jenny decreed, and so we spread out, stooping, reaching, and craning between the stacks, kneeling, poring over, and studying the selections, absorbed and happily torn over which new treasures we would add to our collection.

I loved *Just William,* Robert Westall, Peter Dickinson, Rosemary Sutcliff, Robert Louis Stevenson, and Biggles, and the wonderful nature writing of "BB," Denys Watkins-Pitchford, whose stories, told from the perspective of wild geese and foxes and runaway boys living in forests, chimed exactly with my imagination.

Many of my heroes were tearaways, Red Indians, highwaymen, pirates, bandits, and other outlaws, and I always thought I would make a good one. Never in my daydreams did I place myself in the position of a terrified householder, menaced by a marauding brigand; I never considered the awful fear of the unarmed, law-abiding citizen when a barbarian came down from the mountain, looking for plunder and who knew what else, until one hot summer night, when an outlaw came for us.

9

Intruders

THE MAN APPEARED IN THE VEGETABLE GARDEN, WEARING emerald green shorts. Jenny jumped when she saw him, standing still between the neat rows of Jack's beanpoles, watching her, and her first reaction was anger.

"Can I help you?" she demanded in the brisk and confrontational voice she used when her hackles were up, an attitude she would describe as "shirty."

The man continued to look at her, and said nothing. He was big, barrel-chested, with dark hair in a ponytail.

"That's not the way to the mountain, you know," she continued.

"I know," the man replied, slowly. "I'm trying to get away from *them.*"

Oh my God, she thought, wishing the dogs were not shut in the house, and immediately became more conciliatory.

"OK, well, if you come down the steps and follow the path up around there, behind the barn, you'll see the gate to the hill on the other side of the trees. It's just there . . ."

The man said nothing, but after a moment he descended and disappeared behind the barn. Jenny fled inside and watched from the windows as he reemerged, climbed over the hill gate, and began to walk away slowly, up the hill. It was a bright June day; the bracken was high and bursting green, tall enough to conceal him when he sat down, which he did, before he reached the skyline. She lost sight of him then, and waited a while, watching, but he did not reappear.

"Has he really gone, dogs?" She let the hounds out. They rambled around, sniffing and peeing, but neither of them more than glanced at the hill.

She went about the business of the day, wondering whether she was being watched. She topped up the water trough in the Patch with a hose from the yard and gave one of the oldies a drench. She fed the orphans bottles of milk and patrolled, looking for signs of maggots. Her suspicion fluctuated but did not dissipate. Sometimes it was a thin, paranoid whisper, but at intervals it came as a conviction, which sent her scurrying back to the kitchen to scan the hillside through binoculars. There was no movement. There were a few of Brown's sheep scattered across the ridges, but they were grazing quietly. Perhaps she was imagining it. At half past three she collected us from school.

"Funny thing," she said. "Some weirdo turned up in Jack's garden!"

"What did he want?"

"He said he was trying to get to the hill. Didn't like the look of him much."

"Mmm." Walkers were common in the summer; as far as Alexander and I were concerned most of them were weirdos, so we thought nothing of it. We ran about and played outside as usual, making the most of a lovely evening, until Jenny called us in.

"Time to feed the dogs! I think we'll have them in tonight."

The dogs were moved between the barn and the sitting room, depending on the weather and occasional hygiene campaigns. Feeding them was our job: they lived on a yellow mixture of lumps and flakes, which was served with water in precise proportions, because any uneaten mulch caused Mum almost as much despair as our leftovers: "Look! Look at the waste! And it's so expensive, too!"

It was an iron rule that animals ate before humans. "How can you be happy, how could you enjoy your supper, knowing an animal is hungry?" she demanded when one of us, lazy or ravenous, objected. "The animals must come first."

"But why?"

"Because they rely on us. It's our duty."

So we all ate, then Alexander and I withdrew to the attic, which smelled of warm wood and stone, and mucked about until the shout came from downstairs that it was time we had our bath. We ran to it and climbed in together, fitting easily into the great iron-footed tub, which stood on planks intended to stop it falling through the floor.

Shortly before midnight Jenny checked that the back and front doors were bolted, collected her radio, and came upstairs. She shot the bolt on the bedroom door, turned out my light, and went to bed.

At quarter to two she heard the first bark downstairs. Toss and Lark often barked, especially if they were quartered in the sheds, where they could hear all the night's noises. We were accustomed to their various sounds: droning, repeated barks if they had heard another farm dog somewhere; suspicious growls for a rat rustling in one of the outhouses; long howls in answer to a keening fox.

Tonight they began with a couple of interrogative, questioning barks, then paused, in a listening silence: you could clearly picture them with their heads tilted sideways, mouths slightly open and ears cocked. Then suddenly it came, a volley of furious sound that escalated, both dogs baying.

There was a brief pause, and now came a fusillade of noise, each cry tearing open the night, driving all sleep, all comfort, all gentleness out of the dark. I lay still, hoping it would stop, praying for deliverance, wishing that whatever it was would go away, but the dogs were incensed; they hardly paused for breath between their outraged arias. Their meaning was clear—Enemy! Enemy! Kill! Kill!

I climbed out of bed, and Jenny turned her light on.

"What is it, Mummy?"

"I don't know," she said. She was shaky, alarmed and small in her pale nightie.

The noise downstairs was ferocious.

"I think there might be someone outside," she said. "I'm going to call the police."

It was a warm night; all the bedroom windows were open. The

upstairs phone was on the windowsill. Jenny dialed 999 and spoke loudly into the handset, projecting her voice into the yard in the hope that the intruder would hear her.

"Police, please," she said clearly.

She was put through to an exchange in Brecon, and then handed on to the station in Newtown, a good hour's drive away.

The officer who finally answered said he had two cars available: one in Brecon, which was busy, and one in Newtown.

"He'll be with you as soon as he can," the officer said.

Jenny said, loudly, "Good, see you soon then," and hung up. She backed away from the window. "They're coming, but they're coming from Newtown!" she whispered.

My heart seemed to jump at every bark, and my stomach tightened.

"Who do you think it is?" I asked.

"I don't know, it could be the man who was in Jack's garden."

"Have we got Jack's gun?"

"No. He took it back."

I thought about the rule of threes. The rule of threes was one of Jenny's. Three slips or misfortunes, she said, would take a life. One: a vicious easterly, flailing the ridges with rain, catching some of the flock in the wrong field, exposed. Two: among them, a ewe with a poor udder and a weak lamb, which you thought you saw drinking yesterday. Three: you hoped that udder might be better, but you forgot to check the lamb today. The rule of threes would deliver a little cold body tomorrow. And now there was the man in the garden, the missing shotgun, and the policeman in Newtown.

The barking intensified suddenly, and it was no longer coming from the front of the house.

"It's moved—he's gone round the back," Jenny hissed.

We stared sightlessly through her doorway, into Alexander's dark bedroom, and listened. Both dogs were now jumping against the door to the kitchen: whatever was outside had circled the house.

"Christ," she said, quietly, with a terrible, sober certainty. "He's trying the back. How's Twinks?"

"Still asleep."

"That's a miracle, anyway."

"I'm scared."

"So am I," she answered. "But if he tries to get in Toss will make mincemeat of him. I suppose it *might* be nothing . . . a fox . . ."

We knew it was not a fox. Toss was hysterical. His barks were interrupted with ripping, savage growls, as if he had the enemy in his sights, and frantic whines, longing, frustrated sounds. I sat beside my mother on her bed, and we waited, listening for the sound that was not barking, for splintering wood or breaking glass.

"What are we going to do if . . . ?" I whispered.

Jenny shook her head. "Pray he doesn't," she said.

Everything in my panicked sight—the warm light of the bedside lamp, the soft sheets, the entwined flowers on the wallpaper—all now looked appallingly vulnerable, terrifyingly gentle and feminine, as if their fragility invited their desecration. We would hear him fighting Toss. And wrenching open the stair door. And coming up, and kicking in the bedroom door, as we cried and yelled, and Alexander looked at me and screamed, and I could do nothing, and we looked at Mum and screamed . . .

Minutes scratched past on Jenny's little bedside clock; half an hour, an hour, and still the policeman did not come. The barking downstairs retreated from its worst frenzy but did not stop. Toss sounded certain now. I know all about you, his tone seemed to say, and you know I know. Bark, bark, bark. As another half hour passed the dogs fell silent for periods. Each time they stopped I began to think it might be over, but each time they started again. We stared out the window, willing car headlights to appear.

"It's very strange." Jenny frowned. "He can't still be there, can he? Why are they still barking? How long can they keep it up?"

"It's getting light," she said, later. It was twenty past three when suddenly there was another avalanche of noise from downstairs.

"Oh no," Jenny muttered, then "There!" She jerked. "The police! Thank the Lord! Oh, thank heavens for that."

The car came along the lane with extraordinary reluctance, its blue light flashing.

"He's taking his time!" she exclaimed. "Giving anyone who might be around a chance to get clear so he doesn't have to cope with them, I should think."

At last the policeman reached the yard. Jenny was too relieved and exhausted to be angry about the response time. "Over an hour and a half on a 999 call," she noted wearily. "We'd all be goners by now."

It felt to me like a strange parallel of Christmas, as we went down to the shadowy sitting room to calm the dogs and welcome the longed-for arrival. We invited the officer in, strictly instructing Toss not to bite him. Jenny offered a cup of tea and the policeman had a look around. He went out the back and flashed his torch at the larch trees and the lightening hill.

"Look!" Jenny exclaimed, when he had given that up. "Look at the window frames!"

All the wooden sashes and struts between the downstairs window-panes had been gnawed and chewed right through. Little remained of the white-painted bars but strips of wet splinters. In his determination to reach and slay the enemy, Toss had almost broken out.

"What's going on?" Alexander inquired as we returned to our bed-rooms and the constable drove away.

"Hello, sweetheart." Jenny laughed. "Have you just woken up?"

"Yes, what's happening?"

"And I slept through all of it!" he exclaimed when the story had been told, as amazed at this as by what had gone on.

He gave Toss a hero's adulation the next morning. Toss was Alexander's dog, and the adoring, beguiling, small-eyed savage had saved our bacon, everyone said.

"Good dog, clever dog!" we lied, lovingly, as Toss ducked and wagged under the weight of all this pleasure, his tale whipping joy-fully. He flopped over onto his back, inviting a belly scratch. When it came he expertly grabbed Alexander's wrist, nipping another hole in the sleeve of his sweater.

"Ow, Toss! Get off." Alexander laughed, tugging. The sweater stretched, threads popped, Jenny sighed, and Toss grinned, his little eyes traveling upside down from face to face, the sleeve locked fool-ishly in his incisors. A couple of weeks later he landed us in court.

"Mrs. Clare," the clerk said, and my mother stood up. The policeman closed his notebook, skeptically. One of the magistrates had given me a gently encouraging smile as I sat behind Jenny, praying. "Look ago-

nized," she had instructed me, on the way in. "Look as though they're
going to kill your pet!" It seemed likely enough: I had been pulled
from school to play the part of Alexander, the dog's best friend, while
Alexander remained there so that he would not have to hear the death
sentence from the magistrates. There were three of them, two kindly-
looking men and a sterner woman. They had all directed appreciative
nods at the police officer, for his bloodcurdling tale of unprovoked
assault on a lady from Birmingham by a berserk dog; when they
looked at Jenny, however, their expressions seemed to still somewhat.
Her story, of a marauding brigand who did not attack, a valiant dog,
and a policeman who did not turn up, had made them frown and shift
in their seats. The chief magistrate had the unblinking look of an
annoyed headmistress. She leaned forward.

"You did say you let the dog out at night, to run around, uncon-
trolled?"

"Erm . . ." Jenny dropped her gaze for a second, realizing the mistake. "Um, yes, but . . ."

"Well, we can't permit that. We do accept that you have a need for
a good guard dog, as you say. . . . And if the police are unable to
respond to an emergency like the one you describe, in our view it is
reasonable for you to retain the dog."

"Oh! Wonderful . . . !"

"But we absolutely cannot allow the dog to run around out of
control."

"No . . . no, of course . . ."

"So we are not going to issue a destruction order in this case, but
we are going to order you to keep the animal under close control at all
times. He's been very lucky, this time, Mrs. Clare. Very lucky indeed!"

"Yes! Yes, he has. Thank you so much . . ."

"You did it, well done!" I exulted as we scurried away.

"Trust your mother," she said, risking a rascally wink. "I can't
believe we got away with it! Quick, let's get out of here and tell
Twinks before they change their minds."

We retreated back up our hill. Close control at all times, I thought.
What did that mean?

❖   ❖   ❖

That evening Alexander and I took Toss for a walk in the rain. It was a soft fall, a thickening of hill mist; tickling the hazels, patting the dock leaves, making the nettles shiver and darken. We went down the green lane, listening to the birds; something in the warm mizzle and the approach of dusk was thrilling them. Thrushes floated notes across the Hill Fields; flycatchers and warblers threaded thinner calls through the spinney. Blackbirds threw comments after us as we wandered down the tunnel of trees.

Toss ranged around as usual, checking roots, holes, boles and stumps, sniffing, spraying, scenting. We watched him, calling him back when he pulled too far ahead, though it seemed pointless. There was no one for miles. We skipped from side to side across the track, keeping to the larger stones and the drier patches, heading through the spinney to the point where the trees stopped and the lane met the Hill Fields in a splashy patch of mud. On the bank above it, under the holly tree, was a fox's earth, and here suddenly Toss paused and tensed.

"The fox lives there, you foolish animal . . ." I began.

"No," Alexander said. "Look what he's found."

Then I saw it too: dangling from the holly, on a long string, so that it nearly scraped the ground, was a single glove, tied by the tip of its middle finger.

We stopped dead.

"Let's rip it down," Alexander said crossly. He knew how Jenny would take it, as did I, but in a quixotic burst of responsibility, I decided we should show her.

"Poacher!" she hissed when she saw it. "Look at it, right by the earth. Look at the way it's tied. A noose! And the middle finger! Up yours, baby! Well, sucks to you, too . . ."

Toss barked gruffly and ran a circle around the bush. "Good dog, Toss! Kill the blasted badger baiters!"

"Perhaps someone just found it and hung it up to be helpful," I suggested.

"Nonsense. Tied with a noose! It's some creep . . . some Mad Bomber."

Mad bombers were a generic menace. We could see Jenny mentally shuffling suspects: it was a sign from the poacher; it was a message from one of the hunt followers; it was Idris, or the Norsters; it was another weirdo; it was the same weirdo in green shorts!

"You're being paranoid, Mummy," Alexander said, calmly. "It's nothing . . ."

"I sure hope you're right," Jenny replied, darkly, with a look of bleak prophesy. "It's hard enough without Mad Bombers."

The suggestion of threat, the air of intimidation, was much more disturbing than overt menace. One bright morning as I strolled out into the yard my eye caught a brown, huddled shape by the gate. Soft feathers stirred as I drew closer; I bent over two large speckled ducks, not long dead, tied together by their feet with string. There was a cardboard label attached to the string, bearing a single handwritten line: "A present from Brer Fox."

This seemed so crude and silly that I did not show Jenny, but disposed of the corpses in the stream. It was a perfect day; the ravens flew very high, throatily discussing some distant prospect, and pied wagtails bowed and flitted in the yard, bobbing suddenly, as if they meant to catch out their shadows. So some lunatic held us responsible for the nature of foxes—so what? It was a relief to find a grievance so clearly expressed; much less worrying than the glove. I told Mum about it a week or so later, and she shrugged and rolled her eyes. We could not be hurt, frightened, or even worried like that: we were much more vulnerable to our own imaginations than anyone else's.

The oil pump had been playing up: we yanked and heaved until our arms burned, for barely a dribble of oil. After one brutal spell of pumping, Jenny vomited blood in the night. Cancer, she thought. But the doctor diagnosed a stomach ulcer and called for the surrender of the whiskey bottle. The patient invested in a powdered drink called slippery elm and checked her treasured *Dictionary of Symptoms*. "Ulcers," she murmured, turning the page to the light. "I love this book, because it says things like 'probably not serious' and 'don't panic.' . . . Here we are, treatment . . . Oh! Hops!"

"Hops?"

"It says that hops are good for stomach ulcers!" she cried, joyfully. "What's hops?"

"Hops? Hops are beer! Hurrah!"

A can of cheap lager replaced the nightly slug of Bells. There was no surrender to the situation, but there was a feeling that we might be prepared to negotiate with it.

"This would not be a good place to be if I got ill," Jenny said, looking out of the windows at another green dusk. She had the lights off in the kitchen to save money; it was almost dark inside, tenebrous as a cowshed. "Oh, I hate making decisions," she moaned. "I loathe it!"

The sheep sensed it. The next morning one of her favorites, Arabella, came up and leaned against her, really leaned, pressing her warm, soft weight against Jenny's legs.

I do not remember a moment in which we first discussed leaving the farm. It became part of the background that just as we would not be driven off our mountain, neither would we stay there indefinitely. Contained within our feelings of being custodians and adventurers was the hazy prospect of departure. Jenny had many thoughts about where we might go—farther into Wales; somewhere near the sea; Somerset; Oxfordshire; or just lower down the mountain, somewhere safer—but we had no idea when: one day, we said, one day.

"We should keep our eyes out for somewhere round here," Jenny said, "because there's nowhere more beautiful, is there?" And so began the never-ending house hunt. Her curiosity seemed more urgent than any desire to go; we toured the district as if for pleasure, meeting farmers, inspecting their dwellings, and attending farm sales. These were heartbreaking. When farmers gave up, their neighbors helped them move the entire contents of their house, barns, and fields into the best meadow, where it was arranged in neat lines. On the day of the sale, somewhere among the tractors, sagging double beds, cutlery drawers, hayracks, sheepdogs, tables, clocks, and chickens, apart slightly from the milling crowd, would be the stunned, still figures of the farmer and his wife, staring numbly across their entire lives.

It was enough to put us all off, and the idea of leaving would recede again.

"But I can't stay here forever," Jenny sighed. "All alone up this tump, especially when you're away at school."

I swallowed. We had decided that once I had finished primary school I would try for an assisted place: a government scheme that would sponsor me to go to a fee-paying school. I dreaded the thought of leaving the mountain and my family, and feared for the two of them, isolated up there.

"The winters are so hard, that's the thing. I don't think I could stand it when Twinks goes off as well."

"You couldn't stay here then," I said firmly. "So far from everyone and alone."

"No. So we need to find somewhere lovely, nearer people, south-west-facing and with a few acres for my sheep."

Guy and Jill suggested a long, low farm near their house. It was haunted, thick with spirits; its barns, pigpens, cowsheds, and walled garden were all frozen, agape, in the moment of their abandonment. It had too few acres for sheep farming: could we manage cattle?

"I don't know anything about cows," Jenny said. "How do you make them do something they don't want to?"

I knew about cows from one of her stories, about a bull who leaned, crushing his farmer slowly and inexorably against the wall of his byre, while the farmer's son screamed and jabbed with a pitchfork, and the bull took no notice. While I imagined being the son, Jenny imagined being the farmer. "It hasn't got any sun, anyway," she said, and we let it go.

She mentioned the night of the prowler to Guy. He listened, stooping slightly, his head inclined, that he might catch every word. He took it very seriously.

"It was all right in the end," she concluded. "The police were hopeless, but what can you do?"

"Do you think you are well defended?" Guy asked. "I mean, if he came back, do you think he could get in?"

"Well, there's a bolt on the front door, and I screwed one onto the back of the bedroom door. I don't know. . . . Thank goodness for the dog, that's all!"

She was a little surprised by his concern; her own fears had faded, though she slept very lightly, alert to any sound outside.

Guy said he would come up the mountain the next day, and inspect our defenses.

It was late June. In the meadows scarlet cardinal beetles flew low above a sea of seed heads. There was a yellowhammer by the Far Meadow gate and buzzards wheeling and mewing in the blue. In the distance the mountains looked like the hills of East Africa, eternal and kind under the sun. Guy's sleek car bumped cautiously up the track. Jenny greeted him with huge gratitude and pleasure: how kind it was of him to come. She offered coffee, which they took sitting on logs out the back. Then Guy began his inspection. Doors, windows, skylights in the attic, the roof, internal and external walls were examined. Jenny accompanied him, talking. Her first impressions, months ago when they first met, had been of a rich and ineffective romantic, but she had been wrong: he was a practical man, "a doer," she knew now. And she found him extraordinarily easy to talk to. It was as though she did not have to try.

She had tidied up, of course, but to a man who loved to work with his hands, who had taught himself masonry and woodwork, whose eyes were quick and scrupulous, the farm appeared as it was: old and primitive, cool verging on cold, even in the summer, and fragile—wormy, brittle, unkempt.

He was careful not to show it, but he took it all in with amazement, and thought the living conditions awful: it was a chaotic dump. The walls only faintly divided stock from humans, he noted. Nothing had been done, as far as he could see, to improve or civilize it in any way. They went out the back, and it was markedly colder up there than it was in the valley, a completely different climate zone, he realized. But there was something else, too, something that seemed to make his eyes open wider, and his spirits lift. It was almost a physical sensation. He looked all around, and said nothing. This astonishing woman, in this stunning, desperate place. It was romantic and very beautiful. Free, most of all—it had a feeling of freedom, not just physical, an atmosphere of spiritual freedom that he recognized in himself but had rarely encountered before. It was absolutely striking, and deeply attractive.

The next day he came again, with wood and a serious box of tools. Jenny offered him coffee again and they took it outside. She sat in the grass and he lay down, stretched out, his eyes shut against the sun. He asked her about living there: how did she manage? She chattered away, happy but anxious. To have someone to talk to, a friend her own age, someone kind, it was wonderful. . . . All at once she caught herself and paused.

"I thought 'Wait!'" she said, telling us the story. "I thought, 'You hardly know him. You are a desperate, boring woman, wittering on about your worries.'"

He lay very still. Jenny looked at him, watched him breathing, and in that moment, suddenly, with a swoop of a feeling like fear, she saw him for himself. Not as a friend, and not as Jill's husband: she saw *him*. She jumped up, almost physically shook herself. He opened his eyes, stood, smiled, and began work.

He was still working when Jenny brought us home from school. There were little heaps of curly shavings and piles of sawdust scattered around the top of the stairs. There were saws and drills and boxes of bright screws. Guy was quick and unhesitating, chatting as he worked. I thought he was wonderful. He never asked any of the questions adults always asked, there was none of the old "And how was school?" routine. He asked about what you were up to, and what you were interested in, and he listened to what you said. He had a way of squeezing his eyes, narrowing them slightly and nodding slowly when you made some point; it made you feel original, as though you were worth following closely. He seemed to place you on the same level as him, which was a huge compliment.

The bedroom door was transformed. There were thick wooden shields fixed to the back of the old planks, and hefty crossbars, and instead of one rickety bolt there were now three shiny new ones, screwed in tight, braced against reinforcing spars.

"It's really good," I gawped, tremendously impressed. He was the first man since my father who had shown any sign of taking things in hand. He knew I had been fretful since the bad night, and now he meant to allay my fears.

"Well, it looks all right, but will it work? Let's see. You go in there," he instructed Jenny. "Lock up, and I will try to break it down. It's called destruction testing," he told me, with a look that seemed to promise all kinds of excitement. He backed onto the landing.

"Are you ready? Standing back?" he called.

"Yes!" Jenny cried, and then he charged the door. There was an impressive thump and nothing gave.

"Good," he said, turning to me with a grin. "If anyone wants to get through that they'll need a hand grenade."

The way he said it convinced me that he had seen a hand grenade go off, and I knew from playing with Jill's boys that he had a sword-stick among the umbrellas in the stand by his front door. Around the edges of his tall, distinguished frame, and lurking in the vaults of his arched, aristocratic voice, was an impish mischief, something conspiratorial and amused. When he laughed a certain laugh you could see in his face the schoolboy he had once been; an odd one out; a curious, wide-eyed child, giggling with delight and surprise.

He swept up the shavings and sawdust and we all went down for tea. Twinks and I were on our best behavior, taking our cues from our mother. After tea he measured the upstairs windows for a set of iron bars, which he said we should order from the blacksmith in town. We had no idea there was a blacksmith in town. We waved him off as he left, and that night we shot all the bolts and felt so much more secure that we laughed as if in victory. It seemed that help had come at last, and that we had found a wonderful new friend.

A few days later he came back to install the bars. At the Middle Meadow gate he was ambushed by Hansel, a recently weaned orphan, begging for a bottle of milk. Hansel would not leave him alone, stumbling around his feet, bleating, pleading up at him; Guy could not get the car through the gate without Hansel coming too. Jenny watched, smiling, from the farm, as he appeared to negotiate with the lamb. It did no good. Guy abandoned the car and walked up the track. Jenny noticed his walk: long, slightly uneven strides, head back, very determined.

She kept her distance while he worked. When he had finished he gathered his tools, quietly. He seemed to be leaving quickly. On the way out he stopped suddenly and fixed the garden gate's wonky hinges, and then Jenny accompanied him back to his car. She told us what happened next.

"I walked him down to the Middle Meadow gate after he had put the bars in. I said, 'Good-bye, then, Guy. Thank you so much for everything you have done. It is incredibly kind of you.'"

He had gone very quiet. As they walked down the track he put his arm around her shoulders. She was holding a spare iron bar, which she dropped, so that she would have to move away from him. But when she straightened the arm was there again.

"We got to the gate, and he looked at me very directly and said, 'May I come again?'"

She paused as she recounted this, trying to remember precisely, to get it right.

"I was a bit taken aback. I said, 'Yes, Guy, you are always welcome here, we'd always love to see you.' But then he said, 'I want to get this quite clear: may I come and see *you* again? Would *you* like me to come back?'

"Well. I couldn't believe it. We gave each other a hug, and he said, 'I admire your courage so much. And I admire the way you are bringing up your children.' And he said he thought of me—too much, he said. And I said I thought I could fall in love with him but I wasn't sure I could take it all in."

They sat down, she recounted, at the edge of the hayfield to talk about it. The grass was high and hot.

She said, "I don't have affairs with married men. It is not my style. I'm always so careful. And I've given up sex, anyway."

"What *do* you mean?" he said, and pulled her down to him, beside his car.

She laughed suddenly. "Is it right? Is it proper? To be lying with Guy in a hayfield?"

"It's quite all right," he said. "I'm just making sure the exhaust system is functioning."

"Oh, it was funny! We laughed and laughed, and it was all right. Then he looked at his watch and said, 'Help! It's five to one and we're having people to lunch!' He leaped up and off he went."

He turned his car and drove away, raising his hand. Jenny leaned against the gate, raised hers, and watched him go. She walked back to the farm. She felt extraordinary, warm and excited, and peaceful, and happy and panicked; definitely panicked. And fearful: vulnerable again, she thought, after all this time.

"I hadn't felt like that for years—fifteen years!" she told us. "I didn't know what to do!"

There was an amazement about her as she spoke, a genuine inability to account for what had happened. She hunched slightly, her hands clasped in front of her. It was a position she took instinctively when she heard about something terrible on the radio, or some surprise had struck her, as if she were physically trying to hold herself together. It made her look like a tensed rabbit, unsure of which way to leap.

"I never dreamed of meeting someone like that, it never crossed my mind!" she exclaimed. "Why would it? I've given it all up. How on earth could it happen, up here in the sticks—in the nettles!"

She pulled her hair up with her fingers and let it fall, befuddled. She wanted to see him again, and she wanted to run away.

He telephoned the next day. Could he come and see her? "No! No. Not for a week at least, it's too fast. . . ."

A letter arrived and she pounced on it. She read it over and over again. She was happy, she was dreamy, she was busy, she was skittish. It was a summer enchantment, she told herself, a brief encounter. She liked his writing so much. He couldn't possibly love her, not really. Why her? She was tired, she wasn't pretty, wasn't loveable, had no chin . . .

She went to church and gave thanks for her happiness, and asked for wisdom to deal with it. It was a madness that would pass, she told herself. Midsummer magic. It would not affect Jill and Guy, not really.

❖ ❖ ❖

The next time he came they went up the mountain. Jenny never climbed it for pleasure, but now, suddenly, she wanted to go higher. He lay down on short, nibbled turf at the bottom of the first tump. She sat near him, afraid to be too close. He talked about his past loves. A first wife, several relationships. He had been in a muddle, she decided. He had made compromises, and tried, but was still not happy— Like me, I suppose, she thought.

They talked about time, about how precious and ephemeral it was, and how terribly swift. He helped her bag up loose hay in the barn. She tried to be busy, and to keep her distance. Then an arm shot out and held her. "Is it wise to come so close to me?" he teased.

"Do you always get what you want, Guy?" she asked him.

"Always," he said.

Then he had to go again. He changed his clothes.

"What on earth are you doing?" she asked. He was supposed to be somewhere else, at a meeting somewhere, he explained. She thought it was funny, at first, but then it was terrible. They were into lies.

It was a hot July. One Sunday we dipped three hundred sheep; the next day Guy took Jenny out for lunch. She rose early, washed her hair a second time, to get rid of the smell of dip, and went through every piece of clothing she had, leaving them in heaps around the bedrooms. She put on makeup, took us to school—"Does my breath smell awful?" she asked. "My teeth are so rotten"—and they went off up the border for a picnic.

"It's terrible what happens to your confidence when you're in love," she sighed. "We were in a health food shop and there was this lovely girl serving us, she was wearing a lovely sweater and sexy shorts and her hair was all beautiful golden curls like a Botticelli angel and I suddenly thought that's the kind of girl he'd really go for, and I found myself desperately wishing I looked like her—wishing I was her! Awful, really."

Get a grip, she thought, I am me! Later, on a mountainside, she wanted to shout her happiness; instead, she rolled over and over, dizzier and dizzier, down a long green slope. Guy rolled too. How happy I am, she thought, how happy! I can't believe it.

Thoughts would just pop into her head, and, given any excuse, out of her mouth. Gosh, he's handsome. A real knockout. And so kind, so unbelievably sweet! "He's one of those people who just love to help. He can't see something that needs doing and not do it. . . ." And so good at everything. A Renaissance man. Her type, all right. And so silly. Thought Shakespeare dreadfully overrated. Oh, he made her laugh. . . .

I saw them sitting out the back one morning. Every day seemed awash with light now; the long grasses were bent and gilded. Jenny and Guy leaned their heads toward each other, discussing something, close together on the lip of the huge blue view. They looked beautiful, in the crisp sunlight, and I played at being their child, in my mind, and thought how that would be, how strong and unusual it would feel.

Between his visits she talked to us, of course.

"The awful thing is, darlings, I think I do love him, I do—I love him! But he's married! He's married to Jill!"

"But he loves you, doesn't he?"

"Yes, I think he does. He says he does. I believe he does. But he's married—it's not right."

"Does he love Jill?"

"He says not. He says it was a mistake to have married her. He says they aren't happy but he cares for her very much and he desperately doesn't want to hurt her, and nor do I."

"Well, I think he's great," Alexander said, pulling one of Toss's ears.

"Yeah, me too, Mummy. He is."

She hugged us both, but when she stopped there was desperation in her face.

Alexander and I had no trouble understanding it: they were in love, but not free to love; they had to steal their happiness from themselves as much as from the world.

There is one morning, with swallows diving like thrilled swimmers, sheep nosing up through bracken toward the heights and a sky like a swelling hymn, when every bright thing seems to proclaim itself, as if all existence is in salutation to the day. Jenny is going to meet Guy while we are at school. She has not dressed up, wears a T-shirt and jeans, but there is an air, a swish about her, as she herds us into the car, something vivid and pretty and breathless. She waits for him by a reservoir. When he arrives they hold hands. She feels joy like a deep gulf, something enormous, bottomless, beneath them; as they walk back it seems to carry them, to bear them up and glide them along.

He comes again on a Sunday afternoon. Alexander and I play in the larch trees; holding the swing above our heads, with the ropes tight, we hurl ourselves off the old wall, flinging out in a wide arc, like a horizontal parachute jump, blurring the valley miles beneath us. Jenny and Guy wander across the meadows and down to the badger setts. They sit together in the bracken for a while, then scramble down to the stream. She wants to show him all of her kingdom: the dog roses; the old trees with their ears of fungus; the dark pebble pools and the silver falls of the brook. They climb back up the Patch, lean on the gate at the top, and gaze at it all, at the late afternoon and the sun-dusted valley, at the cloud shadows and shafts of light, like God's fingers, playing over the hills.

"You may have to come and live here," she says.

"Yes," he says. "I've thought of it."

Guy tells Jill what has happened. They talk about divorce. Jill is distraught and furious. She fights every way she can, in love and hurt and anger. She attacks our terrible squalor, Jenny's cooking, her poverty, her emotional indulgence, and the way she has brought us up.

It is as though everyone in town knows: "Half the High Street is on my side and the other half is against me," Jenny says.

"You're imagining it, Mummy."

"Am I? I'm not sure. I don't blame them anyway—I don't blame them! It's a terrible, terrible predicament. Poor Jill! We could never be happy if she's miserable, anyway. I could never be happy."

Guy says he will leave Jill. Jenny says, "Are you sure? Perhaps you should put this aside and try again with your wife."

"I know what it's like to be left," she agonizes. "We know, don't we, children?"

Guy says he could do that, he could try again, but would she still be there, at the end, if it did not work?

"Of course," she says. "Of course I will wait for you."

Guy vacillates. Does Jenny love him enough? Will she put him before her children, will she put him before her farm? He tells her to think about it: Think about losing your independence, he says, and your autonomy. Think about losing your farm.

"Whatever happens, you simply can't stay up there," he insists, gently, but looking her hard in the eye.

"It's not safe, it's not healthy. . . ." She is making faces. He smiles sternly and grips her hand. "It's not sane! You will become more and more lonely. You're going to send the boys off to school. What then? You absolutely must come down."

But she resists. One cold, wide evening, under a luminous lemon sky, she watches storm clouds gathering in flocks over the Beacons, and wonders how she will ever leave.

They each fear the other has "cold feet." That is the phrase they use, "cold feet," as if they are standing in the edge of the sea.

Now he says they will need money, to buy another house for Jill. Jenny calculates how many acres she can sell without destroying the farm. The Far Quoiker and Ty Newydd, she decides. Twenty acres will bring in £30,000; she will give him that. He says he is going to talk to Jill and finish it one way or another, but he does not.

They turn over and over, trapped at the confluence of their hopes, her responsibilities, and his fears. He studies her, and us.

But it is not all anguished debating: they are in love, and how they laugh and kiss and court! At last she has a true friend, a confidant, a partner: in photographs from this time she looks radiant, laughing; someone has found her, at last.

And he loves to help, to make improvements. A cassette player appears in the kitchen: Mozart greets the morning. He spends hours installing a second water system, to augment our supplies. He lugs a thick barge rope up to the attic and ties it over a beam. Thrown out of the skylight it will reach the ground: we now have a fire escape. He gives me an air rifle and teaches me how to shoot it. He buys tools for us, fits us up with a workbench in the attic, and gives Jenny a silver ring.

"It's fallen off!" she cries that winter. "I went up the Quoiker to check the tank, and it's fallen into the snow!" We go looking for it, with a torch, following her footprints. Beside every second pace is a circular trace from the tip of her stick, but there is no sign of the ring.

When Alexander and I go to stay with our father, Jenny and Guy go to Scotland together, and then in the summer to France.

"Oh, boys, we had such a funny time, such a wonderful time. And oh, it was a gas, he does make me laugh. There was one morning . . ."

I want them to be happy, I tell myself and Jenny, I want it to work, but my neediness and jealousy add to the great weight against them. One night after he has been to dinner I suddenly cannot bear the time it takes them to say good night at the Middle Meadow gate. I work myself into a lather.

"Why are you panicking?" Alexander frowns up from his book as I peer out of the windows. "There's nothing to worry about."

"But I don't know what she's doing!"

"It doesn't matter." He shrugs. "She'll come back!"

I ignore him and charge down the track, cursing and wailing in a brutal, self-induced tantrum: seeing the lights of his car poised at the edge of our realm has tipped me into a kind of insanity.

"I don't mind the love affair," I shout, "but I can't stand all this creeping about!"

"You don't have to be jealous!" Jenny cries when she returns, her voice rising to a pitch of disbelief, as though this hysteria in a boy whose mother obviously loves him is the most absurd thing in the world, and I can see that it is.

"I'm not, I'm not!" I shout, "I'm just worried when I don't know where you are and what you're doing."

But I am; I am terribly jealous, and torn: I want him to make her happy, but I fear displacement, a shuffling of my position.

All four of us went on holiday together, to a rented house in Somerset. Between the gentle slopes of the Quantock Hills little oak-wooded valleys wound down toward the Bristol Channel. From rocky beaches we stared back across the sea to Wales, humped, blue and hazy behind its cliffs. We had never seen our mother so happy; it was as if she and Guy were in an open conspiracy that everyone was invited to join. Laughter burst out of nothing: a twitch of his nose; her sidelong glance; every shop assistant, tea waitress, hiker, and holidaymaker was offered a part in the play. A tractor driver grinned and winked as we passed him in a lane. We walked miles, over hills and along cliffs. They held hands, and teased each other about her map reading, his appetite, her walking speed, botany (Guy never admitted not knowing the name of a plant: "You're making it up!" Jenny would cry), and architecture, competing to date houses to the nearest year. Both seemed to have met their match in the other, and it was as though they could not quite believe it.

They dived into churches, swept in and out of shops, and led us beachcombing for fossils. At supper Guy held long conversations with my brother and me, discussions on everything from nuclear power to ghosts. I started to adjust to the sight of our mother beside his tall figure; it was like remembering a half-forgotten formula. We had lived as three, two boys plus one mother; now I began to see how we could live as four, simultaneously composed of three plus one (us and Guy), and two plus two (Alexander and me, and Jenny and Guy). In this adjustment were echoes of memory from the time when Alexander was a baby, and the two of us traveled in the backseat of Dad's car, while he and Jenny talked in the front, and I daydreamed, my attention drifting in and out of their conversation, and it did not matter, because I did not have to listen or respond.

We returned to the mountain full of hope: Guy and our mother were in love; we had had a wonderful holiday; we could all be happy together. Alexander and I knew that with Guy as with all adults, we were on Best Behavior: "Do me proud, please, boys," Jenny would say, and she let us know when we had, with marks out of ten, and blasting reprimands if we had not. The week in Somerset had been a success: we got ten out of ten, and it had been easy; we had had a lovely time. If it was a glimpse of our future then there was nothing to worry about; we were all blessed.

"Here we are, home again," Jenny said, gunning the car up to the top of the yard and hauling on the brake.

"Doesn't it look green! And look, the sheep haven't got in and eaten my tubs for once, since Guy fixed the gate."

It did look green. After fifteen years of her stewardship, nothing had been cut back. Trees and hedges bustled with growth. Gorse rambled across the Quoiker, bracken rolled down from the hill, skirmishing across the fence, sidling ever closer to the house. Armies of thistles bristled proudly in the Patch, jaunty under their cockades of purple and white, and all around the buildings the nettles crowded, waist high. Moss made bright cushions of the roof tiles and the clematis swung from blocked guttering, pushing its tendrils into the upstairs windows and peeling flakes of whitewash off the walls.

Inside, the house smelled of summer: cool stone, bracken, old plaster, and must. Motes of dust danced in shafts of low sunlight. Along the collapsing shelves at the back of the living room, hundreds of children's books bulged and leaned against one another. On the pegs, coats from my father's time moldered. There was a faint acrid tang from the fireplace, where rain had fallen on the ashes, and from the back door came a buzzing sound: large wasps were nesting in the roof. But out beyond the window the mountain waited, summoning our eyes and attention, calling us away from all that ought to be done, toward everything we wanted to do.

"Right, children, you take the dogs out, I'm going to check on the rams and the yearlings, see what's died while we were away."

It was as though the farm was beyond repair, beyond our wills, our strength, and finances: it was so fiercely itself, in its beauty and dilapidation, and its reflection of our willful carelessness, that it seemed unchangeable. Did Guy really think he might live here?

He tried to persuade her to come down from her mountain to

somewhere softer, more peopled. He found she had a fluctuating degree of freedom. One day she was lonely; the next, anyone was an intruder. She appeared to be overrelaxed about things, but also she had a steely something with which he would not argue. He hyped the weather aspect, the snow and the danger and the loneliness, hoping she would come down. But she never did.

He thought about joining her there, but he realized it was not his life. He imagined terrible claustrophobia. Travel was in his blood, and then there was the collapse of his marriage, and he felt he had to try and keep his family together, and himself on the move, and he began to feel he was being pulled in too many directions.

One day, a year after the holiday in the Quantocks, a year of inconclusive discussions, informal trials, and unmade decisions, he packed a bag, put it in his car, stroked his dogs, left a note for Jill, and drove away to France. He wrote a long and loving letter to Jenny, with "good-bye" so gently between the lines that she could scarcely read it.

"What's happened, Mummy?" I asked her. We were walking across the meadows.

"I waited for him, but he didn't wait for me," she said. She spoke slowly, forming the sentences carefully, precariously, like someone tiptoeing along a log over a fast, deep stream. "He wanted me to sell the farm and go away with him, but I wasn't quite ready to. I didn't want to dump you both in schools and sell our safety net. I wanted him to wait, until you were settled and I was ready, but he couldn't."

"Why not?"

"I don't think he wants a woman with children and animals. But that is what I am! I could sell the sheep, and the farm, but there's still you two. I wasn't ruthless! I just wasn't! I wanted him to sort his marriage out properly, without rushing off and just abandoning Jill, but when he was ready I wasn't. And he didn't wait. He was off."

❖   ❖   ❖

I remember it ending in the same weather it began in, in the yellow-grass days of summer. Jenny still dressed the way she had for him, elegantly, in long skirts. She wore sunglasses all the time; behind them her eyes were red. She pored over his letters, and wrote, and walked the sheep, and took us on trips to the reservoir, where they had had their happiest day. And though she noticed everything, as she always had, her gaze did not seem to linger: it slid to the side, stared off, away somewhere. She tried hard to be gay with us, and to worry about the sheep, to be brave and to hold it and hide it. "I'm just fine," she would say. "Just fine!"

But she carried a desolate silence with her, cradled and covered, half hidden, but never not there. And so it was not hardship, or poverty, or Mad Bombers, or illness that finally undid her hold on the hill. It was not the misbehavior of children, our needs and demands, nor the death or the agony of animals. It was not the weather, nor the isolation, nor the state of the house that ultimately drove us away.

It was love, and the terrible beauty of the place, its heartbreaking view and its sky. It was all the wonder of the mountain that did for us, its colors and wild bright days.

"It was the end of the farm for me, really," she said. "After he went, I couldn't stay there. It wasn't the loneliness or even the winters. It was having been there with him."

We began to look for somewhere else in earnest. Jenny thought about a little terraced house on the edge of town, but it was too near people and traffic. She was tempted by a little cottage farther down the valley, halfway up the hillside, and we looked at a farm up a hill above our school, but nowhere we saw had anything to replace or compensate for the magic that we knew. There was also the question of to whom we should sell: Jenny was determined that whoever came after us should farm the land, not break it up or fertilize it to death.

Too quickly, it seemed, a couple were interested, and they fitted all her criteria. They would farm, they would not fertilize, they said; they would plant trees, and have cattle as well as sheep. It fell to me to walk them around the land, and I did so, feeling like a traitor. As we came to the badger setts there was a noise just under our feet. We stopped.

There, just beneath us, were three tiny squeaking cubs. I watched as the husband and wife looked at each other, their faces delighted and amazed. This is how it was for my parents, I thought as the land cast its old spell again. I was jealous and forlorn.

In the end we found a large old house, half derelict, half comfortable, which had not been much messed around. It had the thick walls and the old-ship feeling of the farm. It had an old apple orchard, and there were kind neighbors nearby. Jack's cottage was just across the garden.

"We'll be able to wave to you, Jack!" Jenny said. "It will be wonderful!"

But Jack was ill, sunk, and rarely smiled now. "Don't know if I'll see the cuckoo," he said. "Oh, of course you will," she said. "You always say that, and you always do!"

Before we made the move he died; he succumbed to the rule of threes. He had pneumonia; his relatives did not tell Jenny when his condition worsened; and "they," the doctors, did not help him. "I could have saved him," Jenny wept, "if I'd only got there in time and made a fuss."

Jack's funeral was in the chapel. Higher up the valley, under a swell of the mountains, the chapel stands in a combe above a dark stream. Its situation lifts your eyes up to the hills behind it, and in the sharp line of the highest horizon, and in the nearby sky, which starts at the top of the steep fields above the graveyard, you feel the presence of an austere and watchful God. The chapel was full of men in dark suits and smart overcoats; their shoes shone brighter than water. Women and children went upstairs, into the gallery. The singing was high and strong; thinned voices raised the notes in a tribute that was honoring and acknowledging and bleak all at once; old men saluting one of their own and the end of a life of their time.

We followed the coffin down the lane to the graveyard, which is on a steep slope, and climbed up through the tussocks and headstones. There were sheep cropping the field above; the farmers looked them over as the minister said the last words, instinctively making sure they were all right.

David Hughes was there: he looked up at the mountain, its high prow forging on, always, across the clouds. He squeezed Jenny's arm. "Lucky Jack," he said, quietly. "Yes." Jenny nodded. "Lucky Jack."

When she knew we were leaving Jenny walked around the fields with her camera. It was an autumn afternoon. The mountain was on the turn; brown die-back showing through the green. In the distance the hills were hazy, over the tops of trees still heavy with fading leaves. By the Far Meadow gate the rose hips were blood bright in the hedgerow, and as she walked through the fields, taking pictures, the sheep turned toward her and stared.

Moving day passed in a haze, frantic and unreal. As we boxed our things, all our books and bits, the walls were revealed, stripped bare. As we exposed the collapsing plaster and the rotting boards, the mouse holes and cobwebs and centuries of dust, the old house seemed to age and shrivel. We packed, stuffed, and carried, hurrying madly, trying not to take it in. Jenny hit the same peak of adrenaline and desperate matter-of-factness with which she sent old sheep to the slaughter. We copied her, working like mad. It was as though we were trying not to acknowledge what we were doing; refusing to hear the voices of the farm and the mountain; too miserable to attempt a proper farewell.

I wrote a note, like a short love letter, and stuffed it into the space behind the wallpaper of my bedroom, where no one but the mice would find it.

A friend came with a circular saw to liberate the fridge from the sideboard. He cut straight through the work surface as my brother watched him, transfixed. It was, Alexander says, as though his childhood ended there: common sense, efficiency, and a snarling machine slicing through the heart of the house.

"Well, good-bye, little farm," Jenny said as the removal men struggled to shut the back doors of their van. It sounded strange and unconvincing, as though neither she nor the place really believed she was leaving. I do not think any of us believed it. It was as though we were going, but not as if we were moving on. It reminded me of the great snow, of being forced off for a while, but I still felt I belonged to the farm, and it to me. No one else would grow up there, as we had. No one else would know every foot of it, every inch, as we had. We did not believe it would speak to anyone as it had spoken to us, for no one else would exist there as we had, in the ancient way, after the fashion of its builders, in harmony with their approving ghosts. *Unspoiled* was a word my mother used when we had looked at old farms, and it referred, I realized, to more than fabric, the forms and materials of old places. It was about continuity, an unbroken note, which gently denied all the narrow, pedestrian fashions in which our age approaches time, the way we assume it can be counted and measured in straight lines.

When we reached the new house she handed one of the men the sledgehammer, and asked him to batter down a blocked-up door.

"Are you sure?" he said.

"Quite sure," she replied. "It's going to be the new way in."

"Well, I never saw anyone move into a new house like this," he said. "Stand back!"

That night, our first in our new home, I plugged in the television. The great compensation of civilization delivered three channels of fuzz and one quite clearly.

"Mum! Television! It works! One channel does, anyway."

"Oh, really," she said, tiredly. "What's on?"

"*Death on the Nile!*"

"Oh. Peter Ustinov. Jolly good." It was the tone she used when things were not jolly good, and we sensed the film was a hoary old repeat even then. But we all sat on boxes of books, jammed between sofas, and stared at it nevertheless.

With time, Jenny cast her spell over the house. It is a simple system of tolerance and consideration, of not destroying things, not cutting things down or meddling unless there is absolutely no choice. Swifts nest in the eaves, butterflies hibernate on the windowsills, and there is—despite my protests—an ant colony in the kitchen. Swallows and house martens come annually to the yard, and robins and wrens live in the garden. Sometimes a sparrowhawk ambushes the crowd around the bird table.

A hedgehog used to appear in the kitchen, scoop up slugs, and slurp away at the milk bowl, to the bemusement of the cat. On the ridge of the roof is a starling that does a perfect imitation of a buzzard. Every spring the jackdaws fill the chimney with twigs and wool, rear their young there, and depart, leaving a pillar of sticks blocking the flue. In the autumn the chimney sweep comes and pulls it all down, advising Jenny to have the birds shot. But then there would be no chatting voices in the chimney, and no bright pale eyes watching her comings and goings, and she would have to gather kindling for winter fires herself. In her relationship with nature is a minute appreciation, born of attention and observation of its details, coupled with a passionate engagement with its great patterns. Her stance is political as much as spiritual: behind the simple creed of live and let live is the belief that "let live" is an active process, involving effort, sacrifice, and love.

Long after we had unpacked all our boxes and settled into our rooms we were still discovering how much we had brought with us from the farm. Our eyes were still full of the long, wide views: we stood motionless before them, to drink them in; we were forever calling one another outside, to stare at clouds or moods of light. We still opened the curtains in the morning and gazed up at the hill, measuring the temper of the day. We felt strange to be surrounded by people; our mountain had made us shy. We missed the privacy of isolation: I was forever dashing defiantly out into the garden, "out the back," to pee, as I always had. Alexander and I got into trouble once or twice, running wild with the dogs in someone else's fields, provoking stampedes of bullocks. We could not believe the amount of "tidying up" that went on around us; the cutting of hedges, the felling of trees, the scrubbing and sweeping of birds' droppings. "It's all too neat," Jenny growled from time to time. "Why can't people just let things be?" We could not get used to how much everyone knew and noticed about us, now that we lived in a village. We still saw ourselves as separate, peculiar people of the mountain: we related better to the hill farmers, their brevity and bashfulness, than to the valley dwellers, with their sociable chat. It took us years to get to know all our new neighbors; we were too used to our own company. Often we failed to find ease in the valley, and had to go back up, somewhere high, to feel that we could breathe again. At home we fell heavily into the traps of civilization. We all watched far too much television, allowing ourselves to be hypnotized by it for hours. Alexander and I became obsessed with adverts: soon we could reel them off, their jingles and dialogues, by the score. In our beds at night we all thought about the farm. When the wind blew hard we remembered the way the house used to sing; when the snow came we worried about black ice on the pitches. At night, sometimes, Jenny says, she still walks around the house in her mind, and goes out, into the yard or across the fields.

Jenny and Guy are great friends and barely ever meet.

She is philosophical about it. "It was a good thing I didn't marry him, really," she says. "Trouble is, he's ruined everyone else for me. No one will ever compare."

"You were lucky to have had those times," I say as we watch two greenfinches attacking the bird feeder.

"Yes," she says. "I was."

"When you met him, you said it was the first time you had been in love for fifteen years—since Dad?"

She shakes her head.

"I don't think I was ever in love with Robert. I loved him, but I wasn't in love with him."

That strange feeling comes over me again, a kind of shock without surprise.

"So why did you marry him then?"

"Because he has a wonderful, golden side to him, and I was very fond of him, and because he wanted to, really," Jenny says. She is smoking cigars now, like a retired pirate.

"When you were here and he was in London you must have realized it wasn't going to work—so why did you keep going back there? Why were you surprised when it ended?"

"Well, I used to say to Ursie perhaps it will be better in our forties. I thought we might just settle into it."

She looks rattled now, and I know this is unfair, but I can't resist one more: "But how could it have got better when you didn't love each other?"

"I don't know! Maybe I thought that's what marriage was, because my parents' marriage was so rotten and miserable, I think I thought that that was what it was supposed to be like!"

Part of the answer I had been seeking is there. Having wrestled for so long with the idea that the rupture in our childhood stemmed from my father, and having been so puzzled that he could not keep loving my mother, though she seemed to me so lovable, it is a kind of relief to hear that it was mutual; that her behavior was as singular, willful and yet will-less, as his. It makes them seem more compatible, somehow, and since even now I cannot escape the urge to push them together, perhaps I have finally found a way of joining them: they were perfectly, heroically mismatched. They were doomed, and everything they had and did was miraculous, a romantic defiance of their fate. When they meet now there is a gentleness between them that could be an acknowledgment of that; an ease, a kind of fondness for the other's humor and strangeness, and a respect for their steel. They are both romantics, and though I have learned of the dangers that attend and await romantic people, that bipolar breed, the certain failure, the heartbreak—theirs and others'—and the loneliness, I cannot quite wish they, or I, had been otherwise. If life is hills and valleys, then let the hills be high.

So we came down from our mountain, but we did not quite let it go. We kept one field, the Far Quoiker, which adjoins the hill. Eleven acres of hummocky ground, with a spring, and anthills, and gorse. Green woodpeckers live there, probing the humps for insects, and there is a family of kestrels in the ash. There are squirrels' drays, and a March hare and a hundred miles of view.

From certain parts of the field you can see the farm. It is much changed now. All the sheds have been incorporated into a large, comfortable house. The green lane is gone. The spinney was cut down, the gorse bushes plowed up, and the great ash tree behind the house was felled. The fences do not sag; there are businesslike sheds in the First Meadow and there are fewer animals in the fields. It has all been rebuilt and smartened up, transformed into a fit and conventional dwelling for twenty-first-century tenants. It had to happen, of course. Without a great deal of money and work everything would simply have fallen down.

But the wonder of existence on the edge of that ruin, the fragile and reverent way we lived, patching up rather than replacing, in slow step with time and weather, preserved mysteries and a particular magic of which only traces remain.

Only the Quoiker has not been improved in any way. The gate at the top leads to the mountain, and Mum still puts a few sheep through. In the summer she follows along behind them, high-hearted, up ridges like a giant's stair, just as she used to, as all the tenants before her did, following the animals to their grazing under the great wide air. Near the gate there is an ancient stone wall, constantly collapsing, which she has repaired for years. She says it makes the perfect therapy, if she feels troubled, to unearth and sort the stones. You cannot hurry, you have to try things, let the parts show you how they join. In the weight of the rocks, in their shapes and relationships, are patterns as old as time. You enter a kind of reverie, she says, as you lift them and fit them together.

Acknowledgments

Many thanks to Tina Bennett, for her quite wonderful backing and help and care. I have been hugely blessed by the attentions and efforts of my editor at Scribner, Nan Graham, and her associate Alexis Gargagliano: no one could hope for more astute readers or acute critics. Thank you both.

For the book's existence in the first place, all my thanks to Tif Loehnis of Janklow and Nesbit UK and Roland Philipps and Rowan Yapp at John Murray.

For the diligent examination, herding, and demaggoting of my grammar and syntax, and for effectively translating the book from Anglo-Welsh English into American English, many thanks to John McGhee.

For putting me up and putting up with me for so long, with such patience and care, all my thanks to David, Elizabeth, Merlin, and Anna Rose Hughes.

For their wisdom, friendship, and kindness, I would like to thank Kevin Bohnert, Nathan Hill, Ben Hardiman, and Anne Garwood, in America, and in Britain, Robin Jenkins, Toby Lynas, Chris Kenyon, Jane Matthews, Fliss Morgan, Jane Rafter. Mike White, Roger Couhig, Julian May, John Wilson, Claire Paterson, Alison Finch, and Richard Coles.

Love and special thanks to Sally Spurring.

And for their great help, trust, and faith, and everything else, I would like to thank my parents and Alexander. This is for you, with love.

About the Author

Horatio Clare was born in London in 1973 and raised in Wales. A former BBC radio producer, his journalism has appeared in various newspapers and magazines. He left the BBC in 2005 to edit a collection of writing about Sicily, and is currently working on his second book.